From

the Library

of Emma

from Grandmary

this can be a reference for you

FIFTY FAMOUS COMPOSERS

FOR KIDS OF ALL AGES

BY

DR. CAROLYN WATERS BROE

INKWELL BOOKS
Writing-Publishing-Printing

ISBN 978-0-578-84662-0

Library of Congress 2020945758

Published by Inkwell Books

10632 North Scottsdale Road, Unit 695

Scottsdale, AZ 85254

Tel. 480-315-3781

E-mail info@inkwellbooksllc.com

Website www.inkwellbooksllc.com

Printed in the United States of America

FIFTY FAMOUS COMPOSERS
FOR KIDS OF ALL AGES

BY

DR. CAROLYN WATERS BROE

Dr. Carolyn Waters Broe

ACKNOWLEDGEMENTS

This book was sponsored in part by a generous grant from the Music Teachers National Association. I wish to acknowledge my viola teachers Rene Breggozo, Jerry Epstein, Thomas Hall, Robert Becker, Louis Kievman, Adriana Chirilov and William Magers who believed in me and for inspiring me to become a professional musician. I also want to acknowledge Dr. Christine Forney, who was the chair of my committee when I earned my Master of Fine Arts degree in Music History. Dr. William Magers was the chair of my Doctor of Musical Arts degree committee in Viola Solo Performance. Many thanks to my Husband Dr. Steve Broe for supporting and encouraging my career in music and writing. I also wish to thank my parents Lois and Warren Waters for supporting my music education.

DEDICATION

I wish to dedicate Fifty Famous Composers for Kids to the great composers who have inspired my love of music. My first biography of a composer, at the age of eight, was of Johann Sebastian Bach. Learning about his life and music motivated me to pursue a lifetime performing music, teaching, and my love of music history. This book is dedicated to all the music teachers who have inspired me and to all who wish to inspire their students in the love of music. I wish to dedicate this book to parents and grandparents who want to introduce great music and composers to their children and grandchildren. I am also dedicating this book to the generations of children who want to learn more about the Classical composers, their music, and their lives. By telling the stories of these men and women I hope to bring them and their music alive for the reader.

PROLOGUE

Most people lived vastly different lives than we do now. Girls were expected to get married, have children, and take care of the family home. If a woman did not get married, or was widowed, she would often become a nun. Boys were expected to follow in their father's footsteps and learn his trade. The son of a brick mason would become a brick mason. Some of the men and women composers in this book had a father or mother, who was a composer or musician. This is how many historic composers learned how to write music, from a family member. Music was passed down from one generation to the next. The composers who are listed in *"Fifty Famous Composers for Kids"* were exceptional people for their time. Several of these fifty plus composers came from wealthy families. So, they were given an education in music, and other subjects, when most children were not educated at all until recent times.

Western music has inherited a great deal from the ancient Sumerians who lived in Mesopotamia. The ancient Sumerians used string instruments such as the lyre and the harp around 2,500 B.C.E. The Babylonians are credited with inventing music notation. The earliest known Middle Eastern composer whose music has survived is Enheduanna, who was an Akkadian high priestess of Ur (Grout 2006, pg. 7). She composed hymns to the Moon god Nanna and the Moon goddess Inanna around 2,300 B.C.E. Only the text survived on a clay tablet in cuneiform. The oldest completed piece of music found was a hymn to the god Nikkal's wife on a clay tablet in cuneiform from c. 1,400-1,250 B.C.E.

The ancient Greek philosophers such as Plato (ca. 429-347 B.C.E.) and Aristotle (384-322 B.C.E.) believed that music was one of the four main subjects for the education of a young statesman including poetry, mathematics, gymnastics, and music. The Greeks played instruments such as the aulos, lyre, kithara, harps, panpipes, horns, an early organ, and various percussion instruments. The lyre was a seven stringed instrument that was strummed or plucked. This instrument was used to perform hymns in honor of Apollo, who was the god of light, learning, art, music, and prophecy. The lyre was considered essential as accompaniment for reciting epic poetry, dancing, singing and for education.

50 Famous Composers

The Greek philosophers wrote about music in their philosophical doctrines and their theoretical doctrines. They considered music to be inseparable from mathematics and astronomy. The Greek philosopher Pythagoras (d. ca. 500 B.C.E.) is considered the father of Greek music theory. He discovered the music overtone series through the mathematical ratios when the string of a lyre is divided. The octave has a 2:1 relationship, the fifth is 3:2 and the fourth is 4:3 (Grout 2006, pg.13). Plato wrote about music in his *Republic* and his *Timaeus*. He felt that music was immensely powerful and should be practiced in balance. He did not appreciate the complex music that was being performed in music competitions. Plato felt that some music was too vulgar for the young statesman and could have a negative effect on his character. Other music was more suitable to developing the proper *ethos*. In Aristotle's *Poetics* he gives the elements of poetry as melody, rhythm, and language.

Greek philosophers viewed music as a reflection of the order of the Universe. Music, mathematics, astronomy and *harmonia* were linked together. Claudius Ptolemy (fl. 127-148 C.E.) was a leading astronomer and an important writer about music. He discovered that mathematical laws and musical intervals are linked. However, the Greeks had ideas about the correspondence between musical intervals and heavenly bodies that are not widely believed in modern times. This is the basis for Plato's theory of the "Harmony of the Spheres". Musical intervals and heavenly bodies, certain planets and their distances from each other and their movements were believed to correspond to particular notes, intervals and scales in music (Grout 2006, pg. 13). This was all part of early astronomy and major and minor conjunctions of the planets in our solar system. The revolution of the planets was thought to produce unheard music.

The Music of the Spheres was echoed throughout the Middle Ages in their writings about music all the way to the Renaissance in Shakespeare's play the *Tempest* and Milton's *Paradise Lost*. The Renaissance writers and composers were inspired by the Greek legends about the gods, their heroes, the nine muses and the famous singer Orpheus. They based many of their works on these stories. The Classical composers were inspired by Greek architecture and balance and incorporated this balance into their music. Many of the Greek theories about music are still held today by modern music theorists and serve as the foundation of music. We have inherited a great deal of our western music practice and culture from the Greeks.

However, since the time of the Greeks many new voices have added tremendous variety to Western music. From Gregorian chant, to madrigals, opera, orchestral music, concertos, musicals, jazz, and twelve tone all the way to modern music we have made incredible innovations. Yet not all those voices have been celebrated. Publishers only focused on a few select individuals and their music. Women composers were left out of the music history books entirely. It was as if they never existed. During my graduate work I took a class on the music of women and was incredibly surprised to discover that there were over 6,000 historic women's biographies in Aaron Cohen's *International Encyclopedia of Women Composers*. Inclusion is the key to diversity in education.

I was recently asked to teach music history at a charter school for children aged seven to eleven years old. Like the ancient Greeks, music is considered a core academic at this Classically based school. Each week I needed to prepare a forty-five-minute lecture on Classical composers for the students and play examples of their music. I was delighted to find out that these students were eager to learn about music and soaked everything up like a sponge. They were required to do a book report on a composer and give a presentation in class with a poster. There was a list of composers for them to choose from, however no women were listed. I decided to do an experiment and added about fifteen famous women composers to the list. I was amazed by how many of the girls decided to do their book reports and speeches on the women composers.

I learned many things from these young students. They have no preconceived ideas about the Classical composers. One composer is just as good as the next. Yet, when I asked them to include at least two reference books on their composer in their bibliography I got many panicked calls from their parents. The local library had almost no reference books on music. The few books on the individual composers were checked out by the first of my 180 music students to get to the library. They told me that the library had mostly computers and dozens of copies of CD's by the Canadian singer Justin Bieber. That is when I knew that I needed to write "Fifty Famous Composers for Kids". It is a shame when young people only know of the Classical composers and their music from cartoons. I hope that this book brings a lifelong love of music to all my readers.

TABLE OF CONTENTS

MEDIEVAL COMPOSERS

(Approximately 800-1400)

HILDEGARD VON BINGEN (1098-1179)

Hildegard von Bingen (1098-1179) – She was a **German** abbess of Ruperts-berg, writer, artist, Christian mystic, and composer. Hildegard was the first Western composer ever to have their named attached to their music com-position. She was a **Medieval composer** who founded a monastery on the Rupertsberg, in the Rhine Valley near Bingen. Hildegard was a visionary, who painted, composed music, and wrote about what she saw in her visions. In recent years, her music, writing, and paintings have become famous.

Hildegard composed *Ordo Virtutum* which is the earliest surviving morality play. In this play, she wrote single line melodies for the part of *Anima* (the human soul), which she probably performed herself. She also composed songs for the Sixteen *Virtues* (probably played by the other nuns). There is also a speaking part for the Devil, which may have been played by a monk.

Sixty-nine of Hildegard's many music compositions survived each with its own poetic text. Many of these works are monophonic liturgical songs that she collected in her book *Symphonia armoniae celestium revelationum*. **Monophonic** means that there is only one melody line. Hildegard's music is highly **melismatic**, which means it had soaring melodies that were beautifully ornamented by stretching out each syllable with various notes. She set songs from her *Symphonia* to her own texts including antiphons, hymns, sequences, and responsories. (Maddocks 2001).

It is not known exactly when Hildegard was born, but records place it close to 1098. She was born to Mechtild of Merxheim-Nahet and Hildebert of Bermersheim, a family of lower nobility. Hildegard was sickly from birth and experienced her first visions by the age of three. She was about eight years old when she went to live with a visionary woman named Jutta, who taught her to read and write. They both went into the abbey when Hildegard was about fourteen. Hildegard learned to play the ten stringed **psaltery**, which was a Medieval instrument that was plucked like a dulcimer. The monk Volmar helped Hildegard to write down many of her visions. She wrote over 400 letters to important people like the Pope. The nuns of Rupertsberg elected her *magistra* in 1136. She also wrote about cures and early medicine. Some scholars feel that Hildegard was the founder of scientific natural history in Germany. (Jöckle 2003). Hildegard passed away on 17 September 1179 after a long illness. The nuns there said two streams of light crossed over the room where she died. On 10 May 2012 Pope Benedict XVI declared Hildegard of Bingen a canonized Saint. On 7 October 2012 he named her a Doctor of the Church.

Title: The antiphon "O gloriosissimi" from Hildegard of Bingen's Symphonia armonie celestium revelationum, 1170s.

Genre: In traditional Western Christian liturgy, an **antiphon** is a short sentence (or its musical setting), which is sung, recited, or played alternately by two groups.

YouTube: https://www.youtube.com/watch?v=-u_5SKBCJqQ

"O gloriosissimi" from Hildegard of Bingen's Symphonia armonie celestium revelationum, 1170s.

YouTube: https://www.youtube.com/watch?v=Ei88J4lERbk Canticles of Ecstasy – Sequentia

Birthday: Born 1098 Bermersheim, Holy Roman Empire.

Death Date: 17 September 1179 Bingen on Rhine River, Holy Roman Empire (aged 81)

Fun Facts:

1. Even as a child Hildegard saw visions, and with the aid of the monk Volmar, she felt compelled to write them down.
2. Hildegard was the first composer to have their own name attached to their music composition. Virginia Woolf said, "For most of history, anonymous was a woman," from her lecture essay "A Room of One's Own" (1928).
3. Hildegard was the first composer of music for a morality play.

RENAISSANCE COMPOSERS
(1400-1600)

JOSQUIN DES PREZ (C. 1450/1455-1521)

osquin des prez (C. 1450/1455-1521) – was a **Franco-Flemish** composer of the **Renaissance** era (now France). Josquin, as he was known, was praised as the most famous European composer of his time. He is considered the central figure of the Franco-Flemish School of music. He was a master of the **polyphonic** vocal music style of the high Renaissance during the 16th century. He became so famous for his mastery of technique and expression, that many people copied his style, and tried to sell their works under his name. So, it is difficult to tell which of his 370 compositions are really by Josquin or an imposter (Reese, Grove).

Even though Josquin had a giant reputation, little is known about his biography or his personality. He remains a mysterious and shadowy figure. We do know that he worked for the Duke of Anjou, the Sforza family in Milan, Pope Innocent VIII, and the Borgia Pope Alexander VI in Rome. Josquin wrote both sacred and secular music. He composed in all of the vocal forms of his age, including eighteen masses, sixty-one motets, sixty-one *chansons* and three *frottole*. During the 16th century, he was praised for both his melodic gifts, and his use of clever technical devices.

Josquin grew up in Flanders which is now part of Belgium and Northern France. It was ruled by the Dukes of Burgundy, so his style is often referred to as Burgundian. The first definite record of his employment is dated 19 April 1477 as a singer at the chapel of René, Duke of Anjou, in Aix-en-Provence. He remained there at least until 1478. Josquin worked at several courts in Italy including Milan, papal courts in Rome and in the court of Ferrara. He was a member of the papal choir from 1489-1495 under Pope Innocent VIII and later under Pope Alexander VI, the Borgia pope.

Title: *Missa L'homme armé super voces musicales* (four voices) The L'homme armé (armed man) theme was extremely popular during the Renaissance. Josquin composed two masses on this theme.

Genre: A **mass** is a vocal piece on sacred Latin texts that is usually in four voices. In the Renaissance, composers often wrote a single mass movement, instead of the five to seven movement masses of today.

YouTube: https://www.youtube.com/ watch?v=BKhSYH27Cr4
Missa L'Homme armé super voces musicales

Birthday: born c. 1450/1455, near St. Quentin, Flanders (now Northern France)

Death Date: 27 August 1521, died St Condé-sur-l'Escaut, Flanders (now France) (aged approximately 71)

Fun Facts:
1. Many people copied Josquin's style and tried to say their music was by Josquin, so they could get more money.
2. Josquin is widely considered by music scholars to be the first master of the high Renaissance style of polyphonic vocal music.
3. Josquin is usually considered to be the central figure of the Franco-Flemish School.
4. Graffiti of the name "Josquin J" was found by workers, who were restoring a wall in the Sistine Chapel at the Vatican in Rome. It was a common practice for papal singers during the 15th century to sign their name in the Sistine Chapel, so it is thought to be an authentic signature by Josquin de Prez.

CLAUDIO MONTEVERDI (1567-1643)

Claudio Monteverdi – **(1567-1643)** was an **Italian composer**, choir master, and string player, who was a key figure between the **Renaissance and Baroque eras**. Monteverdi was a pioneer in the development of the **opera** which combines singing with drama, art, instrumental music, plays and poetry. He composed both sacred music for the church and secular music for courts. His nine books of madrigals are considered by many to be the high point of Renaissance vocal music. He worked primarily for the court of Mantua. Claudio made significant developments to musical form and melody through what he called the *"Seconda Pratica"* meaning the second practice, which was different from the earlier more orthodox *"Prima Pratica"*.

Claudio was born in Cremona 15 May 1567, which is now in Northern Italy. Cremona was under the control of Milan, which was in the possession of Spain at the time, so he was technically a Spanish subject. Claudio was the first child of Baldassare Monteverdi an apothecary (pharmacist), and his first wife Maddalena (born Zignani). His brother Giulio Monteverdi also became a musician. He had two other brothers and two sisters born of his mother Maddalena. Cremona was a center for music close to the borders of both Mantua and the Republic of Venice where Monteverdi eventually made his career. There are no records of his early training in music nor any proof that he ever trained with the Cathedral choir or studied at the University of Cremona.

Monteverdi's first set of **motets**, *Sacrae cantiunculae* (Sacred Songs) for three voices, was published in Venice in 1582 when he was only fifteen. In this publication and later works Monteverdi says that he was the pupil of Marc'Antonio Ingegneri, who was the *Maestro di Cappella* (choir master) of the Cremona Cathedral from 1581-1592 and possibly earlier. Musicologist Tim Carter states that Claudio may have learned composition and counter point from Ingegneri (Carter and Chew, "Cremona"). He may also have learned the instruments of the *viol* family which were bowed string instruments such as the *viola da gamba,* which was played between the knees like a cello, and the *viola da braccio,* which was played on the arm like a violin or viola. These older stringed instruments had frets like a guitar and a flat back.

Monteverdi is known for his brilliant use of the Renaissance polyphonic style. **Polyphony** is a musical texture that uses two or more simultaneous lines of independent melody. A single melody is called **monophony**, and a single melodic line accompanied by chords is called **homophony**. Most of our contemporary music is written in the "homophonic" style. Monteverdi was a master at blending multiple melodic lines into his madrigals and motets. Monteverdi also composed the earliest opera, which is still performed today *L'Orfeo*, (1607) which is a tragedy about the famous Greek musician Orpheus who loses his wife Euridice to the underworld and tries to rescue her by singing to the God Hades. He also composed other stage works that have been lost. Two of his works were written for the Venice Theater, including *Il Ritorno d'Ulisse in Patria* and *L'incoronazione di Poppea*. He also wrote large scale sacred music such as his *Vespro della Beata Vergine* (Vespers) of 1610.

Monteverdi was a court musician for Duke Vincenzo I Gonzaga of Mantua between 1591 and 1613. In the dedication page of his second book of madrigals he describes himself as a "*Vivuola*" player. This was probably a *viola da gamba* or a *viola da braccio*. He also composed music for the Duke. Vincenzo admired Monteverdi and had him accompany him on military campaigns to Hungary in 1595 and Flanders in 1599. It was in Flanders that he learned the French style of writing songs, which was different from his settings of Italian poetry with lines in 9-11 syllables. He may also have accompanied Duke Vincenzo to Florence for the Medici wedding in 1600, and heard Jacopo Peri's opera *Euridice*, which was the earliest opera ever written. In 1601 the Duke named Monteverdi his *"maestro di capella"* or choir master.

Monteverdi married the court singer Claudia de Cattaneis in 1599. They had three children. His brother Giulio Cesare joined the court of Mantua as a musician in 1602. Duke Vincenzo made his court into a center for music. He attracted many famous musicians such as violinist Salomone Rossi, his sister the singer Madame Europa, and the choir master Giaches de Wert. The court at Mantua became famous for its music and musicians.

Unfortunately, Monteverdi's method of composing in modes and his use of harmony was attacked in a book by theorist Giovanni Maria Artusi called *L'Artusi, overo Delle imperfettioni della moderna musica* (Artusi, or On the Imperfections of Modern Music) of 1600 (Carter and Chew (n.d.), §2 "Mantua"). Artusi preferred the older polyphonic style or **"Prima Pratica"**. Without naming Monteverdi, Artusi used examples from his madrigals which were later published in Monteverdi's fourth and fifth books of madrigals. Monteverdi did not respond to Artusi, but his brother Giulio defended him and explained that his **"Secunda Pratica"** came from earlier sources.

Duke Vincenzo's heir Francesco commissioned Monteverdi to compose the opera *L'Orfeo* in 1606 for the carnival season of 1607. The libretto was by Alessandro Striggio. The **libretto** is the script for the spoken and staged part of the opera. Monteverdi set the dialogue of the opera to music. In most operas the music includes an **overture** of the main musical themes of the opera at the beginning, solo and duo **arias**, *recitatives*, and songs sung by a chorus. There are often dances in an opera which are accompanied by music and sometimes music in between acts. Monteverdi did not invent the recitative and other elements of the opera but blended them together brilliantly. He had sixteen years of experience writing and arranging music for the stage before writing his opera *L'Orfeo*.

Monteverdi had a series of tragedies fall on him. His wife died in 1607. Then the singer Caterina Martinelli, who was going to sing the title role of his new opera L'Arianna (Ariadne), died of smallpox in March 1608. Monteverdi was tired of so much work and so little pay from the Gonzagas. He decided to retire from the court of Mantua in 1608. After he composed his *"Vespers"* in 1610, Monteverdi went to Rome hoping to get his son Francesco a job at the seminary. He dedicated this work to Pope Paul V. The Gonzaga family hired Monteverdi back and increased his salary. However, after Duke Vincenzo died in 1612, Monteverdi had great difficulty working with the new Duke Francesco and other members of the Gonzaga family. They decided to cut costs, so Francesco fired Monteverdi and his brother Giulio sending them back to Cremona penniless. Even though Duke Francesco died of smallpox in 1612, Monteverdi could not regain his post.

Monteverdi auditioned for his post as **maestro** (music director) at the basilica of San Marco in Venice. He submitted his beautiful mass to the committee. Monteverdi was appointed as maestro in August 1613. The church gave him 50 ducats for his expenses. Unfortunately, he was robbed of the ducats, and all his other belongings, by highwaymen at Sanguinetto on his return to Cremona. When Monteverdi returned to Venice he reorganized and modernized the music organization at San Marco Basilica. Many of Monteverdi's sacred works for churches were published in Venice. He was required to compose a mass every year as well as music for Christmas Eve and Holy Cross Day. He also composed several cantatas for the Venetian Doge, who was the ruler of Venice. He was allowed the freedom to compose music on commission from other churches and nobles as well. The church procurators were so happy with Monteverdi that they raised his salary from 300 to 400 ducats a year. Later when the court of Mantua wanted him back, he said no to them, because he enjoyed the freedom the Republic of Venice allowed him without all the politics.

Monteverdi did accept commissions from the new Duke Ferdinando of Mantua. Ferdinando had formally renounced his position as Cardinal in 1616 to take on the duties of state when Duke Francesco died. These music works included the "*Balli Tirsi e Clori*" (1616) and "*Apollo*" (1620), an opera *Andromeda* (1620) and an *intermedio*, *Le nozze di Tetide*, for the marriage of Ferdinando with Caterina de' Medici (1617). The opera *La finta pazza Licori*, to a libretto by Giulio Strozzi, was completed for Fernando's successor Vincenzo II, who succeeded to the dukedom in 1626 after Ferdinando died. Most of these works are now lost. Monteverdi composed music for other city states as well including a *Requiem Mass* for Cosimo II de' Medici (1621) in Florence and music for the Feast of St. Charles Borromeo in Milan.

The Habsburg army invaded Mantua in 1630 which led to a plague. The plague was carried to Venice by an emissary which led to the deaths of 45,000 Venetians. The chaos that followed meant that Monteverdi was unable to get work composing for the next seven years. Monteverdi's brother Giulio may also have died of the plague. During this dark time Monteverdi turned to the church for comfort and became an ordained priest in 1632. The opening of the Opera House of San Cassiano in 1637 helped to bring music in Venice back to life. It was the first public opera house ever opened in all of Europe. Monteverdi had a burst of musical activity. He composed and published his eighth book of **madrigals** and revised his "*Ballo delle ingrate*". He also published a large collection of his church music including "Selva morale e spiritual". Monteverdi also revised his earlier opera *L'Arianna* in 1640. He wrote three new works for the stage including *Il Ritorno d'Ulisse in Patria* (The Return of Ulysses to his Homeland, 1640, *Le Nozze d'Enea e Lavinia* (The Marriage of Aeneas and Lavinia, 1641, now lost), and *L'incoronazione di Poppea* (The Coronation of Poppea, 1643).

Monteverdi became ill in 1643. He had hoped to gain his long-disputed pension from the court of Mantua and wrote a letter to the Doge in Venice to ask for his help. The pension never arrived, and Monteverdi died in November of 1643. He is buried in the Basilica of Santa Maria Gloriosa of the Frari. His contributions to the development of the madrigal, opera and to sacred choral music were monumental.

50 Famous Composers

Title: Overture and Prologue to the opera *L'Orfeo* (1607) . The instrumentation includes strings, brass and *continuo*. The strings included two kit violins (piccolo violins), two double basses, and the *viole de brazzo* or violin family (in two five-part ensembles made up of two violins, two violas, and a cello). The brass included four or five trombones called *sackbuts*, three trumpets and two cornetts. The continuo included two harpsichords, a double harp, two or three *chitarroni* (a long lute-like stringed instrument called a theorbo), two pipe organs, three bass *viola da gamba*, and a *regal* or small reed organ. There are also parts for two recorders and possibly one or more *citterns* (a stringed instrument like a mandolin).

Genre: An **overture** introduces all the main melodies and themes in the opera performed by the orchestra or an instrumental ensemble.

YouTube: https://www.youtube.com/watch?v=TROsH4jwomg Ausschnitt aus der DVD L'Orfeo

Birthday: 15 May 1567 (baptized) in Cremona, Italy (under Spanish rule)

Death Date: 29 November 1643 in The Republic of Venice (aged 76)

Fun Facts:

1. Monteverdi composed nine famous books of madrigals which are part songs sung by several singers, which are considered the pinnacle of Renaissance music.
2. Monteverdi composed one of the first operas called *La Favola d'Orfeo* (The Legend of Orpheus) in 1607. He is often called the "Father of Opera" for developing many of the musical and staging concepts.
3. Monteverdi developed the "*Secunda Pratica*" or Second Practice in music which revolutionized a new theory of melody and harmony which ushered in the Baroque Era in music.

BAROQUE COMPOSERS
(1600-1750)

FRANCESCA CACCINI (1587-C. 1638)

Francesca Caccini – (1587-c.1638). She was an **Italian Baroque** composer and singer of Florence, and the first woman known to have composed an opera. Francesca was the most prolific woman composer of her time. Francesca was the daughter of Renaissance/early Baroque composer Giulio Caccini (1551-1618). She was also a poet and played the **lute**, which is a plucked stringed instrument. She performed with her parents, her half-brother Pompeo and her sister Settimia, and other Caccini pupils, as the ensemble Le Donne di Guilio Romano.

Francesca Caccini was born on 8 September 1587 in Florence, Italy. Her father Giulio Caccini was a composer and taught her how to perform and compose music. She was also given a classical education in Latin, Greek, languages, and mathematics. Her opera *La Liberazione di Ruggiero d'al Isola d'Alcina*, is a comic-opera premiered on February 3, 1625 in Florence. The plot is an allegory about a good sorceress and an evil sorceress (Julie Anne Sadie, New Grove Women 1995). The *Liberation of Ruggiero* was the first Italian opera to be performed outside of Italy for carnival in Warsaw, Poland (1628). She wrote music for sixteen staged works, but only *La Liberazinone di Ruggiero* survived.

Francesca was also the chief musical ornament (and highest paid composer) at the Court of Tuscany under three Grand Dukes: Ferdinando I, Cosimo II, and Ferdinando II of the Medici family. She was nicknamed "La Cecchina" which is probably short for Francesca. When the consort of family singers organized by her father, Giulio Caccini, visited France in 1604, Henry IV said, "She is the best singer ever heard in France." He asked the Grand Duke to let her enter the service of the French court, but Ferdinando I would not let her go. Monteverdi heard her play three different instruments and sing in 1610, when he visited her father.

Giulio Caccini along with **Jacopo Peri**, who were members of the **Florentine Camerata**, are credited with inventing opera. They wanted to combine drama, music, painting,

dance and poetry into one genre. Francesca Caccini trained a whole school of singing disciples. She wrote five operas called *ballettos*, and a large volume of sacred and secular songs, set to her own poetry. Only one of her operas *La Liberazione di Ruggiero* and her *Primo Libro* of 1625 have survived ("Aria of the Shepherd" is from this opera). Her music shows influences of not only her father, but also Claudio Monteverdi and Jacopo Peri. She composed in the **recitative style** and included *canzonettas* in the style of the concerto *delle donne*. She wrote all the female parts of this opera in flat keys and all the male parts in sharp keys. There is a charming trio of recorders in this opera.

Francesca Caccini served the Medici court as a virtuoso singer, teacher, chamber singer, rehearsal coach and composer of both chamber and stage music until early 1627. She was the highest paid court singer of her time due to her beautiful voice. In 1618 Giulio published a collection of thirty-six of Francesca's vocal solos and soprano/bass duos in her *Il primo libro delle musiche*. She married Giovanni Battista Signorini. They had a daughter Margherita in 1622. After he passed away in 1626, she quickly got remarried to a nobleman in Lucca, Tommaso Raffaelli in 1627. They had a son who was also named Tommaso in 1628. Her second husband died in 1630, which left her a rich landowner. She tried to return immediately to the Medici court, but was delayed by the plagues of 1630-33. Francesca returned to court with her two children and became the teacher for her daughter Margherita and the Medici princesses. She also composed entertainment for the women's court at the Medici palace. Not much is known about the later part of her life. After 1641 she disappeared from the court records.

Title: Her opera *La liberazione di Ruggiero dall'isola d'Alcina* (*Eng.* The Liberation of Ruggiero from the island of Alcina) is a comic opera in four scenes, which was premiered in 1625. This opera talks about the relationship of women, weddings, and power. It features a good sorceress and an evil sorceress.

Genre: An **opera** is a large-scale staged vocal work with orchestral accompaniment.

YouTube: https://www.youtube.com/watch?v=WYfM65BSodA Pro Musica Camerata

Birthday: 8 September 1587 in Florence, Italy.

Death Date: After 1641 (probably 1645 in Florence, Italy) (aged approximately 58)

Fun Facts:

1. Francesca Caccini's opera was the first ever to be performed outside of Italy in Warsaw, Poland in 1628.
2. Francesca Caccini is the first woman known to have written an opera in 1625.
3. She performed with her parents and siblings as the ensemble known as "*Le Donne di Giulio Romano*". Her nickname was "*La Cecchina*".

ÉLISABETH JACQUET (1665-1729)

Elisabeth-Claude Jacquet de la Guerre – (**1665-1729**) was a **French Baroque** composer, and virtuoso harpsichordist (a **harpsichord** is an early keyboard instrument). Élisabeth Jacquet was born on 17 March 1665. She was celebrated at an early age for her brilliant improvisations. Élisabeth's family were noted harpsichord builders and musicians. Her father taught her how to sing and play harpsichord as well as the organ. She performed for Louis XIV, the Sun King, at an early age. At the age of ten, Élisabeth was mentioned as a prodigy in the July 1677 issue of the *Mercure galant* (J.A. Sadie, Grove Women). Later as a teenager, she enjoyed the king's continued protection at court. Her early education was supervised by the Marquise de Montespan, who was also in the king's court. Élisabeth dedicated most of her compositions to Louis XIV. She was married to the organist Marin de la Guerre on 23 September 1684.

Élizabeth Jacquet was remarkable in several ways. She wrote in almost every form then popular, and she was instrumental in introducing the new Italian style to France. One of her earliest works was the five-act opera *Céphale et Procris*, which was premiered at the Académie Royale de Musique on 15 March 1694 and published the same year. It was revived in 1989 with great success in France. Some of her early trio and solo sonatas, from around 1695, were the first to be composed in France. Jacquet de la Guerre was equally a pioneer in the new French

cantata. She wrote a **ballet** *Les jeux à l'Honneur de la Victoire* in 1685 (now lost), two books of biblical cantatas, three mythological cantatas, a set of six sonatas for violin, and fourteen movements for harpsichord solo. Her first book of harpsichord pieces was published in 1687 and is one of only a few harpsichord collections published in France in the 17th century. Jacquet's set of trio sonatas is one of the earliest French examples of the **sonata** (Cessac, Grove 2015).

Her only son and husband died in 1704. She decided to remain in Paris when the rest of the court moved to Versailles. She gave a series of concerts at her home to which many nobles came to hear her beautiful keyboard improvisation and fantasies. She also performed at the *Théâtre de la Foire and* composed one comic scene and some songs for them. Towards the end of her life she returned to composing vocal pieces. After her death in 1729, Jacquet's possessions included three harpsichords: a small one with black and white keys, one with black keys, and a large double manual Flemish harpsichord.

Title: *Cephale e Procris*, her opera *tragedie lyrique*, may have been begun as early as 1687, but was not staged until March 15, 1694. The plot centers on a pair of tragic lovers: Cephalus and his betrothed Procris. The gods decree that Boreus, Prince of Thrace is to be wedded to Procris. Cephalus engages him in a terrible battle. When Procris tries to separate them, she accidentally receives a fatal blow from Cephalus' sword. She dies in his arms with the words "Know you, that my last breath is a sigh of love."
Genre: An **opera** is a large-scale vocal work, with orchestral accompaniment.
YouTube Audio: https://www.youtube.com/watch?v=TOzeeL9PdvA
https://www.youtube.com/watch?v=3qzdpnAS7-k
https://www.youtube.com/watch?v=Di2Et3hKT1A
https://www.youtube.com/watch?v=uKKuRoRreu4 https://www.youtube.com/watch?v=30AuvKoI4to
https://www.youtube.com/watch?v=jVnowGcILB4
Four Seasons Orchestra, Carolyn Waters Broe conducting
Birthday: 17 March 1665, Paris.
Death Date: 27 June 1729, Paris (aged 64)
Fun Facts:
1. Elisabeth was a child prodigy and virtuoso harpsichordist (a keyboard instrument that came before the piano).
2. She was called "the marvel of our century," and favored by Louis XIV (the fourteenth).
3. After her death he struck a commemorative medal in her honor in 1729. It was stamped with her portrait and the words, "I contended with the greatest of musicians." (Library of Congress, Who Was She?)

ANTONIO VIVALDI (1678-1741)

ntonio Lucio Vivaldi – (c. 1678-1741), who is known as the 'Red Priest', was a famous **Italian Baroque** violinist, composer, and cleric. He was born on 4 March 1678 in Venice the day of an earthquake. His father, Giovanni Battista Vivaldi, was a barber, wig maker, and a respected violinist. His mother was Camilla Calicchio, and he had eight brothers and sisters. Vivaldi was one of the most famous and prolific composers of the Baroque era. He wrote over 700 **concertos**, which are mostly for solo violin, or for two solo instruments. Fifty of these works are *sinfonia* concertos for chamber orchestra or strings without any soloist. The *Four Seasons Concertos* are his most famous violin solos. These four concertos are from his *Opus 8* (1725) and show off a variety of colors and textures. They are based on a poem; which Vivaldi may have written himself.

Vivaldi was also regarded as a **virtuoso** violinist. In 1707 Vivaldi was asked by Prince Ercolani, the Ambassador to Venice from Austria, to compete in a violin competition with Giovanni Rueta at his palace in Venice, as an entertainment for some of his guests at a party. Rueta was the official violinist of His Majesty the Emperor and known to be the finest violinist in all of Europe. The audience decided the winner with their applause. Vivaldi amazed the audience and won the competition with Rueta.

As a child, Antonio may have suffered from asthma (a breathing disorder). This may be why the midwife baptized him immediately at birth. He had trouble breathing and was sick much of the time. His father taught Vivaldi how to play the violin at an early age, and they toured around Venice performing. Vivaldi may have studied composing with Giovanni Legrenzi, who was the choir master at St. Mark's Basilica in Venice. It is also possible that his father taught him to compose, as there is an opera listed under Giovanni Battista Rossi, the name Vivaldi's father chose when he joined the Sovvegno di Santa Cecilia.

Antonio Vivaldi started studying for the priesthood at the age of fifteen. He was ordained as a Catholic priest in 1703 at age twenty-five. Vivaldi was a teacher of violin, director of concerts, and choirmaster at a girl's orphanage called the *Seminario Musicale dell' Ospitale della Pietà* in Venice from 1703 to 1715, and again from 1723 to 1740. This was a combination of an orphanage, a musical conservatory for girls, a nunnery, and a convent school. Many of the girls in Vivaldi's orchestra were the abandoned children of wealthy Italian merchants. They were brought up by the state and trained solely to excel in music. Venice boasted four of these schools in all.

The virtuosity of Vivaldi's orchestral works implies that many of these female musicians had achieved tremendous mastery of their instruments. The French jurist Charles de Brosses wrote of this orchestra,

> "The transcendent music is that of the asylums...they sing like angels and play the violin, the flute, the organ, the oboe, the cello, and the bassoon; in short, there is no instrument, however unwieldy, that can frighten them. It is they alone who perform, and about forty girls take part in each concert...There is nothing like the sight of a young and pretty nun in a white habit, with a bunch of pomegranate blossoms over her ear, conducting the orchestra and beating time with all the grace and precision imaginable." (Robbins Landon, 1996)

However, Vivaldi's relationship with the board of the school was strained due to his frequent travels. They had to vote to keep a teacher every year and voted him out in 1709. After one year, the board realized their mistake, and gave him a unanimous vote to come back in 1711. He was responsible for composing numerous concertos for the music school. He published his *Opus 1* in 1705, a collection of twelve sonatas for two violins and basso continuo, and a second set for the same instruments in 1709. His Opus 3, *L'estro armónico* is a set of twelve concerti for one, two, and four violins and strings. This collection was published in 1711 in Amsterdam and was a huge success in Europe. His Opus 4, *La stravaganza* is a collection of concerti for solo violin and strings published in 1714.

Vivaldi was offered a position as the *Maestro di cappella* (choir master) at the prestigious court of prince Philip of Hesse-Darmstadt, governor of Mantua in 1717 or 1718. So, he moved to Mantua and composed three operas. During this time, he composed his famous *Four Seasons Concertos*. So, his inspiration may have been the countryside of Mantua. They were published in his Opus 8, *Il cimento dell'armonia e dell'inventione,* in 1725 as the first four concertos in a collection of twelve, in Amsterdam by Michel-Charles Le Cène. The *Four Seasons Concertos* are programmatic works depicting streams, singing birds, barking dogs, buzzing mosquitoes, calling shepherds, storms, dancers, hunting parties, silent nights, frozen landscapes, ice-skating children, and warm winter fires. He also met the young singer Anna Tessieri Girò in Mantua, who became his student, and his favorite *prima donna* (leading lady singer). In 1722 he moved to Rome and was invited to play violin for Pope Benedict XIII. After this time, he composed four more operas.

Vivaldi claimed to have composed 90 operas, but it was probably closer to 40. Many of them were staged at the Theater St. Angelo in Venice where he was an impresario. His *Four Seasons Concertos* were the rage in Europe. Many nobles and royalty commissioned Vivaldi to write music, including King Louis the XV of France through the French Ambassador to Venice. Vivaldi's Opus 9, *La cetra,* was dedicated to Emperor Charles VI of Bavaria. In 1728. The Emperor was so impressed with Vivaldi's music, that he made him a knight, gave him a gold medal, and invited him to Vienna. Vivaldi traveled to Vienna and Prague in 1730 with his father. He staged his opera *Farnace* there to great success. Later, Vivaldi decided to return to Vienna, possibly to stage more operas. Unfortunately, the Emperor died from poisoned mushrooms shortly after Vivaldi arrived. This left him without income or royal patronage. Soon after he died in poverty from stomach ailments, in the home of a widow near Vienna on 28 July 1741. Vivaldi's name disappeared from history until the late 19th century when his name was rediscovered on some of Johann Sebastian Bach's manuscripts. Vivaldi's music was finally recognized through the work of musicologists such as Marc Pincherle and the British poet Ezra Pound in the 20th century. Today Vivaldi's music is performed and recorded world-wide by the finest orchestras and soloists.

Dr. Carolyn Waters Broe

Title: The *Four Seasons Concerto* No. 1 in E major, Op. 8, RV 267, *"La Primavera"* (Spring) for solo violin, strings, and harpsichord (an early keyboard instrument). Listen for the chirping of various birds in this concerto, and the dancing of peasants.

Genre: Concerto: an orchestral piece for a solo instrument(s) and a larger group of musicians that accompany the soloist. Concertos are usually three movements long.

YouTube: Four Seasons Orchestra – Audrey Wang violinist

Spring Movement I Allegro: https://www.youtube.com/watch?v=Kr4U8UeGjV0

Spring Movement II Largo e pianissimo sempre: https://www.youtube.com/ watch?v=V26xnxJjFtQ

Spring Movement III Danza Pastorale: https://www.youtube.com/ watch?v=89UwRIrAIRA

Birthday: 4 March 1678 in Venice.

Death Date: 28 July 1741 in Bavaria (age 63).

Fun Facts:

1. Vivaldi was known as "The Red Priest" because he had red hair.
2. Vivaldi was born the day of an earthquake in Venice, and he was not expected to live. So, they baptized him immediately on 4 March 1678.
3. Vivaldi had asthma which prevented him from saying mass. He was often ill and had to be carried around Venice in a litter, which was carried by two men.
4. Vivaldi was commissioned to write a wedding piece for King Louis XV through the French Ambassador to Venice. He performed for Pope Benedict XIII in Rome, and he was knighted by Emperor Charles VI of Bavaria. Some scholars believe that Antonio Vivaldi was also a spy, and that he was murdered for this.
5. **Opera in Venice** could get a bit rough in the 18th century. Vivaldi was one of several theater managers and composers. A soprano of another theater in Venice broke her contract. That manager decided to have her thrown into the canal. Several of the theaters burned down due to the use of candles as stage lighting. Many of the patrons, who sat in the balcony liked to eat oranges, and spit the seeds down on the wealthier patrons, who were standing in the orchestra section on the floor of the theater. Many of the audience members were eating and talking during the performance. People who could afford a box seat ordered lavish catered dinners, while they were listening to the opera. If they liked a particular aria, they would demand that the soloist sing it over and over. Venetians would come to an opera every night, while it was being performed, even if it ran for six weeks. This was the way they socialized and did business in Venice.

GEORG FRIEDRICH HÄNDEL (1685-1759)

eorg Friedrich Händel – (1685-1759) was a **German,** and later **British Baroque** composer, who became famous for his operas, oratorios, anthems, and organ concertos. He was born on 23 February 1685 in Halle, Duchy of Magdeburg, to Georg Händel and Dorothea Taust. His father was a barber and surgeon, who served the court of Saxe-Weissenfels and the Margrave of Brandenburg. Friedrich's father wanted him to go into Civil Law. So, when it was discovered that Friedrich had a strong ability in music, his father strictly forbade him to study any musical instrument. He even refused to let him go to school as music was a primary part of learning there.

There is a story about the young Händel, that he found a way to get a little clavichord (keyboard instrument) up to the attic room on the top floor of his house. Then he secretly stole up to this room to practice when the rest of the family was asleep. The heavy timber in the attic helped to silence his music. His mother encouraged Friedrich to become good at music and said, "Here my little boy can play the harpsichord to his heart's content and no one will be the wiser." (Hawkins 1776). So, he became very skilled at the keyboard. You can imagine his father's surprise when he stalked into the attic, followed by the family, and found Friedrich playing so beautifully.

Later, when Friedrich was seven, his father was going on a trip to Weissenfels to visit a family member, who was a valet to the Duke Johann Adolf I. Georg Friedrich begged to go along, but his father said he was too young. So, when he started the journey, Friedrich ran after his carriage until he let him come along. When they arrived at the castle, the young Händel was lifted onto an organ's stool, where he surprised everyone with his keyboard playing. This performance helped Handel and the Duke to convince his father to allow him to take lessons in musical composition and keyboard. The Duke said, "The world should have the good of your son's great ability" (Schoelcher 1857). So, he was sent to study with Friedrich Wilhelm Zachau (Zachow), the organist of Halle's Marienkirche (cathedral). Händel learned to play organ, violin, oboe and harpsichord. One day Zachau said, "The boy knows more than I do." So, at the age of eleven, he was sent to Berlin to study with other teachers. He also studied in Hamburg and Italy before leaving for London, England. In 1710, Händel became **Kapellmeister** (conductor) to German prince George, the Elector of Hanover. Prince George wanted Handel to stay in Germany, but Händel insisted on moving to England in 1712. As fate would have it, Prince George would become King George I of Great Britain and Ireland in 1714 and moved to England. Händel wanted to convince the King to hire him on as his court composer in England. So, he composed a special piece for his coronation called the *Water Music Suite*. This set of twenty-five pieces was performed by the court musicians on a boat that followed the king's boat on the Thames River (pronounced *Tems*) after the coronation. The king wanted to know who composed this music and invited Händel onto his boat. With this work, Händel won the king's favor again.

Händel also wrote famous pieces for King George II such as the *Music for the Royal Fireworks*. It was composed to celebrate the end of the War of the Austrian Succession and the signing of the Treaty of Aix-la-Chapelle (Aachen) in 1748. King George II preferred drums and military wind instruments, so there were no strings. Handel sold tickets to the rehearsal at half a crown as a benefit concert. There was a three-hour traffic jam of carriages on London Bridge when Händel was rehearsing this piece in London's Green Park as people rushed to hear it in 1749. 12,000 people attended the first performance of the *Music for the Royal Fireworks*. 101 cannons were used for this event. It is said that when the fireworks started, the right stage caught fire and all the musicians had to scramble to safety. Several audience members and soldiers were hurt by stray rockets that were flying around wildly.

During his life Händel composed over forty operas, twenty-three organ concertos, and twenty-eight oratorios as well as many other pieces. *The Messiah* is Händel's most famous **oratorio**. At the first performance in 1742, the king rose at the words "For the Lord God Omnipotent Reigneth." Ever after that it became a custom for people to rise during the "Hallelujah Chorus". Händel became a naturalized British subject in 1727. He loved children and conducted *The Messiah* for a benefit concert for a children's hospital, donating large sums of money at that event. At the end of his life, he became blind, but he could still play the organ beautifully. His last performance was conducting *The Messiah*. A few days later, on Good Friday, 14 April 1759, he passed away. The English people loved him so much, that they buried him in Westminster Abbey.

Title: *The Messiah* "Hallelujah Chorus" was written for SATB chorus, vocal soloists and orchestra. For the first performance, the small orchestra included strings,
two trumpets, timpani, organ and harpsichord continuo. Händel added more instruments (oboes and bassoons) for later performances.

Genre: An **Oratorio** is a musical work for chorus and orchestra based on Biblical texts.

YouTube: https://www.youtube.com/watch?v=71NCzuDNUcg London Philharmonic (complete full concerto)

Birthday: 23 February 1685

Death Date: 14 April 1759 (age 74)

Fun Facts:

1. Händel was the boy who practiced in the attic.
2. The *Water Music Suite* was performed by musicians on a boat floating down the Thames River as part of the King George II's coronation celebrations.
3. When the *Music for the Royal Fireworks* was first performed, the stage caught fire. There was also a three-hour traffic jam of carriages on London Bridge when Händel was rehearsing this piece in a nearby park as people rushed to hear it.
4. In 1704 Händel got into an argument with another composer (and friend), Johann Mattheson, over which musician had the right to play the *continuo* part in the pit orchestra of an opera. A duel ensued, and Mattheson won. Handel's life was spared when the large button on his coat broke the nearly fatal blow from Mattheson's sword.

THE BACH FAMILY

JOHANN SEBASTIAN BACH (1685-1750)

ohann Sebastian Bach – (1685-1750), was a **German Baroque** composer. Bach was much more famous during his life as an **organist**, than he was as a composer. Most people do not know that he was also an excellent violinist, violist, harpsichordist, and singer. He was born on 21 March 1685 in the town of Eisenach, Germany where his father, Johann Ambrosius Bach, was a court musician in Eisenach and a director of musicians. His mother was Maria Elisabeth Lämmerhirt daughter of a furrier. He was the last of eight children born in a family with a long history of musicians. He attended the same Latin school that Martin Luther had gone to. Johann had an exceptionally fine soprano voice as a boy, so at the age of eight he was admitted into a choir for

poor boys in Lüneburg (Christoph Wolff 1985). His father taught him how to play violin and harpsichord, and his uncle taught him to play the organ. His family was so poor, that Johann, sang in the streets as a boy, begging for money.

Johann's parents passed away when he was only ten years old, so he went to live with his older brother Johann Christoph Bach, who was the organist at the church of St. Michael's in Ohrdruf. His brother taught him how to play the music of the great German, French and Italian composers on the organ and clavichord. Johann Sebastian loved to practice all day long on his keyboard. His brother became concerned and decided to lock up the music in a cupboard. But Johann Sebastian was clever, and he secretly copied all his music books. Then when his brother was out working, he could practice all day again. He may have learned how to compose in this way.

In 1700, Johann Sebastian Bach was accepted into the prestigious St. Michael's School in Lüneburg, Germany for choir boys. It was there that he was exposed to a wider selection of European music and culture. In January of 1703 Bach took his first job as a **violist** and servant at the court of Duke Johann Ernst III of Weimar (Blume 1968, pg. 15). His reputation as a brilliant organist soon spread. During Bach's lifetime, he held five important musical posts: Arnstadt (1703-1707), Mülhausen (1707-1708), Weimar (1708-1717), Cöthen (1717-1723), and Leipzig (1723-1750) (Broe 1984, pg. 83). In August 1703, Bach accepted the position of organist at the New Church of Arnstadt. Later, the church elders became unhappy with Bach for leaving on a long journey to hear the great organist and composer Dieterich Buxtehude without permission. So, in 1707, Bach took a post as organist at the Blasius Church in Mühlhausen. There he married his second Cousin Maria Barbara Bach.

In 1708, he returned to the court at Weimar, and was promoted to the role of *Konzertmeister* (Principal First Violinist and Director of Music) in 1714. However, in 1717, when the previous *Kapellmeister* (Conductor) passed away, Bach applied for the job. He was furious when the Duke gave the position to his nephew. Bach stormed out of the court, but Duke Johann Ernst had him arrested. He was put into jail for almost a month, and spent the time writing his *Well-Tempered Klavier* books. Afterwards, Bach left to accept another post as the *Kapellmeister* for Prince Leopold of Anhalt-Köthen. He was incredibly happy and wrote many of his most famous concertos and chamber music works there. His first wife died suddenly in 1720 while he was away. A year later he married Anna Magdalena Wilcke, who was a very gifted soprano at the Court of Köthen. Between his two wives, Bach had a total of twenty children. Many of them died in infancy. However, four of his sons became famous composers.

Bach took his last post at the St. Thomas Church in Leipzig in 1723, where he was the **cantor**, and taught both math and Latin to boys at the Thomasschule. It was there that he composed most of his famous **cantatas** (of over 200 cantatas), vocal works like his *Magnificat*, the *B Minor Mass*, and his two famous passions. There is evidence that Bach may have written as many as fifty concerti, unfortunately only a few of these masterworks have survived. Bach's concerto legacy includes: *The Six Brandenburg Concertos*, fifteen harpsichord concertos that he revised from earlier violin (and possibly viola) concertos, the four violin concertos, and the *Concerto for Two Violins and Orchestra in D Minor*. He also composed *Six Cello Suites*, and his *Three Sonatas and Partitas for Violin*.

It is very curious that there are no surviving organ concertos by Bach considering he was the most famous organist in Germany. If he did compose any, they are now lost. Some of his cantatas have extensive organ solos however, and he wrote pieces like the *Toccata and Fugue in D Minor* and the *Chromatic Fantasy*. Bach was a master of the art of the **fugue**, which is a complex imitative contrapuntal form of composition. Bach invented the **keyboard concerto** with his "*Brandenburg Concerto No. 5*". The violin was king during the Baroque era, so it makes sense that he wrote so many of these works. The piano was still in its infancy when Bach was very old. He traveled by stagecoach to play on one but found it extremely lacking. After years of composing and copying music by candlelight, Bach was becoming blind towards the end of his life. Unfortunately, two eye surgeries failed. Johann Sebastian Bach died on July 28th, 1750 in Leipzig at the age of sixty-five.

50 Famous Composers

Title: *Toccata and Fugue for organ in D Minor* by J .S . Bach

Genre: Solo keyboard toccata and **fugue.**

YouTube: https://www.youtube.com/watch?v=Nnuq9PXbywA
Hans-André Stamm the Trost-Organ of the Stadtkirche in Waltershausen, Germany

Birthday: 21 March 1685 in Eisenach, Germany near Wartburg Castle (Christoph Wolff, The New Grove Bach Family 1985). Some scholars say his birthday was 31 March 1685.

Death Date: 28 July 1750 in Leipzig, Germany (aged 65).

Fun Facts:

1. Johann Sebastian Bach was the inventor of the keyboard concerto with his "Brandenburg Concerto No. 5".

2. In 1705 J.S. Bach walked 280 miles from Arnstadt to Lübeck to hear the famous organist Dieterich Buxtehude and take four months of lessons from him. Bach hoped to succeed Buxtehude as the organist at Lübeck, but marrying one of his five daughters came with the deal, so Bach declined.

3. When J.S. Bach was hired to be the organist at Arnstadt, he did not know he was supposed to teach a student choir and orchestra. One day the twenty-year-old Bach got so mad at a bassoonist, who kept making mistakes, that he called him a "*Zippelfagottist*" or "Nanny-goat bassoonist". These were fighting words, so Greyersbach the bassoonist came after Bach with a walking stick. Bach pulled out his sword and the fight became so heated that the two had to be pulled apart by other students (Cultural Cocktail Hour 2010). Bach had to go to court over this insult and lost to the bassoonist. He was told he must tolerate less talented musicians. Later, he threw his wig at a musician.

4. Bach was arrested and thrown in jail for a month of house arrest for breach of contract by the Duke of Weimar when he was passed up to be the Conductor of the court orchestra. He spent the time composing the *Well-Tempered Klavier* books.

5. In 1894, a skeleton that was presumed to be that of J.S. Bach was exhumed for examination from the graveyard of *St. Johanniskirche* in Leipzig, but the authenticity has never been fully established. The skeleton was reburied 55 years later in 1949 at *St. Thomaskirche* in Leipzig where he was the canto. More recently Andreas Otte, who is an anatomist and musician, examined a photograph believed to be of Bach's skeleton, and determined that he had exceptionally long fingers that would have been excellent for playing keyboards. Bach's fingers were 8 ½ inches from wrist to fingertips, with a reach of 10 ¼ inches (Ines Bellinger 2019). That is a 12th on the keyboard (the distance between 12 white keys).

WILHELM FRIEDEMANN BACH (1710-1784)

Wilhelm Friedemann Bach – (1710-1784) **German** composer and organist. The eldest son of Johann Sebastian Bach and Maria Barbara, Wilhelm followed in his father's footsteps becoming a genius composer. His father wrote a graded course of keyboard studies for Wilhelm entitled the *Klavierbüchlein für Wilhelm Friedemann Bach*. Thanks to this intensive musical training, he went on to become an organist and taught none other than Johann Gottlieb Goldberg, the man whose name is immortalized in the great J.S. Bach's *Goldberg Variations*. His family called him Friedemann. He had nineteen brothers and sisters, but not all of them survived infancy. He was the first of J.S Bach's five musical sons.

Friedemann was born 22 November 1710 in Weimar at the Court of the Duke of Saxe-Weimar, where his father served as the court organist and chamber musician. In 1720 his mother died suddenly when he was only nine, while his father was under house arrest for breaking his contract with the Duke. In 1721 his father remarried and began training his son in keyboard and composition. His father taught Friedemann how to play the organ by giving him a graded book of studies. His education included the first book of his father's *Well-Tempered Clavier*, his *Two and Three-part Inventions*, *French Suites*, and J.S. Bach's *Six Trio Sonatas for Organ*. Friedemann also learned to play the violin at the age of sixteen by going to Merseburg and taking lessons from Johann Gottlieb Graun. He received a formal education starting in Weimar. When his father took the post of Cantor at the St. Thomas Church in Leipzig in 1723,

Friedemann attended the *Thomasschule*, which was part of the church. After graduating in 1729, he went on to study law at the Leipzig University. Later, he studied law and mathematics at the University of Halle, even though he decided to become a musician. His love of mathematics continued the rest of his life.

Friedemann Bach competed for his first post as the organist at St. Sophia's Church in Dresden by performing his father's *"Prelude and Fugue in G Major"* BWV 541. The judges were impressed by Friedemann's brilliant organ playing, and said he was far superior to the other two candidates. He became a renowned organist and taught many important students. One of those students was Johann Gottlieb Goldberg, the keyboard player whose name was mistakenly attached to Johann Sebastian Bach's *"Aria with Diverse Variations"* of 1742. They were nicknamed the *"Goldberg Variations"* after Goldberg told a story that J.S. Bach composed and performed them for a Russian Ambassador to help him fall asleep. The truth is that J.S. Bach composed them for Friedemann Bach as a virtuoso piece to show off his talent as a keyboard artist. He was brilliant at improvising on musical themes.

In 1746 Friedemann became organist of the *Liebfrauenkirche* at Halle. In 1751, Friedemann Bach married Dorothea Elisabeth Georgi (1721-1791), who was the daughter of a tax collector. She was 11 years his junior and who outlived him by seven years. The taxes from estates that she inherited from her father became a terrible problem for the couple. They had three children, but only one survived infancy. Unfortunately, Friedemann was unhappy at his post in Halle and quit almost immediately. The Cantor of the church cheated him out of money he had earned. The church authorities also reprimanded him in 1750 when he overstayed his leave trying to settle his father's estate in Leipzig. He tried several times to gain another post but failed. He suffered from a changing society in which it became more difficult for a virtuoso organist to gain employment at a church or court position.

Friedemann Bach gained a position as the *Kapellmeister* at the Court of Darmstadt in 1762 but for unknown reasons declined almost immediately. Then he was appointed the *Hofkapellmeister* at Hessen-Darmstadt. Yet, almost as soon as he left his post at Halle, he lost the job in Darmstadt. His finances soon deteriorated.

It is possible that his personality made it difficult for Friedemann to gain or stay employed. He was also unwilling to compose fashionable music that was easy for other people to perform. However, he did increase his output of compositions in both Halle and Dresden. He composed keyboard sonatas, fantasias, cantatas, fugues, and polonaises for the clavier. His style was much more contrapuntal than his two younger brothers. He also composed church cantatas and instrumental works such as the flute duets and the viola duets. He also composed numerous symphonies.

Friedemann Bach moved to Berlin in 1774 where he was hired at the Court of the Princess Anna Amalia (the sister of Frederic the Great). However, he soon lost favor with that court, and began giving keyboard lessons to various students. He gave harpsichord lessons to Sarah Itzig Levy who was the daughter of a prominent Jewish family in Berlin. She was an avid collector of Johann Sebastian Bach's music and other 18th century composers. She was also the great aunt of the composer Felix Mendelssohn. One of Friedemann's students included Johann Nikolas Forkel, who became the first biographer of Johann Sebastian Bach (Forkle 1802). Friedemann Bach also taught Fredric Wilhelm Rust and Johann Samuel Petri who both became famous musicians. Friedeman Bach died in Berlin at the age of seventy-three. He died in poverty.

There are some scholars who say that Friedemann Bach was an extremely poor keeper of his share of his father's music manuscripts. It is thought that he may have passed off several of his father's works as his own, but that was typical for the time. He also sold many of them to Johann Georg Nacke in 1759 to pay debts. Unfortunately, Nacke's daughter later moved to America, and accidentally destroyed some of J.S. Bach's music. Yet many of the Bach family manuscripts were preserved by two composers, Carl Friedrich Christian Fasch and his student Carl Friedrich Zelter, who was the teacher of composers Felix and Fanny Mendelssohn. These scores of J.S. Bach were placed in the library of the Sing-Akademie in Berlin, which was founded in 1791 by Fasch and continued by Zelter in 1800. Princess Anna Amalia donated her collection of scores by Johann Sebastian Bach to the Berlin State Library where they were preserved.

Title: *Harpsichord Concerto in D*, Fk. 41. This early keyboard concerto is accompanied by strings.

Genre: The solo **keyboard concerto** was a new genre when Friedemann Bach composed his two harpsichord concertos. His father J.S. Bach invented this genre.

YouTube: Wilhelm Friedemann Bach's Harpsichord Concerto in D, Fk. 41 https://www.youtube.com/watch?v=cqWdwVFgV-o

Pavao Mašić, harpsichord with the Varaždin Chamber Orchestra (violin solo: Dunja Bontek)

Birthday: 22 November 1710 in Weimar.

Death Date: 1 July 1784 in Berlin (aged 73).

Fun Facts:

1. He was the first of five musical sons of Johann Sebastian Bach out of a family of twenty children with two wives (they did not all live together though as half of his children did not survive infancy or the age of four).
2. Late in his life, he was one of the first self-employed musicians.
3. Wilhelm Friedemann Bach was given unfair treatment by his early biographers. They tended to treat him as the "wayward sheep" of the family when he was really a very honest man.

CLASSICAL COMPOSERS
Bach Family Continued
(1750-1820)

CARL PHILIPP EMANUEL BACH (1714-1788)

Carl Philipp Emanuel Bach – (1714-1788) was a **German Classical** composer and keyboard artist. When Johann Sebastian Bach is your father and Georg Philipp Telemann is your godfather, you are bound to have a very musical upbringing.

C.P.E Bach went on to become a famous composer in his own right, building on the Baroque training he learned as a boy. He developed his skills to become one of the foremost *clavier* players in Europe after studying for a degree in law. He is known as the "Berlin Bach" and later as the "Hamburg Bach" when he succeeded Georg Philipp Telemann as the *Kapellmeister* there. His second name comes from Telemann. C.P.E. Bach's music was dramatic and emotional,

so it is known as the "sensitive style". That is because he fused rhetoric and drama into the structure of his music. His music was very influential in making the transition between his father's Baroque music to the Classical and later Romantic era music. He was one of four of J.S. Bach's children who became a professional musician.

Carl Philipp Emanuel Bach was born on 8 March 1714 at the Court of Weimar, Germany where his father worked. He was the fifth child and second surviving son of Johann Sebastian Bach and Maria Barbara Bach. His father trained him in music composition and how to play various instruments. At the age of ten Emanuel, as his family and friends called him, entered the St. Thomas School in Leipzig where his father started working in 1723. Johann Sebastian Bach knew that it was important for his sons to get a higher education, so that they would not be treated as servants when they became professional musicians. Therefore, C.P.E. Bach and his brothers all studied law. Emanuel went to the University of Leipzig in 1731 and later attended Frankfurt-on-the-Oder in 1735. He received his degree at the age of twenty-four, but

never practiced law. Instead, he decided to become a musician.

Carl Philipp Emanuel Bach was one of the most famous clavier players in all of Europe. A **clavier** is a name for several keyboard instruments which came before the piano including the *harpsichord*, clavichord, and fortepiano. He had already written thirty works for harpsichord and clavier. C.P.E. Bach was able to get an appointment at Berlin to Frederick the Crown Prince of Prussia with the recommendations of the Graun brothers (Carl Heinrich and Johann Gottlieb). The prince would later become Frederick the Great of Prussia (which is now part of Germany). When Frederick became the king in 1740, C.P. E. Bach became a member of his royal orchestra. During his Berlin years (1738-68), Carl met with many important musicians at the Berlin court, including some of his father's former students. Frederick was extremely fond of the flute. So C.P.E. Bach composed his two famous collections of *Flute Sonatas*, the first for Frederick the Great in 1742 and the second for Charles Eugene, Duke of Württemberg in 1744. Bach married Johanna Maria Dannemann in 1744. Only three of their children lived to adulthood. C.P.E. Bach was promoted to the position of chamber musician in 1746. He worked with other renowned composers and musicians such as Johann Joachim Quantz, Carl Heinrich Graun and Franz Benda.

C.P. E. Bach was a prolific composer of keyboard concertos as well as two hundred sonatas and other solo pieces for keyboard. He composed several character pieces for solo keyboard called the "*Berlin Portraits*" such as "*La Caroline*". Bach also wrote an important treatise called *An Essay on The True Art of Playing Keyboard Instruments*. He composed three cello concertos and three quartets for flute, viola, cello, and clavier. C.P.E. Bach wrote one of the earliest solo works for flute after his father's style. He composed several symphonies for orchestra, which are early string works in the Classical style, which were later updated by adding wind instruments. C.P.E.

Bach's choral works include his *Magnificat in D*, an *Easter Cantata*, and various secular cantatas, twenty-one passions, and three volumes of songs. His *Resurrection and Ascension of Jesus* (1774-1782), on the poetic gospel harmonization of Karl Wilhelm Ramler, was given three performances in Vienna with Mozart conducting. One of his most famous vocal works is *Die Israeliten in der Wüste* ('The Israelites in the Wilderness'). He also composed music for mechanical devices such as clocks and music boxes, which were popular in Prussia at the time.

C.P.E. Bach's music composition was influenced by his father, but his style was influenced by his godfather Georg Philipp Telemann as well as George Frederic Handel, Joseph Haydn, and Carl Heinrich Graun. In turn, C.P.E. Bach influenced important Classical composers such as Haydn, Mozart, Beethoven, and Felix Mendelssohn. C.P.E. Bach's style is difficult to classify. His music has elements of the Gallant style, the Baroque, and *Sturm und Drang* (Storm and Stress) style.

C.P.E. Bach's Hamburg years (1768-1788) started when he was finally allowed to go to Hamburg to fill his godfather Telemann's role as the director of music *Kapellmeister* after long negotiations. He became the composer to Frederick's sister Princess Anna Amalia. Her patronage and love of the oratorio encouraged him to compose many large-scale choral works in her honor including twenty-one settings of the passion. Bach composed a set of six string symphonies in Hamburg that were in a difficult style. Later he wrote an important set of four symphonic works which included wind instruments in the Classical style. C.P.E. Bach died at the age of seventy-four. He was buried in the Church of St. Michael in Hamburg.

Title: C.P.E. Bach / *Cello Concerto in A minor*, Wq. 170 (H. 432). This concerto is for solo cello, strings, and basso continuo.
Genre: A **Cello concerto** is a work for solo cello with orchestra. Solo concertos are usually in three movements.
YouTube: https://www.youtube.com/watch?v=-tzLguU_2Dg
C.P.E. Bach / Cello Concerto in A minor, Wq. 170 (H. 432).
I. Allegro assai; II. Andante; III. Allegro assai. Cello soloist – Peter Bruns
Akademie für Alte Musik Berlin (2001)
Birthday: 8 March 1714 in Weimar, Germany
Death Date: 14 December 1788 in Hamburg, Germany (aged 74)

50 Famous Composers

Fun Facts:

1. C.P.E. Bach is known as the "Berlin Bach" as well as the "Hamburg Bach" to distinguish him from his younger brother, Johann Christian Bach, who was called the "London Bach".
2. He was one of the main composers to create the Classical era style.
3. Mozart said about C.P.E. Bach "He is the father; we are the children".
4. He was one of four sons of Johann Sebastian Bach who became a composer.
5. C.P.E Bach was extremely popular during his life, and for a short time afterwards.

JOHANN CHRISTOPH FRIEDRICH BACH (1732-1795)

Johann Christoph Friedrich Bach was a **German Classical** composer and harpsichordist. He was the fifth son and sixteenth child of Johann Sebastian Bach and is often referred to as the "Bückeburg Bach". He was born on 21 June 1732 in Leipzig in the Electorate of Saxony. His mother was Anna Magdalena Bach who was a singer. His father taught him how to compose and play organ and harpsichord. He was also taught music by his distant cousin Johann Elias Bach who lived with the Bach family. Johann Christoph studied at the St. Thomas School where his father taught. He also studied law but had to quit at seventeen when he was offered a job in music shortly before his father died.

In 1750 Johann Christoph Bach was appointed as the court harpsichordist for William, Count of Schaumburg-Lippe in Bückeburg. He became the Concertmaster of the Count's orchestra in 1759. Johann Christoph was an extremely prolific composer. While he was at the Bückeburg court J.C.F. Bach collaborated with Johann Gottfried Herder who provided the texts for six vocal works, of which only four have survived. He composed many other vocal works including operas, eight oratorios, motets, Liturgical choral works, and songs. Johann Christoph also composed twenty-eight symphonies, fourteen keyboard concertos, a concerto for piano and viola, a concerto for piano and oboe, six flute quartets, six string quartets, forty-three keyboard sonatas, ten flute sonatas, three violin sonatas, a cello sonata, numerous trios and other chamber music works. Due to Count William's love of Italian music, J.C.F. Bach had to adjust his style to suit his employer, but he still retained much of his style from his father and his older brother C.P.E. Bach. He was also profoundly influenced by his younger brother J.C. Bach's operas and symphonies after visiting him in London.

In 1755 Johann Christoph married the singer Lucia Elisabeth Münchhausen (1728-1803). They named their son Wilhelm Friedrich Ernst Bach, who was the only grandson of Johann Sebastian Bach to gain fame as a composer. His grandson said later "Heredity can tend to run out of ideas". (Wikipedia 2020) W.F.E. Bach became music director to Frederick William II of Prussia and is believed to be the last famous composer of the Bach family. In 1778 Johann Christoph traveled to London with his son to visit his younger brother Johann Christian Bach. J.C.F. Bach died in Bückeburg 26 January 1795, aged 62. Unfortunately, Johann Christoph Friedrich is the least well known of Johann Sebastian's four famous sons even though he left us with a wealth of Classical music compositions.

Title: Johann Christoph Friedrich Bach *Piano Concerto E Major*
Genre: A **piano concerto** is a work for solo piano and orchestra. The piano concerto made its first appearance in the Classical era. It became one of the most popular musical genres ever.
YouTube: https://www.youtube.com/watch?v=6HW7oE-PBj0 Cyprien Katsaris piano soloist.
Birthday: 21 June 1732 in Leipzig
Death Date: 26 January 1795 in Bückeburg (aged 62)
Fun Facts:
1. Johann Christoph Friedrich Bach is known as the "Bückeburg Bach" because he lived and worked at the court of this small principality in Saxony.
2. J.C.F. Bach was an extremely prolific composer; however, he is the least well known of the four famous sons of Johann Sebastian Bach, who became composers.
3. J.C.F. Bach composed twenty-eight symphonies, fourteen keyboard concertos, eight oratorios, and forty-three keyboard sonatas among many other works.

JOHANN CHRISTIAN BACH (1735-1782)

Johann Christian Bach – (1735-1782) was the eighteenth child and the youngest of Johann Sebastian Bach's eleven sons. His mother was Anna Magdalena Bach. Johann Christian was an excellent **German** composer of **Classical** music. J. C. Bach is also known as the "London Bach" or the "English Bach" because of the time that he spent composing and performing in Britain. He is also credited with influencing Mozart on the concerto style. His style differs greatly from his father even though he composed in many of the same genres.

J.C. Bach was born 5 September 1735 in Leipzig when his famous father was 50 years old and teaching at the St. Thomas School. Johann Sebastian taught his son music and composition until his death in 1750. After that Johann Christian went to live with his older half-brother Carl Philipp Emanuel Bach, who continued his musical training. C.P.E. Bach was the most gifted of Johann Sebastian's sons and twenty-one years older than J.C. Bach.

Johann Christian moved to Italy in 1754 to study with Padre Martini in the city of Bologna. He became the church organist at the Milan Cathedral in 1760. He converted from the Lutheran faith to the Catholic faith and composed two masses, a *Te Deum* and his *Requiem*. His first mass of 1757 received great acclaim and established his career as a composer. J.C. Bach traveled to London in 1762 to première three of his Italian operas. His opera *Orione* opened on 19 February 1763 at the King's Theater. This opera helped to establish his reputation in London and he soon became the Music Master to Queen Charlotte. He had a very promising career in England and performed on tour with the famous *viola de gamba* player Carl Friedrich Abel. It is possible that they knew each other growing up in Germany. J.C. Bach composed beautiful symphonies, orchestra works, chamber music, cantatas, and keyboard music. In 1766 Johann Christian met the soprano Cecilia Grassi. She was eleven years younger than him and they married soon after, but they did not have any children.

In 1764 the child prodigy Amadeus Mozart was visiting London with his father when he was eight years old. He met Johann Christian Bach who spent the next five months teaching the young Mozart how to compose. As part of this training Mozart arranged three sonatas from Bach's Op. 5 into keyboard concertos. Many scholars believe that J.C. Bach was a major influence on Mozart's concerto style, and that Bach was his only true teacher. Mozart acknowledged his artistic debt to him later in life. J.C. Bach's Classical style was quite different from his father's Baroque style. He composed many works for the piano as the harpsichord was going out of fashion. He gave the very first concert of piano music in London in 1768.

J.C. Bach became internationally famous as both a composer and a performer. However, by 1770 J.C. Bach's popularity as a composer was waning and so were his finances. He became more and more in debt, partly due to his steward embezzling his money. The steward stole 1000 British pounds from Bach, which was an enormous amount by modern standards. By the time of his death in 1770, Queen Charlotte had to step in and pay off his debts as well as providing a pension for Bach's widow. He is buried in the graveyard at the St. Pancras Old Church in London.

Dr. Carolyn Waters Broe

Title: J.C. Bach's *Symphonies Nos. 1-2*

Genre: A Classical **symphony** is usually in four movements. The Classical orchestra was much smaller than the modern symphony orchestra. They typically included strings, winds, and French horns.

YouTube: https://www.youtube.com/watch?v=0e38bHW8yo0

J.C. Bach's Symphonies Nos. 1-2

Netherlands Chamber Orchestra, David Zinman

Birthday: 5 September 1735 in Leipzig, Germany

Death Date: 1 January 1782 in London, England (New Year's Day) (aged 46)

Fun Facts:

1. He was known as the "London Bach" because he was the Master of Music to the Queen of England. This nickname helps to distinguish him from his older brother.
2. C.P.E. Bach, who was known as the "Berlin Bach, and the "Hamburg Bach".
3. J.C. Bach is said to be Mozart's only true teacher. He helped Mozart to develop his concerto style. Mozart acknowledged his artistic debt to J.C. Bach often.
4. J. C. Bach wrote a lot of music for the piano and gave the very first concert of piano music in London in 1768.

PRINCESS COMPOSERS

WILHELMINA PRINCESS OF PRUSSIA (1709-1758)

Wilhelmina Princess of Prussia (Sophie Fiederike Wihelmine) – (1709-1758) was a **German Baroque** composer. She was the eldest daughter of King Frederick William I and Queen Sophia Dorothea. She was also a favorite sister of King Frederick the Great. They were both musicians and great patrons of music. Wilhelmina was born 3 July 1709 in Berlin, Germany. Unfortunately, Wilhelmina was beaten and abused by her governess. This went on until the prince's governess told her mother, the Queen, that Wilhelmina would be crippled if the other governess did not stop. The Queen instantly dismissed the abusive governess. Wihelmina later wrote in her memoires "Not a day passed that she [the governess] did not prove upon me the fearful power of her fists." (Wilhelmina, memoirs 1748)

As in all royal families, politics ruled, so there was a great deal of discussion about whom Wilhelmina was going to marry. Her mother wanted her to marry her nephew the British Prince of Wales, but her father preferred the house of Hapsburg and objected. The King did not want to give away great concessions to the British. Wilhelmina eventually married Prince Frederick of Brandenburg-Bayreuth in 1731. Wilhelmina's only child was Elisabeth Fredericka Sophie of Brandenburg-Bayreuth, born on 30 August 1732.

Once Frederick came into his inheritance they moved to Bayreuth, and together they spent the next 30 years developing a culture of music and philosophy there. She and her husband built the beautiful Baroque opera house in Bayreuth that attracted the composer Wagner to their town a hundred years later. The pair also founded the University of Erlangen. Wilhelmi-

Wilhelmina and Friedrick

na's compositions include the opera *Argenore* (1740), six arias for Andrea Bernasconi's *L'huomo*, and a keyboard *Concerto in G minor* (c. 1750). The concerto has string accompaniment with an obbligato flute part. It could have been performed by either her brother or her husband on the flute. Her music shows the influence of J.S. Bach's music, which she loved. This flute concerto also shows the highly ornamented style of French *gavottes* (a dance form). She learned to play the lute from Sylvius Leopold Weiss. She and her brother, King Friedrick the Great, were both pupils of the flautist and composer J.J. Quantz. Her opera *Argenore* was performed in 1740 for her husband's birthday. Wilhelmina and her brother were close friends their entire life. He was broken hearted when she died early. After her death, Friederick the Great built the Temple of Friendship in her memory.

Title: The opera *Argenore*.
Genre: An **opera** is a large-scale vocal work in one or more acts, with instrumental accompaniment that has usually been based on a literary work.
YouTube: https://www.youtube.com/watch?v=pS4X-F5Rgj4
Overture to her opera Argenore with chorus.
Birthday: 3 July 1709 in Berlin, Germany.
Death Date: 14 October 1758 in Bayreuth, Germany. She died the day that her brother lost the war with Austria (age 48).
Fun Facts:
1. She and her brother were both pupils of the flautist and composer J.J. Quantz.
2. Her brother, King Frederick the Great, loved Wilhelmina, and they were close friends their entire life. He was heartbroken when she died early. After her death, he built the Temple of Friendship in her memory.
3. Bayreuth palace was rebuilt by Wilhelmina and her husband in the so-called *Bayreuth Rococo* style of architecture which is renowned even today.

ANNA AMALIA PRINCESS OF PRUSSIA (1723-1787)

Anna Amalia Princess of Prussia – (1723-1787) was a **German Classical** composer. She was both a Princess and the Abbess of Quedlingburg, which made her a very wealthy woman. So, she used her funds and time as a patroness of

music and as a composer. Anna Amalia composed military band music; a genre rarely adopted by women of the 18th century. Princess Anna Amalia was born on 9 November 1723 in Berlin, Germany (then called Prussia). She was the daughter of Sophia Dorothea of Brunswick-Lüneburg-Hanover (1687-1757) and Frederick William I (1688-1740), king of Prussia (r. 1713-1740). She was also the youngest sister of Frederick II the Great and the aunt of Anna Amalia of Saxe-Weimar (1739-1807). There were ten surviving children in this family. Anna Amalia studied harpsichord and piano under Gottlieb Hayne and counter-

point with Johann Philipp Kirnberger, who had been an important student of the famous composer J.S. Bach.

Anna's father, Frederick I King of Prussia, was known to have been a monster to his family. He even dragged his youngest daughter, Anna Amalia by the hair when he went into fits of rage. He did not approve of his children playing frivolous music. After he died when she was seventeen, Anna Amalia was finally able to play music. Her equally talented brother Frederick

II the new King of Prussia, taught her how to play harpsichord, flute and violin, which were all considered to be essential musical instruments in their day. He also started looking for

a proper husband for Anna Amalia. She had other ideas and secretly married one of her brother's soldiers Baron Fredrich van der Trenck.

Her secret marriage could not be kept a secret when she became pregnant. When her brother found out, he became furious and packed her off to the Quedlingburg Abbey for unwed mothers which was also a Protestant convent. It was said that she had twins. Her husband the Baron was imprisoned. He escaped, but then he was captured and imprisoned

again. Baron van der Trenck spent much of his life as a spy after that, but unfortunately lost his head to the guillotine in France during the revolution.

Anna Amalia thrived in the abbey. She had plenty of time to compose. Anna is best known for her smaller chamber music works. Anna Amalia gained powerful authority when she became the Abbess of Quedlingburg in 1755. This institution with its estate was part of the Holy Roman Empire and answered only to the Emperor. She chose to stay in Berlin most of the time.

Anna Amalia received a modest amount of fame composing marches, cantatas, fugues, trios, sonatas, and songs. Her chamber music included flute sonatas. Anna Amalia also composed a chamber concerto for **cembalo** in G, which is a keyboard instrument. She set the text of Ramler's "Passion" to music in her cantata *Der Tod Jesu* ("The Death of Jesus"). This was her favorite piece. Unfortunately, very few of her works survived as she destroyed many of them due to perfectionism. More of her music may be discovered since the archive of 5,000 German 18th century scores of the *Sing-Akademie zu Berlin* were discovered in Kiev in 1999. They have been missing since the end of World War II when the former Soviet Union took possession of them and hid them from the rest of the world. Anna Amalia remained the Abbess of Quedlingburg until she passed away in 1787 at the age of sixty-three in Berlin.

One of Anna Amalia's greatest contributions to music is her vast collection of 600 volumes of 18th century music known as the Princess Anna Amalia collection, which is now at the Berlin State Library. She collected music by Händel, Telemann, Karl Heinrich Graun, J.S. Bach, and C.P.E. Bach. These are pieces that were performed at her court. She is credited with helping to preserve and revive the music of Johann Sebastian Bach. It is obvious that she appreciated the music of C.P.E. Bach as well as there are many works by him in her collection. He was a court composer and musician for her brother Fredrick II of Prussia. C.P.E. Bach owed his Honorary Director title of the Hamburg Orchestra to Anna Amalia. She lent it to him before leaving. Her collection was split between East and West Berlin after W.W. II and reunited in 1990. Her collection is now almost 2,000 scores and it is a treasure trove of music.

Title: *Sonata for Flute in F*
Genre: A **sonata** is a piece of chamber music for a solo instrument and usually a keyboard instrument such as harpsichord or piano. This genre typically has three or four movements. This piece also includes a **basso continuo** part which is usually performed by a cellist.
YouTube: *Sonata for Flute in F*
Pahud Flautist and Pinnock Cembalo https://www.youtube.com/watch?v=tTi-aj1ksBE
Birthday: 9 November 1723 in Berlin, Germany (Prussia at the time)
Death Date: 30 March 1787 in Berlin, Germany (aged 63)
Fun Facts:
1. She was the youngest sister of King Fredrick II the Great of Prussia and he taught her how to play harpsichord, flute and violin.
2. She was a Princess who was born in a castle in Berlin.
3. She was sent to the Quedlingburg Abbey for secretly marrying a soldier against her brother the King's wishes. She later became the Abbess of Quedlingburg, which is the administrator of the convent.

MARIA ANTONIA WALPURGIS (1724-1780)

Maria Antonia Walpurgis – (1724-1780) Electress of Saxony, was a **German Baroque** composer, singer, harpsichordist, and patron. She was a Saxon princess of Bavaria, whose operas were praised by Johann Adolf Hasse, Pietro Metastasio, Frederick the Great, Johann Christoph Gottsched and Antonio de Eximeno. These operas have yet to be recorded. Although there was a long list of female singers and patrons during the era, the number of women composers whose operas have been conserved is small. Maria Antonia Walpurgis was among the most exceptional of these. Her birth was celebrated in the court of Munich with a performance of the opera *Amadis de Grecia* by Pietro Torri, so ever after Maria Antonia was associated with Italian music.

Maria Antonia Walpurgis was born on 18 July 1724 – Nymphenburg Palace in Munich, Germany. She was the daughter of the Elector and later Emperor Karl Albert of Bavaria, and the Archduchess Maria Amalia of Austria. As a member of the royal family, Maria Antonia was taught by some of the leading opera composers of her time including Giovanni Ferrandini, Giovanni Porta, Nicola Porpora and Johann Adolf Hasse. She also took painting lessons from Rafael Mengs. As a poetess, she wrote the libretto for Hasse's *La conversione di Sant'Agostino* (1750), which is considered one of the best Saxon oratorios. She married Friedrich Christian, the heir to the Electorate of Saxony, in Dresden on 20 June 1747. After marrying, she moved to Dresden, where Maria Antonia had nine children with Friedrich Christian, seven whom survived infancy.

But fundamentally, Walpurgis's most important facet was her musical activity as a composer, singer, harpsichordist, and patron. She became a member of the Accademia dell'Arcadia of Rome, which was a significant institution for operatic reform in 1747. She is best known for her operas *Il trionfo della fedeltà* (Dresden, summer 1754), and Talestri, regina delle amazon (Nymphenburg Palace, February 6, 1760). Walpurgis wrote her own libretto to *Talestri*. She also used her vast influence and power to promote and patronize Italian opera in Germany. In addition to her two operas, several arias, a *pastorale*, intermezzos, meditations and motets are attributed to her.

Title: *The* "Queen of the Amazons Symphonia" (1763). This instrumental piece was part of Walpurgis's opera *Talestri, regina delle amazon*. Thalestris was an Amazon queen in Greek mythology. The plot centers on Talestris' relationship with a Scythian ruler (and man), Orontes. Talestri's advisor, Antiope also falls in love with a Scythian man, Learchus. Because of their love, war was averted, as the Scythians and Amazons manage to co-exist peacefully together. The plot ends happily, with each couple united. The depiction of Talestris as the benevolent thoughtful ruler, who becomes a leader, suggests that this opera may be a semi-autobiographical depiction of Maria Antonia herself.

Genre: Opera Symphonia – was an instrumental piece included in an opera.

YouTube Audio: http://www.fourseasonsorchestra.org/SYMPHONIA.mp3 Carolyn Broe conducting the Four Seasons Orchestra. Scottsdale, Arizona USA

Birthday: 18 July 1724 – Nymphenburg Palace in Munich, Germany

Death Date: 23 April 1780 Dresden, Germany (aged 55)

Fun Facts:

1. Her titles include: Her Serene Highness Duchess Maria Antonia of Bavaria (18 July 1724–13 June 1747); *Her Serene Highness* The Electoral Princess of Saxony (13 June 1747–5 October 1763); *Her Serene Highness* The Electress of Saxony (5 October 1763–17 December 1763); *Her Serene Highness* The Dowager Electress of Saxony (17 December 1763–23 April 1780).
2. She sang the leading role in her own opera as Talestris, Queen of the Amazons.
3. During her Regency of Germany, she opposed Franz Xaver, her Co-Regent and brother-in-law's, attempt to get her son to give up his claim to the throne of Poland in 1765.

JOSEPH HAYDN (1732-1809)

ranz Joseph Haydn – (1732-1809) was an **Austrian** composer of the **Classical era,** who became famous for his symphonies. He was born in the village of Rohru in Lower Austria on 31 March 1732. His Father was a wheelwright, a farmer,

and the town Mayor. His mother was a cook before her marriage. She gave birth to twelve children. Joseph and his brother Johann Michael both became respected composers. At the age of five little Joseph's talent for music was discovered and he was committed to a relative who was a schoolmaster, for instruction. He quickly learned to play the keyboard and violin as well as reading and writing. At the age of eight he was taken in as a choir boy at St. Stephen's Cathedral in Vienna. He had a great sense of humor and loved to play pranks. Joseph was well liked even though his face had pock marks from smallpox. Joseph was not always fed well by Ruetter the choirmaster. So, he was very motivated to sing well, so he could get invited to sing at the homes of wealthy aristocrats where the singers received refreshments afterwards.

By 1749 his services as choir boy ended at the age of seventeen when his voice changed. His beautiful high voice was lost, and he was accused of "crowing" instead of singing by the Empress Maria Theresa of Austria (Dies 1810 biography). His younger brother Michael was admitted to the cathedral school and sang so beautifully that he was awarded gold ducats. Shortly after Joseph played one too many pranks, by snipping off the pigtail of another choir boy, choirmaster Reutter had enough of Joseph and kicked him out of the choir and sent out into the streets of Vienna.

Haydn had nowhere to go and no money. His friend Johann Michael Spangler took him in. Here he continued his studies in composition, Italian, and voice. Haydn had the luck of renting the attic room in a house in Vienna where several very influential people lived including the Dowager Princess of the wealthy Esterhazy family, Pietro Trapassi (Metastasio) the poet Laureate of Austria, and an Italian composer Niccolo Porpora. Haydn also taught piano to Maria von Martinez, who was the daughter of one of the residents. After some struggle for an existence teaching music lessons and singing serenades, Haydn was engaged as an accompanist and servant for Porpora.

In 1759 through an acquaintance, Count Furnberg, Haydn was appointed *Kapellmeister* (Music Director) to Count Morzin. Here he wrote his first **symphony** at the age of twenty-seven. The following year Haydn married Anna Keller, a sister of his first sweetheart, who entered a convent. The marriage proved to be an unhappy one. Anna did not share his love of music. They did not have any children. In 1761 Haydn entered the services of Prince Nikolaus Esterházy I and remained in his household for thirty years. Esterházy Palace in Eisenstadt boasted both a beautiful opera house, and a puppet theater. Therefore, Haydn composed and premiered many of his symphonies, operas, string quartets, concertos, music for the puppet shows, and many other works at the palace. During these years, Joseph Haydn and Wolfgang Mozart become intimate friends.

Haydn made two trips to London in 1791 and 1794 where he wrote his last twelve London symphonies, and conducted concerts of them for which he received a handsome payment. It was reported that his symphonies were performed by up to 300 musicians in London. His fame spread rapidly. He returned to Vienna and became ill during the siege by Napoleon. The French general thought so highly of Haydn that he posted guards around his house and said that no harm should come to this great composer. However, on 31 May 1809, the battle was so close, that a cannon ball landed in Haydn's back yard. The cannon ball missed Haydn, but he died later that day of illness at the age of seventy-seven. Franz Joseph Haydn endowed the world with one-hundred-six symphonies, sixty-eight string quartets, twenty-three operas, concertos, sixty-two piano sonatas, thirty-two piano trios, and many other works in various forms. He is known as the father of the symphony and the string quartet. Some of his most famous works include The Creation (1798), *The Seasons* (1801), "*Surprise*" *Symphony*, "*Farewell*" *Symphony*, the Trumpet Concerto, the two *Cello Concertos*, and the "Fifths," "*Emperor*," and "Sunrise" string quartets.

After his death and burial in Vienna in 1809, Haydn's body was dug up by the gravedigger, and his skull was stolen. Rosenbaum, a secretary from Esterházy Palace, bribed the gravedigger to steal it, because he and his friend Peter were trying to prove that the size of the cranium predicts genius (a theory which has now been debunked). In 1820 Prince Nikolaus Esterházy II, the grandson of Haydn's former employer, came to claim Haydn's body, and take it back to Esterházy Palace. He was shocked to find it had been beheaded. Realizing immediately that it must have been Rosenbaum, the Prince sent his men to the secretary's house, but Rosenbaum hid the skull under the mattress, and gave them another skull. Haydn's skull was later willed to a musical society, where it presided over their meetings. The skull was not returned for 145 years, when the Prince's great grandson Paul discovered the deception. In 1954 Prince Paul Esterházy reunited Haydn's skull with his skeleton along with a great parade and ceremony at Esterházy Palace and laid him to rest at the Bergkirche in Eisenstadt, Austria.

50 Famous Composers

Title: *Symphony No. 94, in G Major*, Hob. 1:94 "Surprise" – movement no. 2 "Andante".

Genre: A **symphony** is a large-scale orchestra piece, which is usually in four movements.

YouTube: https://www.youtube.com/watch?v=VOLy6JxEDLw
Mariss Jansons with Berliner Philharmoniker and Emmanuel Pahud

Instrumentation: Flutes (2), oboes (2), bassoons (2), French horns (2), trumpets (2), timpani, strings (typical classical orchestra)

Form: Theme and variations

Birthday: 31 March 1732

Death Date: 31 May 1809 (aged 77)

Fun Facts:

1. His friend and student, Wolfgang Amadeus Mozart, called him "Papa Haydn".

2. Haydn's contributions have earned him the epithet of "Father of the Symphony" and "Father of the String Quartet".

3. Haydn had an exceptionally good sense of humor and liked to play pranks on people such as in the slow movement of his *Symphony No. 94* is nicknamed "Surprise". Some of the patrons at his London concerts were falling asleep during his slow movements. Insulted by this rude behavior, Haydn decided to play a trick on them by opening with a soft passage, and then waking them up with a loud bang a few measures later.

4. After Haydn matured and lost his beautiful voice at sixteen, he cut the pigtails of another boy chorister at the St. Stephen's school, and was caned in public for it, and dismissed from the school.

5. During the premiere of Haydn's *Symphony No. 96*, a huge chandelier fell during the performance, but no one was injured. Hence this piece was nicknamed "The Miracle".

6. In the early days of the string quartet, they were sometimes performed in taverns. Haydn and some of his musicians decided to play a prank in one of those taverns. Haydn came in and pretended to be someone else. He shouted at one of his friends "That Haydn cannot write a string quartet! He could never write music like that. Haydn is a fraud". Hearing this Haydn's friend, who was in on the prank, stood up and raised his fists shouting back "How dare you malign the music of Joseph Haydn!" Then they got into a mock fist fight in full view of the people at the tavern. It was all for show.

7. Haydn's "Farewell" Symphony was performed for the first time in 1772, the composer was gently hinting to his employer Prince Nikolaus that his overworked musicians might like to return home to see their family. In the final movement each musician stands up, extinguishes the candle on their music stand, and leave the room in turn, until only a pair of musicians remain.

8. Haydn's sense of humor is found in many of his pieces, including his *String Quartet in E flat* (subtitled 'The Joke'). There are false endings to try and catch the audience out.

9. Four famous composers played string quartets together with Haydn and Dittersdorf on violins, Mozart on viola, and Vanhal on the cello.

The True Story of Haydn's Head:

After his death and burial in Vienna in 1809, Haydn's body was dug up by the gravedigger, and his skull was stolen. Rosenbaum, a secretary from Esterházy Palace, bribed the gravedigger to steal it, because he and his friend Peter were trying to prove that the size of the cranium predicts genius (a theory which

has now been debunked). In 1820 Prince Nikolaus Esterházy II, the grandson of Haydn's former employer, came to claim Haydn's body, and take it back to Esterházy Palace. He was shocked to find it had been beheaded. Realizing immediately that it must have been Rosenbaum, the Prince sent his men to the secretary's house, but Rosenbaum hid the skull under the mattress, and gave them another skull. Haydn's skull was later willed to a musical society, where it presided over their meetings. The skull was not returned for 145 years, when the Prince's great grandson Paul discovered the deception.

In 1954 Prince Paul Esterházy reunited Haydn's skull with his skeleton along with a great parade and ceremony at Esterházy Palace and laid him to rest at the Bergkirche in Eisenstadt, Austria.

MARIANNE VON MARTÍNEZ (1744-1812)

Marianne von Martínez – (1744-1812) was an **Austrian Classical** composer and pianist of Spanish descent. She was taught singing, piano and composition by Nicola Porpora and Franz Joseph Haydn, who both lived in the same house where she grew up. Wolfgang Mozart asked her to premiere several of his piano concertos. She composed one symphony, a keyboard concerto, three keyboard sonatas, two oratorios, four masses, six motets, psalm cantatas, and secular cantatas. Marianne von Martínez was born on 4 May 1744 in Vienna, Austria. Marianne's father was the major domo at the Papal Embassy in Vienna. The Martinez family lived on the third floor of a large building in Vienna with several floors. As it happened, several famous people also lived there including a Dowager Princess of Austria.

Marianne was discovered at the age of nine by the poet and librettist Pietro Metastasio for her great musical talents. Metastasio, who became the Poet Laurate of Austria, also lived on the third floor of their building, and supervised her training. To this end, he called on Niccolò Porpora, a well-known Italian teacher and composer, and the then unknown Franz Joseph Haydn. Haydn, who boarded in the leaky attic of her home, gave the girl lessons in singing, playing keyboard instruments, and composition, while Metastasio provided her with a general education. Martinez studied counterpoint with Giuseppe Bonno, and probably received informal suggestions and guidance from Johann Adolph Hasse. It was exceedingly rare for any girls to receive a music education from such distinguished teachers.

Marianne's talents quickly attracted the attention of the Viennese court, and an early *Mass* of hers was performed at St. Michael's, the court chapel. As an adult, Martinez was frequently asked to perform at the court of Empress Maria Theresa. Mozart sought Martinez out to perform with him in his piano duets, and singer Michael Kelly paid tribute to her in his memoirs. Martinez composed in the Italian style, which was favored in Vienna during the Classical era. Her compositions for solo voice show that Marianne had an exceptional voice, with a high degree of flexibility, if we consider that she was the most likely person to have premiered these pieces. Her harpsichord performance practice was compared to that of the famous composer C.P.E. Bach.

In 1773 she was made an honorary member of Bologna's *Accademia Filharmonica*, which cited the nobility of expression and the amazing precision exhibited in her works. About the same time, she may also have received an honorary doctorate from the University of Pavia. Metastasio left her and her siblings large sums of money, which she used to create a musical salon and singing school. Martinez was praised during her life as a composer. She is the only woman to have composed a symphony in the Classical era. She also wrote masses, oratorios and cantatas. Only 65 of her 150 pieces survive.

Title: Piano *Concerto in A Major No. 1*, I. Allegro con Spirito
Genre: A **piano concerto** is a large-scale work for solo piano and orchestra.
YouTube Video: https://www.youtube.com/watch?v=tr-r35XkZF8 Judith Valerie Engle pianist and
  conductor
Title: *Symphony No. 1 in C Major*
Genre: A **symphony** is a large-scale instrumental work, which is usually in four movements.
Instrumentation: 2 flutes, 2 oboes, 1 bassoon, 2 horns, and strings.
Birthday: 4 May 1744 in Vienna, Austria
Death Date: 13 December 1812 in Vienna (aged 68)
Fun Facts:
1. The young composer Franz Joseph Haydn, who lived in the leaky attic of her home, was her first keyboard and voice teacher.
2. Marianne von Martinez performed piano duos with Mozart and premiered some of his piano concertos.
3. She never married, which was very unusual for a woman of her status during the Classical era.

CHEVALIER DE SAINT-GEORGES (1745-1799)

hevalier de saint-georges (1745-1799) was a virtuoso violinist, **Classical composer**, a champion fencer, and conductor of the leading symphony orchestra in Paris. Joseph was also an expert at dancing and riding horses. He was born on 25 December 1745 in the islands of Guadeloupe, which was a colony of France located in the Caribbean Sea. Joseph was the son of George Bologne de Saint-Georges, a wealthy married plantation owner, and Anne dite Nanon, his wife's African slave. In 1753 his father took him to France when he was seven to be educated. Joseph also became a champion fencer. During the French Revolution, the younger Saint-Georges served as a colonel of the Légion St.-Georges in the first all-black regiment in Europe. He fought on the side of the Republic. He composed numerous string quartets, symphonies, concertos, and operas. He had several 19th century biographers who dramatized his life.

The Chevalier de Saint-Georges is best remembered as the first known classical composer of African ancestry. He is often referred to as the "Black Mozart".

His father, George Bologne had been a Caribbean plantation owner and a councilor of the parliament of Metz (1711-1774). He was called "de Saint-Georges" after one of his plantations. He had been a commoner until 1757 when George was given the title *Gentilhomme ordinaire de la chambre du roi* (Gentleman of the king's chamber). His son Joseph was not eligible to receive this title as he had an African mother. However, his father took Joseph to France in 1753 and made certain that his son had the finest education including music, history, languages, and fencing. Joseph was enrolled in a French boarding school and then his father returned to Guadeloupe. Two years later his father returned to France with Joseph's mother and they all lived together in an apartment in Paris.

At age thirteen, Joseph's father enrolled him in Tessier de La Boëssière's *Académie royale polytechnique des armes et de 'l'équitation* (a school for fencing and horsemanship). According to *La Boëssière fils*, son of the Fencing Master: "At fifteen his [Bologne's] progress was so rapid, that he was already beating the best swordsmen, and at seventeen he developed the greatest speed imaginable." (la Boëssière 1818, p. xvj) Alexander Picard, a fencing-master in Rouen, had been mocking him as *"Boëssière's mulatto"*, in public (half-black). Bologne was still a student when he beat Picard in a fencing competition. This victory was a great honor for Joseph, but also a victory for abolitionists (anti-slave groups). When Joseph graduated from the *Académie royale Polytechnique* in 1766, Bologne was made a *Gendarme du roi* (officer of the king's body-guard) and a *chevalier* (knight). After that he went by the title "Chevalier de Saint-Georges".

The Chevalier de Saint-Georges was not only a master of the sword, but also of the violin bow. Joseph's father hired famous violinists to teach his son how to play violin. Several noted composers dedicated concertos and other works to him including Antonio Lolli (1764); François Gossec (1766); Carl Stamitz (1770); and Avolio (1778). Some people have claimed that Saint-Georges may have studied with the violin master Jean-Marie Leclair, but that is in doubt. Some of his techniques were said to reveal influence by the violinist Pierre Gaviniès.

In 1769 Saint-Georges performed in Gossec's new orchestra *Le Concert de Amateurs*. In 1772 Saint-Georges created a sensation with his debut as a soloist, playing his first two violin concertos, Op. II, with Gossec conducting the orchestra. The next year he became the concert-master and conductor of this orchestra. When Gossec took over as conductor of the *Concerts Spiritual Orchestra* in Paris, he designated Saint-Georges as his successor as conductor of *Le Concert de Amateurs*. After a couple of years under Bologne's direction, this group became the best orchestra in all of Europe.

Saint-Georges' first compositions, Op. I, were a set of *Six String Quartets*, among the first in France, that were inspired by Haydn's earliest quartets, brought from Vienna by Baron Bagge. These quartets were published by famed French publisher, composer, and teacher Antoine Bailleux. Saint-Georges composed fourteen violin concertos, two symphonies, and eight ***symphonie-concertantes***. The *symphonie-concertante* was a new Parisian genre of which Bologne was one of the chief exponents. This music genre is a combination of the concerto and the symphony and usually features two or more soloists. He wrote his instrumental works over a short span of time, and they were published between 1771 and 1779. He also composed the music to six ***opéras comiques*** (comic operas) and several songs.

Bolonge met the famous composer Wolfgang Mozart through Baron von Grimm, who was a writer, diplomat, and secretary to the Duke of Orleans. Grimm had been astounded by the prodigy Mozart when the musical family from Salzburg visited Paris in 1763. When the twenty-two-year-old Mozart and his mother arrived in 1778, Grimm served as his manager and mentor. But in July Mozart's mother, Anna Maria, fell ill and died. Grimm was living in the ducal palace and now he took the distraught young Mozart to stay with him. Another resident at the palace was none other than the Chevalier de Saint-Georges.

Mozart was at his lowest point without his mother, not good at speaking French, mourning, lonely, and finding it difficult to get paid for commissions. That is when he encountered, under the same roof, Saint-Georges, who at thirty-two was exotic, brilliant, established, at ease, popular with the ladies and close to Queen Marie Antoinette. (Duchen 2016) Moreover, he led one of the best orchestras in Europe, *Le Concert des Amateurs*, Mozart's symphonies received inferior performances at the *Concert Spiritual*. (Duchen 2016) Naturally, Mozart became very jealous of the Chevalier de Saint-Georges. He decided he hated France and left. Yet, several of Mozart's most famous pieces were influenced by the *Chevalier* including his *Sinfonia Concertante in Eb Major for Violin and Viola* composed in 1779. The final run of the third movement matches a run in Saint-George's *Violin Concerto in E Major*.

The eighteenth century was the **Age of Enlightenment (1685-1815)** which brought many important advancements in science and philosophy, but also brought revolution. Unfortunately for Saint-Georges, many of the contributors to *Le Concert Amateurs* started to give their money to send a fleet of fifty ships to the American Revolutionaries in 1781 with the promise that they would return those ships with rice, cotton and other goods. The ships came back empty, so the backers and the orchestra went bankrupt. The orchestra was disbanded. Saint-Georges turned to his friend and admirer, Philippe D'Orléans, Duke de Chartres, for help. In 1773 at the age of twenty-six, Philippe had been elected Grand Master of all the Masonic orders in France. Responding to Saint-Georges's plea for funds, Philippe revived the orchestra as part of his Loge Olympique, an exclusive Freemason Lodge. The Masons were a secret society in Europe and the colonies that had started the American Revolution. They were also men of the Enlightenment movement.

Saint-Georges' orchestra was renamed *Le Concert Olympique*, with practically the same personnel, and performed in the grand salon of the Palais Royal. Later Haydn's *Paris Symphonies* were commissioned by the Masons for this group and the premiers were conducted by Bologne. Queen Marie Antoinette attended some of Saint-Georges' concerts at the Palais de Soubise, arriving sometimes without notice, so the orchestra wore their lavish court attire for all its performances. Saint-Georges played all his violin concertos as soloist with his orchestra.

In 1776 Saint-Georges was asked to conduct the *Académie royale de musique*, the Paris Opera, which was struggling financially and artistically. Bologne was the best and most likely the only qualified candidate. Unfortunately, three of the soprano divas refused to work with a *mullato* (half black) conductor and sent a letter to the Queen. Saint-Georges withdrew his name to avoid offending the queen with a scandal. King Louis XVI responded by taking the Paris Opera back from the city and organizing a few light entertainments exclusively for the Queen and her court. Joseph Bologne was asked to perform with the Queen for these concerts. He was probably playing violin and she accompanied him on the piano. The first of his six comic operas was not well received due to the librettist, but his second was given rave reviews for his music.

Saint-Georges went on tour to England performing in fencing matches in London for George Prince of Wales. The Prince invited him on a fox hunt and to the horse races. Philippe sent Saint-Georges over to London with Jacques Pierre Brissot de Warville, his chief of staff who was an abolitionist. England was experiencing a large abolitionist movement at the time. So, Brissot saw

an opportunity to make a case for freeing the slaves by presenting Joseph Bologne to help build abolitionist organizations in London. A cartoon with the caption "St. George and the Dragon" appeared about him in the Morning Post on April 12, 1789. The dragon represented slavery. A pro-slave group found out about his abolitionist activities and sent five men armed with pistols to assassinate Saint-Georges. He beat them all off with a stick! Afterwards he returned to Paris.

During the French Revolution (1789-1799), Joseph Bologne was one of the first to sign up. He felt that it was unfair that he be denied his father's title because of his mother's color. When the revolutionaries declared on August 16, 1789 that all French people were equal, Bologne signed up for their revolutionary army even though he was part of the French National Guard. In 1792 the Parliament established a light army battalion of 1,000 colored soldiers. Bologne quickly became a Colonel and eventually their regiment became known as the "Légion St-Georges" due to his leadership and bravery. They fought against the Austrian pro-Imperialist army and achieved several victories.

Even though St. George was a hero, he was condemned by critics for being involved in non-revolutionary activities such as funding music events. He was dismissed and imprisoned for eighteen months while facing execution by the dreaded guillotine. Bologne went to trial three times, most likely due to his aristocratic upbringing and his father's wealthy background, which was frowned upon by the revolutionary court. He was saved since his mother was a slave and his African ancestry. Bolonge was later released, due to the support given by his soldiers, but he was not allowed to return to his command, and he was banned from seeing his former comrades. He tried to regain his command by making the statement in a letter to the court "I continue to show loyalty to the revolution. Since the beginning of the war, I have been serving with relentless enthusiasm, but the persecution I suffered has not diminished. I have no other resources, only to restore my original position." (Banat 2006) However, his application failed.

The Chevalier de Saint-Georges spent the rest of his days practicing his violin. He said that he had never played better. In 1796 Saint-Georges went to Saint-Domingue to fight with Toussaint Louverture, a Haitian revolutionary, who led a slave revolt to free the island from French Colonial rule. His friends thought that he had been captured or killed, but two years later Joseph returned to France and composed more music. He also started a new orchestra with a different Masonic lodge called the Circle of Harmony Orchestra. Unfortunately, in 1799 he became ill with a bladder infection and died on June 10th in Paris. Joseph Bologne leaves us with an incredible legacy of six operas, eight symphony *concertantes*, two symphonies, fourteen violin concertos, eighteen string quartets, and many other vocal and instrumental chamber music works.

Title: *Symphony Concertante for Two Violins, Op. 6, No. 1 in C Major*
Genre: A **symphony *concertante*** is a combination of a concerto and a symphonic work. These Classical works are usually for two or more soloists, in this case two violinists and orchestra.
YouTube: https://www.youtube.com/watch?v=CqdmuSC1OLw
This video includes Bologne's *Symphony Concertante for Two Violin* Op. 6 Nos. 1-2 and Op. 9 Nos. 1-2.
Pilsen Philharmonic Orchestra Michal Pospisil, Violin (3,4) Jiri Zilak, Violin (1-4) Miroslav Vilimec, Violin (1,2) Jiri Malát , Conductor (1,2)
Frantisek Preisler Jr., Conductor (3,4)
Birthday: 25 December 1745 in the French colony of Guadeloupe.
Death Date: 10 June 1799 in Paris, France (aged 53).
Fun Facts:
1. Joseph Bologne Chevalier de Saint-Georges was the first Classical composer of African ancestry.
2. The Chevalier de Saint-Georges was a master of the sword and the violin bow. He won fencing championships and was hailed as one of the finest violinists in France during the Classical era.
3. Joseph Bologne composed the first string quartets in France.
4. Joseph Bologne was one of the main developers of the French *symphonie concertante* genre which featured two or more soloists with orchestra.
5. The Chevalier de Saint-Georges was a Colonel in the French Revolutionary army and the leader of the legion de Saint-Georges, which was the first all-black legion in France.
6. Saint-Georges was the conductor of *Le Concert des Amateurs*, which became the finest orchestra in Paris under his direction and the finest in Europe. He was also the violin soloist with this orchestra.

HENRIETTE DE BEAUMESNIL (1748-1813)

enriette Adélaïde Villard de Beaumesnil – (1748-1813) was a **French Classical** composer and singer, who performed under the stage name Mlle. Beaumesnil. She was born on 30 August 1748 Paris, France. From the early age of seven she was on stage and performed numerous roles as an opera singer. She specialized in *soubrette* roles in comedies. Henriette made a successful debut at the Paris Opéra in 1766 in the title role of *Silvie*. She was overshadowed by other singers such as Sophie Arnould and Rosalie Levasseur.

She married the tenor Philippe Cauvy (1754-ca 1820), a celebrated member of the comic opera (also known as *comedie Italienne*). When Arnould left the Paris Opera, Henrieitte was passed over for the role of lead singer by Levasseur, who was the favorite. Henriette protested with a letter to the Journal de Paris on 27 December 1778 and threatened to quit the Paris Opera. She later retired from the Paris Opera in 1781. Her first composition, the one act opera *Anacreon*, was given a private performance in 1781, but it was not officially accepted. Beaumesnil then achieved public success with her *acte de ballet Tibulle et Délie, ou Les Saturnales,* which was given at the Paris Opéra on 15 March 1784 after a court première the previous month. She was the third woman ever to have her work performed at the Paris Opera. She was also hailed for her two act *Opéra comique Plaire, c'est commander* of 1792. The libretto was by the Marquis de La Salle. She also wrote an oratorio, *Les Isrealites poursuivis par Pharaon*, which was performed in 1784. After she passed away in 1813, her memoirs were published by her son in 1837. Her music library is preserved at the Napoleon Museum in Arenenberg.

Title: Sinfonia from Tibulle et Délie: Allegro Moderato, Andante Gracioso and Allegro.

Genre: A **Sinfonia** is an instrumental work, which usually proceeded an opera, cantata, or an oratorio. Sinfonias were later performed without being attached to a vocal work.

YouTube Audio: https://www.youtube.com/watch?v=aEvx52kBZE4

Allegro Moderato – Four Seasons Orchestra, Carolyn Waters Broe conductor

https://www.youtube.com/watch?v=iwTT-JGBPwQ

Andante Gracioso and Allegro – Four Seasons Orchestra, Carolyn Waters Broe conductor

Birthday: 30 August 1748 Paris, France

Death Date: 5 October 1813 Paris, France (aged 65)

Fun Facts:

1. Henriette was known to have a bad temper. Émile Campardon tells the story (maybe a legend) of her getting into a '*duel au pistolet*' with the dancer Mlle. Théodore. Fortunately, the Paris Opera orchestra conductor Jean-Baptiste Rey, showed up at the scene of the duel and took their pistols away and put them on the grass. But the two ladies got the pistols back and decided to fight the duel anyway. Fortunately, the pistols had gotten moist with dew and misfired. Henriette and Emile decided to bury their differences by throwing their arms around each other's neck and making up.
2. She was performing on stage at the early age of seven and specialized in comic operas.
3. She was the third woman ever to have her work performed at the Paris Opera.

THE MOZART FAMILY

WOLFGANG AMADEUS MOZART (1756-1791)

Wolfgang Amadeus Mozart – (1756-1791) was an **Austrian Classical** composer, virtuoso pianist, and violinist. Wolfgang was a famous child music prodigy who was born on 27 January 1756 in Salzburg (which was a separate country from Austria at the time). His father, Leopold Mozart, was a violinist, teacher, and a minor German composer, who taught Wolfgang how to compose and perform as a solo keyboard player and violinist. His mother was Anna Maria born Pertl. He had an older sister Maria Anna, who was nicknamed

Dr. Carolyn Waters Broe

"Nannerl". Wolfgang loved to watch his sister Nannerl practicing her keyboard lessons when she was seven. He copied the thirds she was playing on the keyboard when he was only three. Later she remembered,

> "*He often spent much time at the clavier, picking out thirds, which he was ever striking, and his pleasure showed that it sounded good... In the fourth year of his age his father, for a game as it were, began to teach him a few minuets and pieces at the clavier... He could play it faultlessly and with the greatest delicacy and keeping exactly in time... At the age of five, he was already composing little pieces, which he played to his father who wrote them down*" (Deutsch 1965, p, 455).

By the time Wolfgang was five he was composing and by six he was performing with his sister for kings and queens all over Europe. In 1762 they performed for the Austrian court of Empress Maria Theresa and her children in the Hall of Mirrors at Schönbrunn Palace in Vienna. After the performance, the six-year-old Mozart jumped up into the Queen's lap and gave her a hug and a kiss. Wolfgang slipped on the polished floor and the Princess Marie Antoinette helped him up. The young Mozart said "You are good to me. I will marry you when I get older". The future Queen of France was two months older than Wolfgang at the time. This behavior became the talk of Vienna.

Wolfgang and Nannerl Mozart became famous as child prodigies. The Mozart family went on a three-and-a-half-year long concert tour to the courts of Munich, Mannheim, Paris, and London (1762-1766). They performed first at the court of the Prince-Elector Maximilian III of Bavaria in Munich, Germany. They went on to perform at the Imperial courts in Vienna and Prague. After They also performed at The Hague, again in Paris, Zurich, Donaueschingen, and Munich on the way back home. Wolfgang met many famous musicians during this tour, including Johann Christian Bach in London in 1764 and 1765. J.C. Bach taught Wolfgang a great deal about composing during this time. When Wolfgang was only eight years old, he composed his first symphony, which was probably mostly transcribed by his father Leopold.

Wolfgang often performed tricks for the royalty such as performing blindfolded, improvising on a melody given to him by a guest, and turning around and playing the keyboard with his hands behind his back.

While the Mozart family was on tour, their travels were often difficult. They rode in a post coach, which was like a stagecoach drawn by horses. The roads were very bumpy, and the coach was cold inside. They had to wait a long time to get paid by the people whom they were performing for. The Mozart family members often became ill with nearly fatal diseases in a faraway land. Because of these conditions, Wolfgang never grew very tall. He had a pail completion and was sickly much of the time. However, he got to wear hand-me-down silk clothing from princes and meet with all kinds of famous musicians and artists at the courts he was performing at. He got to visit and learn about more countries and cities which other children could only dream of.

The Mozart family went again to perform in Vienna and stayed there from 1767 to 1768. After one year back at home in Salzburg, Leopold and Wolfgang set off for Italy, leaving his mother and Nannerl at home. This tour lasted from December 1769 to March 1771. In the city of Bologna Wolfgang met with Italian composer Giovanni Battista Martini and the Czech composer Josef Mysliveček. Wolfgang was accepted as a member into the prestigious *Accademia Filarmonica*. Mysliveček became a friend and mentor to the young Mozart. He taught him a great deal about the form of Italian serious opera, the symphony, and violin concerto. While in Rome, Wolfgang visited the Vatican. He heard that Gregorio Allegri's piece "Miserere" was a carefully guarded secret. So, Mozart listened to it twice in the Sistine Chapel, and wrote it out from memory. This was the first unauthorized copy of that piece. In Milan, he performed his opera *Mitridate, re di Ponto* in 1770. It was a great success. This was followed by two more commissions for operas premieres of *Ascanio in Alba* (1771) and *Lucio Silla* (1772). He also composed his beautiful solo motet *Exsultate, jubilate* K.165.

Leopold had hoped that their trips to Italy would help to get Wolfgang a job. The Archduke Ferdinand thought about hiring Wolfgang Mozart. However, Ferdinand's mother, Empress Maria Theresa, did not approve of hiring what she considered to be "useless people" (Halliwell, Ruth 1998). She was probably referring to Leopold Mozart as he had been rather pushy with her earlier. After returning from Italy in 1773, Mozart was employed as a court musician by the Archbishop of Salzburg, Prince-Archbishop Hieronymus Colloredo. At first everything went well. Mozart had many fans in Salzburg. He composed in many genres including symphonies, sonatas, serenades, and string quartets. He also composed his five famous violin concertos. Next, he composed several piano concertos including his Eb concerto K. 271. But the Archbishop demanded that Mozart compose religious music such as masses and entertainment pieces like the three *Divertimenti* (K. 136-138) for his parties. Mozart soon grew restless. He wanted to compose operas. The Archbishop eventually gave Wolfgang the liberty to travel again.

In 1777 Mozart resigned from his position with the Archbishop of Salzburg. He traveled to Augsburg, Mannheim, Paris, and Munich in search of employment. There was a famous orchestra in Mannheim, but he could not get a job there. He fell in love with Aloysia Weber who was one of four sisters in a musical family. Mozart left for Paris in March of 1778 with his mother, continuing to look for work. There was a possibility of him becoming the court organist in Versailles, but he did not want that job. During this time, he composed his *Piano Sonata in A minor*, and his *"Paris" Symphony No. 31*.

Unfortunately, his mother Anna Maria took ill and died in Paris in July of 1778. He was devastated. He returned to Munich and again met Aloysia, who was now a famous singer, and no longer interested in him. Meanwhile, Leopold had found a job in Salzburg for Wolfgang as the court organist and concertmaster. He was reluctant to take this position but agreed and returned to Salzburg and took the job. During this difficult time, he composed some of his greatest works including his *"Sinfonia Concertante for Violin and Viola"* K. 364 in Eb of 1779. This is a crossover work between a symphony and a concerto. His friends thought it was unplayable, however this piece has become a standard in the orchestral repertoire of most professional orchestras.

In January 1781, Mozart's opera *Idomeneo* premiered with considerable success in Munich. Later, the Archbishop asked Mozart to travel with him to see Emperor Joseph II crowned. Mozart felt that if only he could get an audience with the Emperor, he could show him one of his latest operas and perform some fugues which he knew Joseph liked. He hoped to get employment with the Emperor. When they returned to Salzburg, the Archbishop did not want Mozart performing for other patrons and denied him a chance to perform for the Emperor at the Countess Thun's home. The fee would have been half his annual salary at the Archbishop's court. This made Mozart incredibly angry. He decided to resign, but the Archbishop would not let him. Later the Archbishop agreed to let Mozart go, but had his steward kick Mozart in the pants on the way out. Mozart decided to move to Vienna to become a freelance performer and composer.

Mozart's career in Vienna started out well. In December of 1781 he entered a keyboard competition before the Emperor between himself and Muzio Clementi. Mozart quickly established himself as the finest keyboard player in Austria. Eventually Mozart did meet the Emperor, who supported his career with commissions and a part-time position. He was also successful as a composer in Vienna. In 1782 Mozart completed his opera *Die Entführung aus dem Serail* (The Abduction from the Seraglio), which premiered on 16 July 1782. This opera achieved a great success and was performed in much of Europe.

During the climax of Mozart's quarrel with the Archbishop, he had moved into the Weber home in Vienna. Aloysia was now married to an actor, so they needed to take on boarders to pay bills. It was there that he met Aloysia's sister Constanze. Their courtship did not go smoothly. At one point she separated from him. Wolfgang had trouble getting permission to marry from his father. Yet on 4 August 1782 Wolfgang and Constanze were finally married. They had six children of which only two survived. Mozart started producing piano concertos for the public in Vienna to great success. He and Constanze moved into a lavish apartment in Vienna and lived a plush life for a while on his earnings.

Mozart was influenced by looking at the scores of Johann Sebastian Bach and George Handel. His friend named Gottfried van Swieten owned a large music library of Baroque composers. Mozart was especially interested in Bach's fugues, which he used in his later works. He saw many of Bach's cantatas while visiting his former church in Leipzig. Mozart also met with the famous Austrian composer Franz Joseph Haydn in Vienna around 1784. When Haydn would visit Vienna from Esterhazy Palace, they would often play string quartets together. Haydn was the inventor of the string quartet. Mozart dedicated six of his string quartets to Haydn. They became good friends and Mozart called him "Papa Haydn". Haydn declared that Mozart was one of the finest composers he had ever met.

Mozart composed more than 600 works, many of which are considered the greatest works of symphonic, concerto, chamber music, operatic, and choral music. Some of his most famous operas include the *Marriage of Figaro, Don Giovanni, Cosi van Tutti* and *The Magic Flute*. He had great success collaborating with the librettist Lorenzo Da Ponte. Mozart became a super star as an opera composer in both the cities of Vienna and Prague. Many of his operas were premiered in Prague. After Mozart's father died in May of 1787 Wolfgang became depressed and worried that his own time was near. Some scholars have suggested that the ghost in his opera *Don Giovanni*, which premiered in Prague in 1787, is a depiction of Leopold. He did not perform much in public anymore and turned to composing some of his best works. The Austro-Turkish war made life difficult in Vienna. The Mozart family finances dwindled, so they moved out of Vienna to the suburbs to reduce the rent. Mozart often found himself asking his friends for money. In December of 1787 Mozart finally achieved his dream when Emperor Joseph II granted him the post of "Chamber Composer" when Gluck passed away. This gave Mozart the funds to do more composing. He was required to compose numerous dances.

Mozart became a Mason in 1784. The Masons were a secret society in Vienna at the time because they believed in Democracy rather than Imperialism. The Free Masons were declared illegal, and the Masonic brothers developed secret knocks at their meetings, so they would know if the police had found their meeting and hide. It is thought that his opera *The Magic Flute* was based on secret Masonic rituals. It was very daring of Mozart to reveal these rituals in public. Some scholars feel that the evil Queen of the Night in this opera was a depiction of the Empress Maria Theresa. Many of Mozart's pieces include knocking motives such as those in his *Piano Concerto No. 21* and his *Jupiter Symphony No. 41*. Only his Masonic brothers would have understood the significance of these knocking motives and rituals at the time.

Mozart also met the famous German doctor and early hypnotist Franz Anton Mesmer in Vienna. He had developed a treatment he called "animal magnetism," which was later called "mesmerizing". He was also a Mason and a talented performer on the glass harmonica. Mozart later composed a piece for glass harmonica. Mozart may have been influenced by Mesmer in his opera *Cosi van Tutti* (1790) and in his tempo markings. Mesmer used a metronome to hypnotize his subjects. Mozart thought this instrument was perfect for keeping time.

Mozart went on a tour to several German cities in 1789 hoping to improve his position. Unfortunately, he found little employment to relieve his family's financial situation. In his last years Mozart completed three of his greatest symphonies Nos. 39-41. He finished composing his last *Piano Concerto. K. 595.* He composed his beautiful *Clarinet Concerto K. 622.* He also finished writing his last *String Quartet K. 614 in Eb.* Emperor Joseph commissioned Mozart to compose *La Clemenza di Tito*, which he premiered the 6th of September 1791 in Prague. He also premiered his opera *The Magic Flute* on the 30th of September of 1791. The stress of so much work may have weakened him, so Mozart became ill.

Mozart returned to Vienna, but by November 20 he was bedridden. He became obsessed with completing his unfinished *Requiem*, which was a commissioned work. Some scholars speculate that he may have dictated some of this work to his student Franz Xaver Süssmayr. Mozart died at home in Vienna on 5 December 1791 at the age of 35 going on 36. At first, he was buried in a regular cemetery plot. It is not known exactly what he died from. Everything from the official diagnosis of "miliary fever" to influenza, rheumatic fever, mercury poisoning, trichinosis (from bad pork) or a strep infection or falling and hitting his head have been suggested. Unfortunately, Mozart was reburied later in a "common grave" due to his wife Constanza not being able to afford the plot fees, and new laws handed down from the Emperor on burials. This does not mean a mass grave, but rather one for a commoner instead of an aristocrat. So, it is not known exactly where his grave is now. There were only a few people in attendance, which was the practice in Vienna at the time. Wolfgang Amadeus Mozart left us one of the greatest musical legacies of his generation.

Title: *The Magic Flute Overture* by Wolfgang A. Mozart
Genre: An **opera overture** is an instrumental work that precedes and introduces the main opera and contains all the musical themes of that opera.
YouTube: https://www.youtube.com/watch?v=vvhlJC04JtM Neville Marriner conducting

Title: "Papageno's Aria" from the opera *The Magic Flute*
Genre: An **opera aria** is a song which is sung by a soloist with piano or orchestral accompaniment. An aria usually depicts the feelings of the character towards someone or something in the operatic story.
YouTube: https://www.youtube.com/watch?v=hbRLJlVliZ0
Opera di Roma's production of *Il Flauto Magico* with Troy Guthrie as Papageno

Title: The Queen of the Night aria from The Magic Flute
YouTube: https://www.google.com/search?q=youtube+mozart+queen+of+the+night+aria&oq=YouTube+Mozart+Queen+of+ the+Night+aria&aqs=chrome.0.0j69i64. 12279j0j7&sourceid=chrome&ie=UTF-8
Diana Damrau soprano with The Royal Opera

Title: Mozart's *Symphony No. 40 in G minor* K. 550
Genre: A **Classical symphony** is a composition for symphony orchestra which is typically in four movements. The Classical symphony was usually scored for a smaller orchestra and may have included two flutes, two oboes, two clarinets, two bassoons, two French horns, two trumpets, strings and timpani (depending on the composer and if the symphony is early or late in the Classical era).
YouTube: https://www.youtube.com/watch?v=p8bZ7vm4_6M Leonard Bernstein conducting the Boston Symphony Orchestra.
Birthday: 27 January 1756 in Salzburg (now in Austria)
Death Date: 5 December 1791 in Vienna, Austria (aged 35)
Fun Facts:
1. Wolfgang Mozart had the ability to hear musical tones in color. This rare trait is called **"synesthesia"**. He could see each key in a different color. D Major sounded orangey, B flat minor was black, and A Major was a rainbow of colors to him.
2. As a child W.A. Mozart proved his amazing abilities as a musician by performing blind folded or by turning around backwards and playing the keyboard with his hands behind his back.
3. W. A. Mozart like riddles. He spoke sentences backwards, wrote letters to his sister in multiple languages, and made-up secret words that only they understood.
4. The court musicians at each palace, where Wolfgang Mozart visited as a child, demanded that he take extremely hard music exams to prove that he was a musical genius. They gave him tests that none of these adult composers could pass themselves. Mozart passed every one of their exams with flying colors.

LEOPOLD MOZART (1719-1789)

eopold Mozart – (1719-1789) **German Classical** composer, conductor, violinist, and writer. He is most famous for being the father and teacher of Wolfgang Amadeus Mozart. His full name was Johann Georg Leopold Mozart, but everyone knows him by Leopold Mozart or "Papa Mozart". He is also known for writing the first treatise on the violin published in 1756.

Leopold was born 14 November 1719 in Augsburg, Germany to Johann Georg Mozart (1679-1736), a bookbinder, and Anna Maria Sulzer (1696-1766). He sang as a choir boy at a young age.

Leopold loved to act and sing in theatrical productions. He also became an excellent violinist and organist. Leopold attended the St. Salvator Gymnasium, which was a Jesuit school. He studied science, theology (religion), and logic graduating *magna cum laude* in 1735. He then moved on to the St. Salvator Lyceum, which was a more advanced school. However, he left this school quickly and moved to Salzburg, where he enrolled at the Benedictine University (now University of Salzburg) in November 1737 to study philosophy and law. Leopold received the degree of Bachelor of Philosophy in 1738. However, in September 1739 he was expelled from the university for poor attendance.

In 1740 he became the violinist and valet to a university canon Johann Baptist, Count of Thurn-Valsassina and Taxis. He also published his first set of six *"Trio Sonatas Opus 1"* and did the copper engraving for the printing himself. In 1743, he was appointed as fourth violinist in the orchestra of Count Leopold Anton von Firmian, the ruling Prince-Archbishop of Salzburg. Leopold married **Anna Maria Pertl** in 1747. She bore them seven children, but only two survived infancy, **Maria Anna** Walburga Ignatia (30 July 1751-29 October 1829) and Johann Chrysostomus **Wolfgang Amadeus** (27 January 1756-5 December 1791). She nearly died giving birth to him. Anna Maria was the mother to two of the most famous musicians in Europe.

Scholars debate weather Leopold was a successful composer. Some say that he was already a well-known composer when his son Wolfgang was born. Leopold was writing his *Versuch einer gründlichen Violinschule, (Treatise on the Fundamental Principals of Playing Violin Playing)* in 1755 while his wife was expecting Wolfgang. In this treatise, Leopold poses the question of whether genius is due to nurture or nature? In other words, is a genius produced by their teachers and environment or are they born through genetics? The treatise was published in 1756 the year Wolfgang was born. Leopold discovered that his two children were both gifted at music in 1759 when his daughter Maria Anna, who was nicknamed "Nannerl", started keyboard lessons. Wolfgang learned a great deal by copying his older sister Nannerl. He started picking out thirds on the keyboard when he was three (From Nannerl's *Reminiscences*, composed 1792 and printed in Deutsch 1965). Leopold called Wolfgang the "miracle that God let be born in Salzburg." (Grove section 1).

Leopold gave up most of his own composing to teach his children all the musical skills they would need to play the violin, keyboard and to compose music. As their only teacher, Leopold also taught his children languages and other academics. He became their manager and took them on tours to perform all over Europe for kings and queens as well as the public. They performed in Vienna, Munich, Presburg, Paris and the Hague, as well as a longer stay in London. Some scholars say that these tours were profitable, however, the cost of travel was extremely high. Most of the time the Mozart family broke even. When they became ill and could not perform, then they made nothing. Some scholars say that Leopold was tyrannical with his children even when they became adults, however others claim that he had to be strict with Wolfgang due to his irresponsible nature. In many ways Leopold felt that it was his duty to share Wolfgang's genius with the world. It was his mission in life.

The Mozart family travels took Leopold away from Salzburg and his duties with his Prince for long months and even years at a time. He had to give up his violin teaching and eventually quit composing to organize these trips. Some of his better-known works include the *Cassation in G for Orchestra*, the *Toy Symphony* (also attributed to others), his *Trumpet Concerto*, numerous symphonies, thirty large serenades, trios and divertimentos for various instruments, twelve oratorios, his *Sleigh Ride*, Turkish music, and hundreds of minuets and opera dances. He liked to include special effects in his music including shotguns in his *Jagdsinfonia* (*Sinfonia da Caccia* for four horns and strings). His *Bauernhochzeit* (Peasant Wedding) includes bagpipes, hurdy-gurdy, a dulcimer, whoops, and whistles (ad. lib.), and pistol shots. His *Toy Symphony* includes bird calls (whistles), triangle, a toy drum, and a ratchet (used to wind up a volunteer from the audience with a giant key). His *Sleigh Ride* includes sleigh bells and a glockenspiel (some editions of this piece use whip cracks and a horse whinny too).

Leopold's wife, Anna Maria, died in 1778 while she was in Paris with Wolfgang. Leopold, Wolfgang and Nannerl were devastated. Wolfgang moved 200 miles away from his father to Vienna to declare his independence. His father felt this was a great betrayal. Leopold went to Vienna in 1785 to hear his son's success there. He heard Joseph Haydn's widely quoted words of praise, upon hearing the string quartets Wolfgang dedicated to him, "Before God and as an honest man I tell you that your son is the greatest composer known to me either in person or by name: He has taste, and, furthermore, the most profound knowledge of composition." (A letter from Leopold to his daughter Maria Anna from February 16, 1785)

Later Leopold became so obsessed with raising another genius, that he undertook raising Nannerl's son, who was also called Leopoldl (which means Little Leopold). There is a letter

Leopold wrote to Nannerl suggesting that Wolfgang wanted him to raise his two children as well. This never happened. Wolfgang, knowing that his father was ill, waxed philosophical about death in a letter to his father. Two months later, on 28 May of 1787, Leopold died, and Wolfgang never got over it. He had missed his chance to get what every son desires from his father, approval. It is speculated that the ghost in Wolfgang Mozart's opera *Don Giovanni* represents his father coming back to haunt him.

Title: *Sleigh Ride* for orchestra. The Orchestration: 2 Flutes, 2 Oboes, 2 Clarinets in Bb, 2 Bassoons, 2 Horns in F, Trumpet in Bb, Percussion (3 players: Sleigh bells (2 different pitches), Glockenspiel). Strings (Violin 1, Violin 2, Viola, Cello, Bass)

Genre: A **programmatic piece** for orchestra is one that depicts a theme or story in sound. In this piece Leopold Mozart cleverly creates the image of a sleigh pulled by horses through the snow. He used sleigh bells and the glockenspiel to make the sounds of the sleigh ride. Some editions of this piece used a whip cracking, a horse whinny and percussion instruments to make the sounds of the horse's hooves.

YouTube: https://www.youtube.com/watch?v=3j4-Ny_DDS4 Leopold Mozart's *Sleigh Ride*

Birthday: 14 November 1719 Augsburg, Germany

Death Date: 28 May 1787, Salzburg, Austria (aged 67)

Fun Facts:

1. Leopold Mozart was writing his *Treatise on the Violin* while his wife was pregnant with Wolfgang Mozart. In this book he asks the question "Is nurture more important than nature in producing a musical genius?
2. Leopold Mozart composed pieces that had shotguns, sleigh bells, whistles, a ratchet, and toy drums for special effects.
3. Leopold was expelled from what is now the University of Salzburg for poor attendance.

MARIA ANNA MOZART (1751-1829)

ria Anna Mozart – **(1751-1829)** was an **Austrian** virtuoso pianist and **Classical** composer. She was also the older sister to the famous composer Wolfgang Amadeus Mozart. Maria Anna was born 30 July 1751 in Salzburg (now part of Austria). She began taking keyboard lessons at the age of seven. Nannerl's little brother sat nearby fascinated by her music. Soon he began to imitate the notes she was playing. Her father Leopold Mozart taught her how to play the harpsichord as well as academics and languages. He discovered that she was very gifted at music. Soon he was taking both of his children on tours of Europe to perform before kings and queens. Maria Anna Mozart became the most famous female keyboard artist in Europe. Reviews of her performances glowed with words of praise such as "prodigy," "virtuoso," and "genius". Her father stated in a letter from 1764 that "My little girl plays

the most difficult works which we have… with incredible precision and so excellently." "What it all amounts to is this, that my little girl, although she is only 12 years old, is one of the most skillful players in Europe." (Family's-first-prodigy smithsonianmag.com)

Maria Anna and her brother Wolfgang were the best of friends. While they were on tour, they played a fantasy game where they became the king and queen of their own country. They called it the Kingdom of Back. When they were separated Nannerl and Wolfgang wrote many letters to each other. They even had a secret language that only they understood. They performed together in 88 cities of Europe during a three-year tour. It was Nannerl who got a piece of parchment paper and wrote down Wolfgang's first *Symphony K. 16* when he was six and their father Leopold became ill on tour. Yet in time she became overshadowed by her brother's fame.

Maria Anna Mozart was born and grew up in Salzburg which at the time was a very wealthy country in Europe. She traveled to many cities with her family including Vienna and Paris, which was not typical for girls living in the eighteenth century. Most girls never had a chance to perform on stage. Yet, Nannerl was often given top billing as a harpsichord player or on the fortepiano, which was an earlier form of the piano. Wolfgang often praised Nannerl for her ability at composing music in his letters to her. Unfortunately, none of her music survived. There were social taboos about women performing on stage during her lifetime. So, in 1769, after she became old enough to get married at eighteen, her father no longer allowed her to perform in public. While her brother Wolfgang was touring Italy with Leopold, Nannerl had to stay home with their mother. While Wolfgang was touring Paris the second time with their Mother, she had to stay home with their father. She spent the time composing. Meanwhile her brother went on to soaring fame as a keyboard soloist and composer. Nannerl fell in love with Franz d'Ippold, who was a captain and a private tutor.

However, her father disapproved of him. Wolfgang tried to get her to stand up for herself, but Nannerl was not her brother, who argued with Leopold constantly. She always did as she was told to by her parents. So, at the age of thirty-two she married a magistrate, Johann Baptist Franz von Berchtold zu Sonnenburg on 23 August 1783. A magistrate is a type of judge which Leopold felt would provide a better living for his daughter than a tutor. He was a widower who lived in St. Gilgen, which was several miles away from her family home. She moved in with him and his five children from previous marriages. She helped raise his children and gave birth to three of her own. Her first child Leopold was born in 1785 and named after his grandfather. She went to Salzburg to have her son. However, her father insisted on keeping her baby and raising him without Nannerl. He delighted in all his grandson's progress. It is likely that Leopold senior wanted to create another musical genius patterned after himself. Not like his son Wolfgang whom Leopold thought had disobeyed him. By taking the younger Leopold away from his mother, he was disregarding all the positive influence Nannerl may have had on her son, and what a great influence she was on her own brother when he was a baby. As a toddler Wolfgang idolized his older sister and wanted to be just like her. That is why he wanted to play keyboard when their father was teaching her lessons. Her father allowed Nannerl to visit her son, but not to raise him. When Leopold senior died on 28 May 1787, Nannerl gained her son back again, who was now about two years old.

Wolfgang had a great respect for his sister throughout his life. He sent copies of his piano concertos to her up to No. 21. He also composed pieces for his sister to perform including his *Prelude and Fugue in C*, K. 394 (1782). They were remarkably close most of their adult life, however the last time he and his wife Constanza visited her was in 1783. After 1788 they no longer wrote letters to each other. She was devastated to learn of Wolfgang's premature death in December of 1791. Nannerl did not know how poor her brother Wolfgang had become until 1800 when she read Franz Xaver Niemetschek's 1798 biography of Mozart. It brought tears to her eyes. Her husband died in 1801 and Nannerl moved back to Salzburg with her two living children and four of her stepchildren.

Later in 1820 Wolfgang's wife Constanza moved to Salzburg with her second husband Georg Nikolaus von Nissen. Nannerl helped Constanza and her husband write a biography of Wolfgang Mozart by lending her the letters her brother wrote to her as well as letters that Leopold and Wolfgang had written to each other. Towards the end of her life Nannerl grew frail and blind. She looked poor but was very frugal. She left behind a large fortune. She died in 1829 at the age of 78 and was buried at St. Peter's cemetery in Salzburg.

The big question is what happened Nannerl Mozart's compositions? There is some very recent evidence that she composed up to twenty pieces in her notebook to help Wolfgang learn to play keyboard. Professor Martin Jarvis, an Australian-based scholar and conductor, believes he has finally identified Maria Anna's "musical handwriting". (Telegraph.co.uk January 13, 2019). The Mozart family handwriting in her notebook was analyzed during a five-year study by forensic document specialist in the United States and an Australian police forensic scientist.

They concluded that of the three scribes who wrote in Maria Anna's notebook, that "Anonymous 1" was most likely her writing. This study confirms that Maria Anna Mozart composed these works to help her bother to learn how to play the keyboard when he was a child under five years old.

We also know that Maria Anna composed for thirteen years during the time between 1769, after she finished touring, and 1783 when she got married. Were her compositions lost, destroyed or were they possibly published for her in secret by her brother? It is likely that Leopold Mozart would never have allowed his daughter's music to be published under her own name. This was not done in the eighteenth century. She was very subservient to him, so she would have obeyed his wishes. Professor Jarvis told The Telegraph: "We have only just opened the crack in the door. Maria Anna has always been this mysterious piece in history. What else we can find? Who knows?" (Telegraph.co.uk January 13, 2019)

Title: Music from Maria Anna's Notebook.
Genre: Solo keyboard works are pieces for one keyboard instrument.
YouTube: https://www.youtube.com/watch?v=AUuPIS0CD94
Music from Maria Anna's Notebook. This book includes pieces that were written by Leopold Mozart and others to teach Wolfgang how to play the keyboard. It also includes the first piece composed by Wolfgang, which was taken down by his father. Gunther Hasselmann soloist.
Birthday: 30 July 1751 in Salzburg (now part of Austria)
Death Date: 29 October 1829 in Salzburg (aged 78)
Fun Facts:
1. Maria Anna Mozart "Nannerl" was the finest female keyboard artist in Europe as a child.
2. Nannerl and Wolfgang Mozart had a secret language together.
3. Nannerl Mozart was a composer whose works were praised by her brother Wolfgang Amadeus Mozart in the letters they exchanged.

MARIA THERESIA VON PARADIS (1759-1824)

Maria Theresia von Paradis – **(1759-1824)** was an **Austrian Classical** pianist and composer. Her father was the Imperial Secretary and Court Councilor to the Empress Maria Theresia, whom she is named after. She was born on 15 May 1759, Vienna, Austria. Unfortunately, Maria lost her eyesight on 9 December 1762, when she was only three years old. It is thought that she had a nervous eye disorder. She was treated by the famous Austrian doctor Anton Mesmer and others. At first his treatments seemed to work and most of her eyesight returned. She found that the noses on people's faces were hysterically funny. Despite their best efforts to save Maria's eyesight, she became blind again. The scandal forced Mesmer to stop his treatments on her, and so Maria's

condition became permanent.

Maria showed an incredible talent for music, so the Empress granted her a stipend to support her musical and general education. Most girls were not so fortunate to receive such a broad education during this time. Her teachers included Leopold Kozeluch for piano, Vincenzo Righini and Antonio Salieri for singing and composition, and Karl Frieberth and G.J. Volger for theory and composition. Maria started performing as a pianist and singer at Viennese concert rooms and solons in 1775 when she was sixteen years old. It was said that she was able to perform sixty sonatas and concertos by memory. Mozart, Salieri, and Haydn all composed pieces for Maria Theresia von Paradis to perform. On 18 August 1783 the librettist Johann Riedinger, who was Maria's friend, invented a composition board for her. She and her mother left Vienna on a concert tour that lasted three years. They visited the Mozart family in Salzburg where it is presumed that Maria commis-

sioned Wolfgang to write a concerto for her (probably K. 456). She performed in Germany, Switzerland, France, and England.

When Maria and her mother reached Paris in March 1784, she performed about fourteen times including the *Concerts Spirituel* in April. She met with Valentine Haüy, who is remembered as the "father and apostle of the blind" (Julie Anne Sadie 1995). Von Paradis assisted him in establishing the first school for the blind which he opened in 1785. She performed Handel's fugues for King George III in London. After leaving London, her concert tour continued to Brussels, Amsterdam and Hamburg where she met C.P.E. Bach. She went on to perform in Berlin and Prague and returned to Vienna in February of 1786.

Von Paradis composed many pieces for piano as well as vocal and piano pieces. Unfortunately, many of them are lost. Her earliest surviving collection *"Zwölf Lieder auf ihrer Reise"* *in Musik gesetzt* was composed between 1784-6 while she was on tour. By 1789 Paradis was devoting more of her time composing than performing. She composed at least five operas and three cantatas. After her opera *Rinaldo und Alcina* failed, she spent more of her time teaching.

In 1808 she founded her own music school where she taught piano, singing and theory (mostly to girls). She continued to teach and give recitals with her students until her death in 1824.

Maria Theresia von Paradis was not a prolific composer. Of about thirty compositions, the authenticity of most of her piano sonatas and Italian *canzonets* have come into question. The famous *"Sicilienne"* is spurious, and was probably the work of Samuel Duskin, who discovered the piece (and is really after Weber's *Violin Sonata Op. 10, No. 1*). She composed music for five staged works, but they are all lost except for part of her *Der Schulkandidat* which was premiered in Vienna on 5 December 1792. It is also a shame that her cantatas and many of her *lieder* (songs), piano concertos and sonatas are also lost. Those works that have survived show the influence of lyrical features from Viennese and Italian styles combined with the dramatic elements from the Berlin School. Paradis did contribute important work on behalf of the blind and young women musicians through her tours as a pianist. She also commissioned several works by other composers including an organ concerto by Antonio Salieri, a piano concerto (probably No. 18, K. 456) by Wolfgang Mozart, and a piano concerto by Joseph Haydn.

Title: *"Sicilienne"*
Genre: Chamber music for solo violin and piano.
YouTube: https://www.youtube.com/watch?v=90z1KgGhtAw Violinist Nathan Milstein, pianist Arthur Balsam 1957 https://www.youtube.com/watch?v=qKFa1xOCpeICellist Jacquline du Pré
Title: Morgenlied eines armen Mannes
Genre: A **lied** is a song that is accompanied by a pianist.
YouTube: https://www.youtube.com/watch?v=hC8cTiQ8R4o Natalia Kawalek & Joelle Bouffa solo artists
Birthday: born 15 May 1759, Vienna, Austria
Death Date: 1 February 1824, Vienna, Austria (aged 65)
Fun Facts:
1. Maria von Paradis lost her eyesight at an early age.
2. Von Paradis commissioned and premiered three keyboard pieces by Salieri, Mozart, and Haydn.
3. Maria Theresia von Paradis was a virtuoso pianist and was able to compose music even though she had lost her eyesight.

LUDWIG VAN BEETHOVEN (1770-1827)

Ludwig van Beethoven – (1770-1827) was a **German Classical** and **Romantic** composer and pianist. He is famous for leading music into the Romantic era and for having composed many symphonies, concertos, string quartets, and an

opera. Ludwig was born 16 December 1770 in the town of Bonn, Germany. Ludwig was named after his grandfather who was a bass singer and *kapellmeister* for the Elector of Cologne, and one of the most important musicians in Bonn. Ludwig began to study piano and violin as a young boy from his father Johann Beethoven at the age of four. His father was a singer at the Chapel of the Elector, but he was too lazy to work enough to make his family comfortable. He wanted Ludwig to become the next Mozart, so he beat him if he did not practice enough. His father was drinking buddies with Ludwig's piano teacher, so his music lessons started at 2 a.m. in the morning when the bar closed. Ludwig worked hard and did become a piano prodigy. His father promoted him on posters as being six years old at his first performance in March of 1778 when he was really seven.

Ludwig started composing music between the ages of ten and twelve. He apprenticed as an organist at the age of thirteen and had a full-time job as an organist by the age of fourteen. He had to support both of his parents, and his two younger brothers Kasper and Nicholas, because his father was an alcoholic. His organ teacher, Christian Gottlob Neefe, encouraged Beethoven to practice and learn composition. Neefe was a member of the local chapter of the Order of the Illuminati. Neefe said of the young Beethoven "If this goes on as he has begun, he will someday be a second Mozart." (The New Grove Beethoven). On his sixteenth birthday, Beethoven decided to go to Vienna, Austria to meet Mozart and take lessons. Mozart said to his friends "Pay heed to this boy. He will surely make a noise in the world someday." (Mozart's Letters). But Ludwig's mother became ill, and he had to return to Bonn. After his mother died, Joseph Haydn convinced Beethoven to come back to Vienna to study composition with him.

Ludwig worked hard on learning counterpoint from Haydn. He also studied counterpoint with Johann Albrechtsberger and other teachers. Ludwig studied violin under Ignaz Schuppanzigh and learned to play violin and viola from Franz Rovantini. The Elector Maximilian Frederick noticed his talent early and encouraged the young Beethoven's musical studies through a stipend of money. Ludwig dedicated his first three piano sonatas to the *Kurfürst* ("Elector") and they were published in 1783.

Beethoven became a great pianist and composer, who was welcomed everywhere in Vienna. He did not like to perform in public though, preferring to play for his friends. Unfortunately, around the age of fifteen Beethoven gradually began to lose his hearing. He had to have a special piano built, so he could hear it. Most of his greatest symphonies were written after he had become deaf. Beethoven composed nine symphonies, six piano concertos, a violin concerto, sixteen string quartets, piano trios and quartets, piano and violin sonatas, other chamber music pieces, choral pieces, songs, and operatic works.

Beethoven was one of the first composers who did not rely on employment from the church or a court to supply his income. He earned his income by performing, teaching piano, from various patrons, and by publishing his works. One of his patrons and life-long friends was Count Ferdinand von Waldstein. Some of his other patrons include Prince Joseph Franz Lobkowitz, Baron Gottfried van Swieten, and Prince Karl Lichnowsky. His friend Anton Hoffmeister published many of Beethoven's works. Beethoven dedicated his first six *String Quartets Op. 18* to Prince Lobkowitz, who had commissioned them. Another patron was Count Andreas

Razumovsky who later became a prince. Beethoven dedicated his *String Quartets Nos. 7-9, Op. 59* to this prince.

As Beethoven's hearing loss became more profound, he performed less in public. After his failed attempt to perform the premiere of his *Piano Concerto No. 5* the "Emperor," he did not perform in public again. That is until 1824 when he helped to conduct the premiere of his *Symphony No. 9*. He was so deaf that at the end of this first performance he had to be turned around to see the great applause from the audience. In 1825, all nine of his symphonies were performed in a cycle for the first time, by the Leipzig Gewandhaus Orchestra under Johann Philipp Christian Schulz and in 1826.

After Beethoven's brother Kasper died in 1815, he went to court against his sister-in-law and won the right to raise his nephew, Karl. His relationship with Karl was often argumentative. After going to the university Karl joined the military. The last years of Beethoven's life he was ill. He became bedridden for several months and his friends came to visit him. During this time, he composed a replacement last movement for his string quartet op. 130. The fourteenth string quartet was his favorite. Beethoven believed in the liberty and the brotherhood of mankind. He expressed his immortal spirituality in his musical works. Beethoven died on the 26th of March 1827 during a thunderstorm. His friend Anselm Hüttenbrenner was with him and said that there was a peal of thunder at the moment of death. Beethoven was only 56 years old. His liver was severely damaged as well as his auditory nerve (Copper 2008). It is not known exactly what he died from. Nearly 20,000 people attended his funeral in Vienna including composer Franz Schubert.

50 Famous Composers

Title: "Moonlight" *Sonata for Piano No. 14, Op. 27 in C# minor* "Quasi una Fantasia"
Genre: A **sonata** is a chamber music piece for one or two solo instruments in four movements.
YouTube: https://www.youtube.com/watch?v=-VmQNKaOeEw Anastasia Huppmann
Title: *Symphony No. 5, Op. 67 in c minor* "Fate" also known as the "Victory"
Genre: A **symphony** is a large-scale work for orchestra, usually in four movements.
YouTube: https://www.youtube.com/watch?v=1lHOYvIhLxo
Leonard Bernstein conducting the Vienna Philharmonic.
Birthday: Born 16 December 1770 in the town of Bonn, Germany.
Death Date: 26 March 1827 in Vienna, Austria during a thunderstorm (aged 56). It is estimated that nearly 20,000 people attended his funeral.

Fun Facts:

1. He ate macaroni and cheese almost every day of his life, and a soup with twelve drowned eggs to settle his stomach.
2. Beethoven's deafness started at the age of fifteen, and he was completely deaf by the age of forty-six in 1816. Beethoven sawed the legs off his piano, so that he could put it on the wood floor and feel the vibrations from the music.
3. Beethoven was paid to walk by his patrons because he did his best composing then.
4. Beethoven was kicked out of twenty-seven apartments for banging on his piano.
5. Beethoven originally wrote the dedication of his *Symphony No. 3* to Napoleon Bonaparte, however when Bonaparte crowned himself Emperor, Beethoven tore off the title page and renamed it "The Heroic" symphony instead *(Sinfonia Eroica)*.
6. Composer and virtuoso Prussian pianist Daniel Steibelt came to Vienna in 1800 and challenged Beethoven to a musical duel by improvisation. Prince Lobkowitz agreed to sponsor Steibelt, and Prince Lichnowsky sponsored Beethoven. The contest took place at Lobkowitz's Palace where Steibelt, as the challenger, went first. Each composer was to improvise on the other's music. Beethoven had been challenged by many pianists in Vienna and beaten them all at this game. But Steibelt had a fierce reputation as a great pianist. So, the day of the contest Steibelt brought in one of his own compositions and tossed it on the floor. He was known to be a "storm" composer and conjured up great thunder in his rumbling bass line. The audience was blown away by his performance and gave him a standing ovation.

All eyes turned to Beethoven, who took a deep breath, exhaled slowly, then trudged to the piano to the relief of the audience. He picked up Steibelt's music, showed it to the audience, then turned the music upside down. He played the four notes that opened Steibelt's piece, embellishing them, and then improvising them. Beethoven imitated Steibelt's "storm," unpicked his playing, put it back together, parodied it, and then mocked it. Steibelt realized that not only had he been outplayed by a great genius of the piano, but he had also been humiliated in the eyes of the Vienna public. He made a hasty exit with Lobkowitz running after him. The Prince returned saying that Steibelt had vowed never to return to Vienna if Beethoven lived there, and he kept his promise.

ROMANTIC COMPOSERS
(1820-1910)

GIOACHINO ROSSINI (1792-1868)

Gioachino Rossini – (1792-1868) **Italian Romantic** composer, singer, and impresario. He was born 29 February 1792 in Pesaro, Italy into a family of musicians. His father, Giuseppe, was a horn player, and his mother, Anna, was a singer.

Gioachino was often left in the care of his grandmother, who was not particularly good at minding him. His father was a Napoleon sympathizer, which got Giuseppe thrown in prison when the French invaded Northern Italy. Giuseppe got out later when the Austrians took Italy back. His mother got a job working in the Bologna theaters, so Gioachino was left in the care of the pork butcher. Later his father joined her by performing in the orchestras at the theaters where she sang. They started Rossini's music training early, so that Rossini was playing the triangle in his father's music group by six.

Rossini's first harpsichord teacher Prinetti had a bad habit of falling asleep while standing up and playing scales with only two fingers. This was cause for ridicule by the young Rossini. Then he got lessons from the music master Angelo Tesei, who taught him how to play piano accompaniments, and sing well enough that he was given solos at church. His early string works show the influence of melodies by Mozart and Haydn, and operatic tendencies to punctuate the notes. He learned to play the horn and cello, and was admitted to the Conservatory at Bologna, where he also learned counterpoint from Mattei. However, he learned more about music from the scoring of Mozart and Haydn's quartets, so he was nicknamed "Il Tedeschino" ("the Little

German") at the conservatory on account of his devotion to Mozart.

Rossini composed his first opera at the age of thirteen or fourteen which was called *Demetrio e Polibio*, but it was not performed until he was twenty after he had written five other operas. He moved to Paris, France in 1855. He entertained guests as an excellent amateur chef. He also spent part of his life in Florence and Naples, Italy and in Vienna and London. Rossini composed thirty-nine operas, sacred music, songs, chamber music and some piano pieces. Among his best-known operas are his Italian comedies *Il barbiere di Siviglia* (The Barber of Seville) and, *La Cenerentola* (Cinderella) and the French-language epics *Moïse et Pharaon* (Moses and Pharaoh) and *Guillaume Tell* (William Tell).

Rossini's opera *William Tell* is based on a Swiss folk hero who was legendary as a strong man and an expert marksman. It is said that he assassinated Albrecht Gessler, who was a tyrannical official of the Austrian dukes of the House of Habsburg. Tell's actions led to an open rebellion by the people and the foundation of the Swiss Confederacy. Rossini went into retirement after composing this opera. The overture is in four parts, which are performed without pause. Franz Liszt created a piano reduction of the "William Tell Overture". This piece has been featured as the theme song in television series such as the UK "Adventures of William Tell" and "The Lone Ranger" in the US as well as in many film scores.

During Rossini's later life he was often sick. He passed away from cancer after an unsuccessful operation at the age of seventy-six. Four thousand people attended his funeral. He left a life estate to his second wife Olympe Pélissier, who was an artist's model. After she passed away ten years later his estate passed to the Commune of Pesaro for the establishment of a *Liceo Musicale*. His estate also funded a home for retired opera singers in Paris (Osborne 1993). He was buried at the Père Lachaise Cemetery. Later in 1887 his remains were moved to the church of Santa Croce, Florence.

Dr. Carolyn Waters Broe

Title: "Finale" to the William Tell Overture – This overture is in four parts that are performed without pause including: Prelude: Dawn; Storm; *Ranz des vaches* "call to the cows" featuring the English horn; and the Finale: March of the Swiss Soldiers

It is scored for: a piccolo, a flute, two oboes (first or second oboe doubles on *"cor anglaise"* or English horn), two clarinets in A, two bassoons, four French horns in G and E, two trumpets in E, three trombones, timpani, triangle, bass drum and cymbals, and strings.

Genre: An **opera overture** is an instrumental work that precedes and introduces the main opera and contains all the musical themes of that opera.

YouTube: https://www.youtube.com/watch?v=YIbYCOiETx0

The Milwaukee Symphony Orchestra, under the baton of Edo de Waart, performs the thrilling finale to Rossini's "William Tell Overture".

Birthday: 29 February 1792 in Pesaro, Italy

Death Date: 13 November 1868 in Paris, France (aged 76)

Fun: Facts:

1. Rossini said, "I know of no more admirable occupation than eating". His favorite dish was Tournedos Rossini, where he would ask his butler to "turn his back" to hide the final ingredients from his guests.
2. Rossini said, "Give me the laundress' bill and I will set to music even that".
3. "I take him [Beethoven] twice a week, Haydn four times, and Mozart every day".
4. *"Every kind of music is good, except the boring kind"*. Rossini

FRANZ SCHUBERT (1797-1828)

ranz Schubert – (1797-1828) was an **Austrian Romantic** composer, who composed over six hundred songs called "lieder," and seven full symphonies before passing away before his 32nd birthday. Franz was born 31 January 1797, Vienna, Austria. Schubert's father, Franz Theodore Schubert, was a parish school master, and the son of a Moravian peasant. His mother, Elisabeth Vietz Schubert, was the daughter of a Salesian master locksmith. She had been a maid servant before marrying his father. He was one of five surviving children out of fourteen. Franz began his education at the age of six with his father. He also learned the basics of the violin from his father, and piano from his brother Ignaz.

At seven he was given piano lessons from the local organist and parish church choir master Michael Holzer. A friend took him to a pianoforte warehouse so that he could practice on better instruments. He played the viola in his family string quartet with his brothers Ferdinand and Ignaz on first and second violins, and his father on cello. Franz composed his early string quartets for this group.

When Franz Schubert was still a boy of only seven, his vocal talents were first recognized by the Italian composer Antonio Salieri. Franz was given a scholarship in 1808 to attend the *Stadtkonvikt* (Imperial Seminary) as a member of the choir. At this school Schubert studied the symphonies of Mozart, Joseph Haydn, and his brother Michael Haydn. Schubert also became interested in songs by Johann Rudolf Zumsteeg, who was the leading composer of *lieder*. His good friend Joseph von Spaun helped to purchase manuscript paper for Schubert when he was low on money. Schubert had several good friends who were very generous with him. When Schubert's talents as a composer began to materialize, Salieri gave him private music theory and composition lessons. Schubert was given the opportunity to conduct the *Stadtkonvikt* orchestra and composed some of his early orchestra music for this ensemble.

When Schubert turned sixteen at the end of 1813, he left the Stadtkonvikt to finish his training as a teacher at the St. Anna Normal School. The next year, he started teaching the youngest students at his father's school. He met the beautiful soprano named Theresa Grob, who was the daughter of a silk merchant, and composed his *"Salve Regina," "Tantum Ergo,"* and *Mass No. 1* for her. Schubert was inspired and composed numerous pieces in 1815. He wanted to marry Theresa but could not pass the strict Austrian law requiring that the bridegroom be able to prove his ability to support the marriage. His attempts at gaining a position as a choirmaster and *kapellmeister* had failed. Distraught, Schubert quit his job as a schoolteacher, and moved in with one of his students, who lived with his mother. Schubert and his close circle of friends, artists and students began to have social meetings called *Schubertiaden* to discuss music and art.

Unfortunately, Schubert and four of his friends were arrested later by the police in Vienna. In the early 1820's the Austrians were extremely nervous about any revolutionary activities due to the French Revolution and the Napoleonic wars. His friend Johann Senn was put on trial and held in prison for over a year. He was released but ordered never to come to Vienna again. Even though Schubert never saw Johann again, he set two of his poems to music, *"Selige Welt" (D. 743)* and *"Schwanengesang" (D 744)*.

Schubert was very prolific during this time composing his unfinished oratorio *Lazarus (D. 689)*, his *"Wanderer Fantasy" in C for piano (D. 760)*, and he staged two of his operas *Die Zwillingsbrüder* (D. 647) and *Die Zauberharfe (D. 644)*. Yet publishers were reluctant to publish Schubert's music. Anton Diabelli agreed to publish his works on commission including his first seven opus numbers. This all changed when the famous singer Vogl performed Schubert's song *"Der Erlkönig"* (The Erl King) (D. 328) from his *Opus 1* in March of 1821. This was a *lieder* based on a poem by Goethe. The concert was very well received, so more of Schubert's music was published after that. It was during this time that Schubert became hopelessly in love with his pupil, the Countess Karoline Esterházy, but the only work he dedicated to her was his *Fantasia in F minor for Piano Duet* (D. 940). Schubert experimented with instrumentation in several works including his *Sonata in A minor for Arpeggione and Piano* (D. 821), and the unconventional scoring of the *Trout Quintet* (D. 667).

Even though Schubert staged twenty of his operas, they were almost completely unsuccessful. His now famous opera *Rosemunde* has many beautiful arias, yet it did not become popular during his lifetime. Part of this is due to the success of the Italian opera composer Rossini. Schubert finished his *Mass in A-flat Major* (d. 678), which is considered one of his mature works. He met both Beethoven and Carl Maria von Weber, who were both successful musicians, but nothing came from this, because they were not familiar with Schubert's music. When Beethoven was on his deathbed, he finally got a chance to look over Schubert's music, and remarked "Truly, the spark of divine genius resides in this Schubert!" We will never know if Beethoven would have helped Schubert if he had recovered from his illness. Schubert was a torch bearer at Beethoven's funeral in Vienna in 1827. Little did he know that his own funeral was so close at hand. He left his *Symphony in B Minor* (D. 759) "Unfinished," yet it became one of his most famous works. The reason why he left this symphony, which has two movements and part of the third, unfinished is still a mystery.

It is a tragedy that during his time of greatest musical activity, Schubert's health began to fail. By the late 1820's he told his friends that he feared that he was near death. In the summer of 1828, he was seen by the court physician, who confirmed that he was beyond help. Schubert died on 19 November 1828 at the young age of thirty-one. The cause of his death is officially listed as typhoid fever, however, there has been much debate about what happened. Some scholars feel that Schubert died from mercury poisoning, which was a common remedy during the 19th century. Five days before his death Schubert said that he wished to hear Beethoven's *String Quartet No. 14 in C-sharp minor*, Op. 131. His friend, violinist Karl Holz, who was there commented: "The King of Harmony has sent the King of Song a friendly bidding to the crossing" (Deutsche 1998, pg. 300).

Dr. Carolyn Waters Broe

Title: The *"Erlkönig"* or Elf King for voice and piano by Franz Schubert, was based on a poem by Johann Wolfgang von Goethe. This *lied*, or song depicts the death of a child attacked by a supernatural being called the Erlking or *"Erlkönig"*. It was originally composed by Goethe as part of his 1782 Singspiel entitled *Die Fischerin*. The Danish legend of the Elf King was later adapted by the Germans. Schubert revised this piece four times, and it was finally published in 1821 as his Opus 1.

Many composers set this poem to music, but Schubert's is the most famous.

Genre: A *"lieder"* or *"lied"* is a type of German song with piano accompaniment that was extremely popular during the Romantic era.

YouTube: https://www.youtube.com/watch?v=JS91p-vmSf0 Daniel Norman – Tenor

Sholto Kynoch – Piano

Jeremy Hamway-Bidgood – Director & designer

Birthday: 31 January 1797, Vienna, Austria.

Death Date: 19 November 1828, Vienna, Austria (aged 31).

Fun Facts:

1. Schubert was nicknamed *"Schwammerl"* by his friends, which means "Little Mushroom" or "Tubby" in German. Schubert was not even five feet tall and a bit chubby.

2. Even though he lived to be only 31 years old, he composed over 1,000 pieces, which is astonishing considering that he composed many operas and symphonies.

3. Schubert was in awe of Beethoven most of his life, but the first time he got a chance to meet him, he ran away. At their second meeting, he was brave enough to speak to the famous composer.

LOUISE FARRENC (1804-1875)

ouise Farrenc – (1804-1875) **French Romantic** composer, *virtuosa* pianist, teacher, and scholar was born 31 May 1804 in Paris, France. She was the daughter of the famous sculptor Jacques-Edme Dumont, and the sister of Auguste Dumont, who was also a sculptor. She came from a long line of French sculptors and Bohemian painters, who were open to women exploring their artistic talents. Louise began piano lessons at an early age with Cecile Soria, a former student of Muzio Clementi. She was accepted later as a student of the piano masters Ignaz Moscheles and Johann Nepomuk Hummel. Louise Dumont showed great talent as a composer incredibly early. So, in 1819, at the age of fifteen, her parents sent Louise to study composition with Anton Reicha at the Paris Conservatoire. It is not known if she studied with

him privately, or attended classes, as only men could take Reicha's composition classes. She performed many of her own compositions in concerts.

In 1821 Louise married a fellow conservatory student and concert flautist Aristide Farrenc, who was ten years older than her. After he got tired of touring around Europe, Louise helped him to start a music publishing firm. Louise Farrenc's earliest compositions for piano were published by her husband's company (between 1825 to 1839) in France. Her "*Air russe varié*" was reviewed favorably by Robert Schumann in his journal the *Neue Zeitschrifdt für Musik*. He praised Louise for her musical charm and romanticism. Farrenc's *30 Etudes*, in all the major and minor keys, were endorsed by the music critic Maurice Bourges in *La revue et gazette musicale* in 1840. He predicted that her etude collection would become a classic for developing technique and taste. Thus, in 1845 the Paris Conservatory required Farrenc's *Etudes* for all piano classes. Louise Farrenc had been appointed by D.F.E. Auber, the Director of the Paris Conservatoire, as professor of piano in 1842. She continued to teach there until she retired on 1 January of 1873. Louise Farrenc was the only woman in the 19th century to hold a permanent chair at the Paris Conservatoire. Even though many of her students won competitions, and went on to become professionals, Louise was paid less than her male colleagues for ten years. One of her most famous students, was her own daughter Victorine Louise, who became ill in her twenties, and tragically died before the age of 33.

Farrenc's large scale orchestral pieces include two sets of grand variations for piano and orchestra, two overtures (1834), and three symphonies (which were completed in the 1840's). One of her earliest pieces was the *Deuxieme Overture*, Op 24, 1834. The famous composer Hector Berlioz wrote that the piece was "orchestrated with a talent rare among women." Even though these works had performances in Paris, Copenhagen, Brussels and Geneva, all remained unpublished during her lifetime. She also composed important chamber music pieces including two piano quintets (composed in 1839 and 1849), and two piano trios (1844). Between 1848 to 1858 she composed two violin sonatas, a cello sonata, two trios, a nonet for wind and strings, and a sextet for piano and wind instruments. The young violin virtuoso Joseph Joachim took part in the 1850 premiere of Farrenc's nonet, which brought her near celebrity status. She also composed vocal and choral works, but unfortunately no operas. Farrenc was twice awarded the *Prix Chartier* of the Académie des Beaux-Arts, in 1861 and 1869 for her contributions to chamber music.

Unfortunately, after the death of her daughter in 1839, Louise Farrenc abandoned her music composition. She decided to help her husband Aristide with his project to edit and publish many historic keyboard pieces for piano and harpsichord. He closed his music publishing firm in 1840 and devoted his time to scholarly research. After his death in 1865, she compiled and edited a 23-volume anthology of historic keyboard pieces spanning 300 years which was published as *Le trésor de pianists* or Treasures of Pianists (1861-74). She and her pupils gave many concerts of 17th and 18th century keyboard compositions.

Through her extensive research, Louise gained an incredible knowledge of performance practices from earlier eras and published this as the forward to her anthology. Her scholarship as a pioneer in music research, helped to bring in a French musical renaissance in the 1870's. After she passed away, the introduction to the first volume of Farrenc's Le trésor de pianists, called "Des signes d'agrément", was later published as a separate volume entitled Traité des Abréviations in 1895. She continued to be remembered as a virtuosa piano performer, however she was largely forgotten as a composer. This was largely due to her not composing an opera during an operatic era in France, and her status as a woman. However, if there is any woman of the 19th century who deserves to be famous, it is Louise Farrenc.

Title: *Symphony No. 3 in g minor*, Op. 36 (1847), 4. Finale-Allegro Instrumentation: 2 flutes, 2 oboes, 2 clarinets, 2 bassoons, 2 horns, timpani, strings.

Genre: A 19th century symphony is a large-scale music work for about eighty-five musicians, which is usually composed in four movements with brass, winds, strings, and percussion.

YouTube Video: https://www.youtube.com/watch?v=R2erXxyX0x8 Insula Orchestra, Laurence Equilbey director.

Title: Piano Quintet No. 1 in a minor, Op. 30 (for piano and strings). Allegro 2. Adagio ma non troppo 3. Scherzo: Presto 4. Finale: Allegro.

Genre: A piano quintet is considered chamber music for piano and four other musicians. Chamber music is written for a small group of two to ten musicians.

YouTube Video: https://www.youtube.com/watch?v=jypbFP89Hng Berit Cardas, Violine; Klaus Christa, Viola; Bjørg Værnes Lewis, Violoncello; Leon Bosch, Kontrabass: Akiko Shiochi, Klavier.

Birthday: 31 May 1804 in Paris, France

Death Date: 15 September 1875 in Paris, France (age 71)

Fun Facts:

1. Louise Farrenc would have been more famous during her lifetime if she had written an opera.
2. Louise Farrenc was the first woman in the 19th century to hold an important permanent music position at the Paris Conservatory as Professor of Piano.
3. The year Louise Dumont Farrenc was born, Napoleon was crowned Emperor of France, so she was born into a time of political upheaval.

SISTER AND BROTHER COMPOSERS

FANNY MENDELSSOHN (1805-1847)

anny Mendelssohn Hensel – (1805-1847) was a prolific **German Romantic** composer, a skilled pianist, conductor, and a respected leader of a flourishing Berlin salon. She grew up in a culturally sophisticated home, where she was exposed to the leading artistic and intellectual figures of the day. Heirich Heine, the author of the text of Hensel's song "*Schwanenleid*" *Op. 1, No. 1*, was a frequent visitor to the Mendelssohn home. She came from a distinguished Jewish family but was not brought up in that faith. Her grandfather was the famous philosopher Moses Mendelssohn Bartholdy. Her father was Abraham Mendelssohn and her mother Lea Salomon Mendelssohn. Fanny Mendelssohn composed over 460 pieces of music, including

a piano trio, a piano quartet, an orchestral overture, over 250 *lieder* (songs), four cantatas, and over 125 pieces for the piano.

Fanny Mendelssohn was born 14 November 1805 in Hamburg, Germany, but her family moved to Berlin, which was then part of Prussia. She was the eldest of four children, including her brother Felix Mendelssohn, who was also a famous composer. Felix and Fanny shared a similar education, however because she was a girl, Fanny was not encouraged to become a professional musician. Therefore, most of her compositions are in genres that were acceptable for women: *lieder* (songs) and piano pieces. In fact, Fanny's first published compositions, three *lieder*, appeared under her brother's authorship. Her husband, the court painter Wilhelm Hensel, encouraged Fanny to publish, while her brother Felix opposed it. It was because of Felix's negative attitude that very few of Fanny's more than 400 compositions were ever published during her brief lifetime. Felix may have felt that he was protecting his sister. However, Felix got in trouble with Queen Victoria for signing his name to Fanny's pieces, when the Queen said she wanted to sing her favorite piece by him, and he had to admit to her that it was really written by Fanny.

Fanny showed great ability in music at an early age. She was taught piano in the Berliner-Bach style by her mother Lea Solomon Mendelssohn, who was a student of Johann Kirnberger, who was himself a student of Johann Sebastian Bach. Thus, at the age of thirteen, Fanny could already play all 24 Preludes from Bach's *The Well-Tempered Clavier* by heart. She performed all of Bach's preludes for her father, Abraham Mendelssohn, on his birthday in 1818. She may also have been inspired by her two great aunts Fanny von Arnstein and Sarah Levy, who were both music lovers. She also studied with pianist Marie Bigot in Paris, and later with Ludwig Berger. Both Felix and Fanny began to take lessons in composition from the composer Carl Friedrich Zelter in 1819. The next year Fanny and her brother Felix joined the Sing-Akademie in Berlin, which was led by Zelter. He favored Fanny over Felix when he wrote to the poet Johann Wolfgang von Goethe in 1816 introducing their father, "He has adorable children, and his oldest daughter could give you something of Sebastian Bach. This child is really something special" (Conway 2012, 171). Later, Zelter again wrote to Goethe describing Fanny's piano playing with the highest praise for a woman of this time "She plays like a man" (Todd 2010).

Fanny Mendelssohn loved to give concerts in her large garden salon, which seated 200 audience members. Many famous people attended her garden concerts including the famous pianists Franz Liszt and Clara Wieck Schumann, the Prussian polymath and naturalist Alexander Humbolt, and his brother Wilhelm Humbolt who was a linguist, Johanna Kinkel who was a composer, and Heinrich Heine the poet, writer and literary critic. (Thompson 2020) At these concerts Mendelssohn would perform many of her latest compositions for piano and chamber music, which were given high praise from her distinguished guests. She also invited singers and other musicians to perform with her.

In 1829, after a courtship of several years, Fanny married the painter Wilhelm Hensel. Fanny had to write the music for her own wedding the night before when Felix failed to keep his promise to compose the music for her. According to Sheila Hayman, a direct descendant of Fanny, she wrote music for special occasions like birthdays, weddings and public events. (Thompson 2020) Every morning Wilhelm would put a beautifully illustrated color manuscript page on Fanny's piano, and every evening she would present him with a new composition on the page. The following year after they married, she had her only child Sebastian Ludwig Felix Hensel. While she was still nursing Sebastian, a cholera epidemic broke out in 1831 in Berlin. Fanny wrote about this extensively in her diary. Fortunately, no one in her immediate family died, but she lost friends. So, in January of 1832 Fanny composed her *"Cholera Musik"* (Cholera Cantata) to honor the fallen victims of this epidemic. (Thompson 2020)

On 14 May 1847 Fanny Mendelssohn Hensel died suddenly of complications from a stroke that happened during a rehearsal of her brother's oratorio *The First Walpurgis Night*. She was only forty-one years old and her death broke her brother Felix's heart. Felix also died of a stroke six months later at an early age (as did both of their parents and their grandfather Moses Mendelssohn). But Felix managed to finish his *String Quartet No. 6 in F minor*, which he dedicated in her memory. Some of the most famous pieces by Fanny Mendelssohn include her *Notturno in G minor for Piano, Piano Trio Op. 11, Oratorium nach den Bildern der Bibel*, and her lieder *"Morgenständchen"*. It is also thought that she composed an *Easter Cantata*, which was published under her brother's name.

Title: *Piano Trio Op. 11 for Violin, Cello and Piano.*
Genre: chamber music, piano trio.
YouTube: https://www.youtube.com/watch?v=oKC-f3zPcV4 Piano Trio op.11 Dvorak-Trio München
Birthday: 14 November 1805, Hamburg, Germany.
Death Date: 14 May 1847, Berlin, Germany (aged 41).
Fun Facts:

1. Each of her pieces was written on colored paper, illustrated by her husband Wilhelm Hensel, and accompanied by a poem.

2. By the age of thirteen Hensel could play the entire first book of Bach's *Well Tempered Clavier* by memory.

3. Felix discouraged his sister Fanny from publishing her music directly. He even published several of them under his own name. However, at the age of 40, Hensel defied her brother by publishing two books of solo songs, several piano pieces and a book of part songs. All these works were given critical acclaim. (Library of Congress, Who Was She?)

4. Felix got in trouble with Queen Victoria for signing his name to Fanny's pieces, when the queen said she wanted to sing her favorite piece by him, and he had to admit to her that it was really written by Fanny.

5. Hensel is now thought by some scholars to have created the musical form *Lieder ohne Worte* (songs without words). (Library of Congress, Who Was She?)

FELIX MENDELSSOHN (1809-1847)

elix Mendelssohn – (1809-1847) was a **German** early **Romantic** composer, pianist, organist, and conductor. He was born 3 February 1809 in Hamburg, Germany (which was a city state then). Felix was a child prodigy, who started piano lessons with his mother, Lea Solomon Mendelssohn, at the age of six. By seven, he was studying with Marie Bigot in Paris. At the age of nine, Felix gave his first public performance with a horn duo. His father, Abraham Mendelssohn was a wealthy banker, and his grandfather, Moses Mendelssohn, was a well-known Jewish philosopher. He was the second child of four children, including his older sister Fanny who was also a child prodigy. Felix loved his sister Fanny and was inspired by her musical abilities. In 1811 the Mendelssohn family fled to Berlin in disguise, fearing

revenge from the French for evading Napoleon's banking block. It was there that all four children were taught piano by Ludwig Berger, who was himself a student of the famous keyboard artist Muzio Clementi. The Mendelssohn family converted to Christianity and added the last name Bartholdy.

Starting in 1819, Felix and his sister Fanny both studied composition and counterpoint from Carl Friedrich Zelter. Zelter was a student of Bach's oldest son, W. F. Bach, and he was a champion of C.P.E. Bach. Felix was greatly influenced in his childhood by the music of Bach, as well as the music of Mozart and Beethoven. He later helped to preserve and revive many of

Johann Sebastian Bach's compositions through the Sing-Akademie of Berlin. Mendelssohn's aunt Sarah Levi was an accomplished keyboard player, who soloed with Zelter's orchestra at the Sing-Akademie. It is likely that Aunt Sarah was the one who recommended that Felix and Fanny study with Zelter. She also had a large collection of Bach family manuscripts, which she left to the academy when she passed away. Felix Mendelssohn's music shows many important similarities with the fugues and counterpoint of the great master Johann Sebastian Bach. His direct access to the Baroque works of Bach gave his music a brilliant clarity and classical formal style, which is unmatched. In 1821 Zelter introduced Felix to his friend, the elderly Johann Wolfgang von Goethe, who was a famous German poet. Goethe was impressed with Felix and compared his talent favorably to that of Mozart. Later, Mendelssohn set several of Goethe's poems to music.

Many of Mendelssohn's early works were performed by private orchestras to entertain his father's wealthy guests at their home. Between the age of twelve and fourteen, Felix composed twelve string symphonies for this purpose. Later, Mendelssohn composed five full symphonies, such as his "Scottish" and "Italian" symphonies. He composed his brilliant *String Octet* at age sixteen, and his famous *Overture A Midsummer Night's Dream* at age seventeen. He also composed concerti including his famous *Violin Concerto*, piano music, oratorios, and chamber music including his string quartets. Mendelssohn composed his "Hebrides Overture" in 1830, after visiting the Scottish Hebrides.

On 28 March 1837, Mendelssohn married Cécile Charlotte Sophie Jeanrenaud, who was the daughter of a French Reformed Church clergyman. They had five children. Over the next few years Mendelssohn traveled widely, including England, Vienna, Florence, Milan, Rome, Naples, and Scotland. After Zelter's death in 1832, Mendelssohn thought that he would become the conductor of the Sing-Akademie of Berlin, but he was passed over by a lessor musician. In 1835 Mendelssohn was named conductor of the Leipzig Gewandhaus Orchestra, even though he could have been the opera conductor in Munich, or the editor of a prestigious music journal. So, Mendelssohn and his family moved to Leipzig. Felix was exceptionally close to his sister Fanny. After she passed away at a young age in 1847, Felix was very depressed. Felix Mendelssohn died at the age of thirty-eight after six months of ill health, following a hectic tour of England, and a series of strokes. His grandfather Moses, his sister Fanny, and both of his parents also died of similar strokes. He was buried in the Trinity Cemetery in Berlin, Germany.

Title: *A Midsummer Night's Dream – Overture*, in E Major, op.21 was written in 1826 when he was seventeen years and six months old. The Overture is scored for two flutes, two oboes, two clarinets, two bassoons, two horns, two trumpets, ophicleide (a brass instrument like a tuba), timpani and strings. The incidental music adds a third trumpet, three trombones, triangle, and cymbals to this scoring. This overture includes wonderful effects such as the scampering of fairy feet in the strings, and the braying of a donkey.

Genre: An **overture** is usually an instrumental piece that precedes another larger work such as an opera or a play. In this case, Mendelssohn was composing "incidental music" for Shakespeare's play.

Mendelssohn wrote his Concert Overture Op. 21 soon after he read a German translation of Shakespeare's *A Midsummer Night's Dream* in 1826. It is said that he was inspired to write the opening chords after hearing a breeze rustling the leaves in the garden of his family home. The effect is descriptive of the scampering of fairy footsteps. You can also hear the donkey braying. Unfortunately, Mendelssohn did not have the benefit of midsummer weather to hear the first performance of his Overture. He had to travel eighty miles through a terrible snowstorm to get to the place where his piece was being performed. Then he performed as the soloist on two piano concerti and performed as a violinist in the orchestra for Beethoven's *Ninth Symphony*. Mendelssohn was only eighteen at the time.

A Midsummer Night's Dream **Op . 61 – "The Wedding March"** was music that Mendelssohn composed in 1842 for a play based on Shakespeare by the same title. It is called "incidental music". This is music that goes along with the play. Mendelssohn's "Wedding March" has become incredibly famous as one of the most popular wedding processionals ever written. This is strange considering that Shakespeare wrote the scene in his play as part of a comedy.

Birthday: 3 February 1809 in Hamburg, Germany

Death Date: 4 November 1847 in Leipzig, Germany (aged 38).

Fun Facts:

1. Mendelssohn was often afflicted with frequent fits of bad temper, which even led to his collapse in some cases. He was nicknamed the "discontented Polish count" because of his aloofness. There was one fit where he scared his family when he started ranting in English. His father spoke sternly to him, which stopped the rant, and sent him to bed for twelve hours.

2. Mendelssohn visited Britain often. He was a close friend of Queen Victoria and Prince Albert, who were great admirers of his music. Queen Victoria even chose Mendelssohn's 'Wedding March' for her daughter's wedding. Which is the reason why the 'Wedding March' is so popular at weddings today! It is frequently played when the bride and groom walk out of church.

3. Felix was a great fan of his sister Fanny's music compositions. He had an embarrassing moment when Queen Victoria asked Mendelssohn's permission to sing one of his *lieder* (songs). He had to admit that the *lieder* was composed by his sister Fanny! Some scholars think that he published several of her pieces under his own name, because it was so difficult for women to get their music published in the 19th century.

HUSBAND AND WIFE COMPOSERS

CLARA SCHUMANN (1819-1896)

lara Schumann – (1819-1896) was a **German Romantic** composer and pianist, and the wife of composer Robert Schumann. She was born 13 September 1819 in Leipzig, Germany. Clara Schumann was a child prodigy on the piano. She was taught by her father and manager Frederick Wieck. Before the age of 21, she composed only works that would be performed at her own concerts. Almost all her 182 performances that were performed between 1828 and 1840, included at least one piano work by the young Clara Weick. Her work was praised by the "new Romantic" composers such as Mendelssohn, Chopin, and Liszt. She was showered with gold and jewels by kings and queens in Vienna. Students sat by her feet to be near this genius.

Clara performed at the age of eight at the home of Dr. Ernst Carus, who was the director of the mental hospital in 1828. It was there that she met her future husband, Robert Schumann, who was nine years older than Clara, and a young pianist. He was so impressed with her performance, that he asked if he could come and study with her father. So, Robert came to live at the Weick home for about a year. In 1830 Clara went on her first concert tour at the age of eleven including Paris and other European cities accompanied by her father. She performed her first solo in Leipzig, Germany at the Gawandhaus. In Weimar, she performed for the famous poet Goethe, who awarded her a medal with his portrait saying, "For the gifted artist Clara Weick". She started writing her *Piano Concerto in A Minor* at the age of thirteen and finished it in 1835 at fourteen.

Robert asked for Clara's hand in marriage in 1837, when she was eighteen, and Clara accepted. However, her father did not approve of Robert. They had to go to court and sue him so they could get married. Her first published works after her marriage to Robert Schumann in 1840, were three songs in a collection entitled *Zwölf Leider*. "*Liebst Du um Schönheit*," with texts by Friedrich Rückert, is the fourth song of the collection. Robert published this collection in both of their names but did not tell the critics which pieces belonged to Clara and which belonged to him. They must have enjoyed the confusion. Clara memorized all her performances, edited Robert's music, composed, taught many students, and raised a family of eight children. Robert and Clara also became good friends with the German composer Johannes Brahms and aided his career.

Robert became mentally ill and Clara sent him to a sanctuary. He passed away at the age of forty-six from a brain tumor. After Robert Schumann's early death, she continued her concert tours in Europe for decades. In 1878, Schumann was appointed the first piano teacher of the new Dr. Hoch's Konservatorium in Frankfurt. She was the only woman on the faculty. She passed away from a stroke at the age of 76 in Frankfurt, Germany and was buried next to Robert in Bonn at Alter Friedhof. During her life, she performed 1,000 public concerts by memory. Her concert piano career spanned sixty-one years. She composed piano pieces, *lieder*, choral and orchestra works, a piano trio and her piano concerto.

Title: *Piano Concerto in A Minor*, Op. 7 for piano and orchestra (1835).
Genre: Concerto – A concerto is a work for one or more solo instruments that is accompanied by a larger group of instruments such as an orchestra.
YouTube: https://www.youtube.com/watch?v=X4rhHiPUltE
Stuttgart orchestra directed by Alexander Adiarte with pianist Diana Brekalo
Birthday: 13 September 1819 in Leipzig, Germany.
Death Date: 20 May 1896 in Frankfurt, Germany (aged 76)
Fun Facts:
1. Kings and queens showered her with gold and jewels for her virtuoso piano concerts.
2. Clara and Robert kept a joint diary together.
3. Clara Weick was called the "*Wunder Machen*" or Wonder Maiden by her patrons.
4. Clara and her composer husband Robert launched a lawsuit against her father to marry without his permission. (Library of Congress, Who WasShe?)

ROBERT SCHUMANN (1810-1856)

Robert Schumann – (1810-1856) was a **German composer**, virtuoso pianist, influential music critic of the **Romantic** era and husband to composer Clara Schumann. He was born 8 June 1810 in Zwickau in the Kingdom of Saxony (now in Germany).

He was the fifth and last child of Johanna and August Schumann. His father was a book seller, publisher, and novelist. Robert began learning piano at an early age from Johann Gottfried Kuntzsch, and wrote his first compositions at the age of seven. However due to his father, much of his early education was focused on literature. Robert wrote an essay about famous men at the age of 14, which was published in a book by his father. He read many works by the German poet-philosophers including Friedrich Schiller, Johann Wolfgang von Goethe, Byron, and the Greek tragedians. He also developed a keen interest in the music of Beethoven, Schubert, and Mendelssohn.

His father died when he was only 16. His mother and guardian did not encourage him to continue his music. So, he went to Leipzig to study law. While he was there, Robert studied piano with Friedrich Weick, who had assured him that he could be the finest pianist in Europe. In 1840 he married his teacher's daughter Clara Weick, against her father's wishes. This caused a great deal of trouble for the young couple. Some scholars have suggested that he used a mechanical device to strengthen his fingers as a pianist, which caused permanent damage to them. However, Clara said that the damage was caused by other problems, and not the device. He had to quit his career as a concert pianist. Robert suffered from a deep melancholic depression which began in 1833 when he was 23 years old. This was a result of the deaths of his brother Julius, and his sister-in-law Rosalie from the worldwide cholera pandemic. His mental illness became worse as he got older. Eventually, he attempted suicide in 1854, and was put into a mental asylum, at his own request, in *Endenich* near Bonn. He died two years later in 1856 without ever recovering from his depression. It was discovered after the autopsy, that he had a tumor at the base of his brain. This may have been brought on by the mercury treatments that were in common practice for another illness he had.

Robert Schumann published only his piano works until 1840. After that, he composed his works for piano and orchestra. His legacy also includes four symphonies; an opera, many *lieder* (songs for voice and piano); and other choral, orchestral and chamber works. Some of his more famous works are *Carnaval, Symphonic Studies, Kinderszenen, Kreisleriana, Violin Concerto, Fantasy for Violin and Orchestra*, and the *Fantasie in C for Piano*. Robert Schumann founded a music journal the *Neue Zeitschrift für Musik* (New Journal for Music), in Leipzig. He wrote many articles for this music publication.

Title: *Concerto in A Minor*, Op. 54 for Piano and Orchestra, I. *Allegro-Affetuoso*. This is the only Romantic piano concerto completed by Robert Schumann. His A Minor Piano Concerto was premiered 1 January 1846 in Leipzig by his wife Clara Schumann as the soloist and the dedicatee Ferdinand Hiller conducting. The concerto is scored for 2 flutes, 2 oboes, 2 clarinets, 2 bassoons, 2 horns, 2 trumpets, timpani, strings, and solo piano.

Genre: The **piano concerto** was a popular composition for solo piano and orchestra during the late 18th and 19th centuries.

YouTube Video: https://www.youtube.com/watch?v=fWDrJT0s1s8 Wiener Symphony conducted by Lorenzo Viotti Vienna Wiener Konzerthaus 1-31-2019 with Yuja Wang as soloist.

Birthday: 8 June 1810 in Zwickau, Germany.

Death Date: 29 July 1856 in Bonn, Germany at age 46.

Fun Facts:

1. While staying at Clara's house, Robert liked to dress up as a ghost at night to scare her. This created a close bond between them.
2. Franz Liszt said of Schumann's *Fantasy in C*, Op. 17 that "It is a noble work, worthy of Beethoven, whose career, by the way, it is supposed to represent". This work was dedicated to Liszt, and he was the one to premier it.
3. He suffered from the condition called tinnitus, which is ringing in the ears.

EMILIE MAYER (1812-1883)

milie Luise Friderica Mayer – (1812-1883) was a **German** composer of **Romantic** music and sculptor. She was born on 14 May 1812 in Friedland, Germany. Even though she started composing late in life, Emilie Mayer was a very prolific composer. Her works include eight symphonies, fifteen concert overtures, numerous *lieder*, and chamber music works. She became the Associate Director of the Opera Academy of Berlin. Emilie was influenced by the Viennese Classical style and later produced music in the Romantic style. Mayer made frequent use of seventh chords, especially with the diminished seventh, which allowed her to make a variety of resolutions. Sometimes she skipped the resolution altogether. Her harmonies are characterized by sudden shifts in tonality and her rhythms are often complex, with several layers.

Emile was the daughter of a well-to-do pharmacist, Johann August Friedrich Mayer and Henrietta Carolina. She was the third of five children, who received a musical education at an early age. Her first piano teacher was an organist by the name of Driver. Unfortunately, the young Emilie had an eating disorder, which caused many issues in her compositions. She did not eat enough food, so she became very thin.

Emilie's entire life changed on 28 August 1840 when her father fatally shot himself, 26 years to the day after he buried Emilie's mother (Aleksandra Maslovaric 2012). She decided to move to Szczechin, Poland in 1841, so she could study composition with Carl Loewe, who was a prominent composer. According to author Marie Silling, he gave Emilie a music test and said that he would like to help her talents blossom. She was a generous person, so "she asked Löwe whether she could share the composition lessons with other female pupils, he answered: *"Such a God-given talent as hers had not been bestowed upon any other person he knew."* This statement filled her with the greatest thankfulness throughout her whole life and obliged her to work extremely hard." (Marie Silling in *Jugenderinnerungen*).

Her first two symphonies (in C minor and E minor) were premiered in 1847 by the Stettin Instrumental Society. Emilie moved to Berlin to study fugue and double counterpoint with Adolph Bernhard Marx, and instrumentation with Wilhelm Wieprecht.

She published several of her *lieder* (songs) in her op. 5-7. Then on April 21, 1850 Emile was given a wonderful honor by Wieprecht. He led his "Euterpe" orchestra in a concert entirely of music by Emilie Mayer at the Royal Theatre. She received great critical and popular acclaim from this concert, so she continued composing works for public performance. Emilie travelled to Cologne, Munich, Lyon, Brussels, and Vienna in order to hear performances of her music.

Emilie Mayer was the most prolific German woman composer of the Romantic era. Many of her works were kept in royal libraries. Yet many of her compositions, which are now in the Berlin *Staatsbibliothek*, have never been recorded. One of her better-known works is the *Faust Overture* of 1880. This piece starts out in a serious and ominous tone. She composed many unresolved seventh chords. Then Mayer introduces a new theme which is energetic and dramatic. She interrupts this dark mood with a much lighter motive. Then she returns to the darker theme. (Incandela, Obscure Music Monday) Her *Piano Trio in D Major* Op. 13 is a four-movement chamber work. She also composed eight symphonies, six piano trios, two piano quartets, seven string quartets, two string quintets, seven violin sonatas, twelve cello sonatas, lieder, and choral works. She was also an excellent sculptor.

50 Famous Composers

Title: *Faust Overture* for symphony orchestra, 1880.

Genre: An **overture** is an instrumental piece which is usually performed at the beginning of a larger work such as an opera. It often includes many or all the themes or melodies of that work. However, a concert overture may be composed as a stand-alone piece that was never performed as part of another work.

YouTube: https://www.youtube.com/watch?v=sWGu3tntNoo
Played by the Neubrandenburger Philharmonie, conducted by Stefan Malzew

Birthday: May 14, 1812, Friedland, Germany

Death Date: April 10, 1883, Berlin, Germany (aged 70)

Fun Facts:
1. She was the most prolific German woman composer of the Romantic era.
2. She started composing later in life after the age of twenty-eight.
3. She had an eating disorder that interfered with her composing.

JOHANNES BRAHMS (1833-1897)

Johannes Brahms – (1833-1897) **German Romantic** composer, virtuoso pianist, and conductor. He was born 7 May 1833 in Hamburg, Germany, but most of his professional life was spent in Vienna, Austria. His father, Johann Jakob Brahms, performed as a string bass player in taverns, and a horn player in the Hamburg militia. His mother was Johanna Christiane Nissan, who was a seamstress. He had an older sister Elisabeth, and a younger brother Fritz. He got his early training in music from his father. When he was seven years old, Johannes went to study with pianist Otto Friedrich Willibald Cossel. At the age of ten, Johannes performed a concert including a difficult Beethoven piano quintet, and a Mozart piano quartet. A musician in the audience recommended an American tour for the young Brahms, however, his teacher decided that he should study with  Eduard Marxsem instead, who gave the boy piano and composition lessons for free.

There are many stories that Brahms' family was poor, so he had to contribute towards the family income at the age of thirteen by playing in taverns, restaurants, and other amusement places. However, most scholars believe that his family was relatively prosperous, and that music and minors were both forbidden in taverns by Hamburg legislation (Swafford 2001 passim) (Hoffmann 1999 pp. 12-14). Brahms did perform a piano concert tour at the age of nineteen. He later learned to play the cello and became a proficient choir and orchestra conductor. During his many concerts, he often performed his own music as the pianist or chamber musician. However, Brahms was always very self-critical and destroyed many of his earlier pieces. In 1853 Johannes sent a package of his music compositions to the composer Robert Schumann, who did not know him, and sent it back unopened. The twenty-year old Brahms tried again, getting a letter of introduction from the famous violinist Joachim to Schumann. On 1 October 1853, Brahms took the train to Düsseldorf to meet Robert and Clara Schumann. After hearing him play piano, they welcomed him into their home, which lead to a long-lasting friendship. Robert Schumann was so amazed with the young composer, that he wrote an article in the October issue of his journal *Neue Zeitschrift für Musik* praising his talents. This caused Brahms to feel even more self-conscious about living up to Schumann's lofty predictions about his future as a composer. A year later Robert Schumann became so mentally ill, that he had to go into an asylum. Brahms stayed with Clara and her family to help her get through this tragedy.

Clara Schumann was a virtuoso pianist as well as a composer. After Robert's death, she helped Brahms by giving him tips on his new compositions. She also premiered one of his piano pieces in public. Later his music became extremely popular and was performed by many famous musicians and conductors. Brahms composed four symphonies, two piano concertos, a violin concerto, a double concerto for violin and cello, two overtures (the *Academic Festival* and the *Tragic Overtures*), chamber music works, songs, and other orchestral and piano works. Joachim performed the premiere of Brahms' *Violin Concerto* on 1 January 1879, and later conducted the premier of Brahms' *Symphony No. 1*. Brahms was later diagnosed with cancer. He managed to live long enough to hear his fourth symphony premiered by conductor Hans Richter. There were long ovations in between each movement. Brahms died a month later at the age of 63. Brahms never married, and had no children, but he left a great legacy in his music to all of us.

Dr. Carolyn Waters Broe

Title: *Symphony No. 4, in E Minor*, Op. 98 movement 4. The score calls for 2 flutes, piccolo, 2 oboes, 2 clarinets, 2 bassoons, contra-bassoon, 4 horns, 2 trumpets, 3 trombones, kettledrums, triangle, and strings. His fourth symphony was composed during the summers of 1884 and 1885 in the tiny Alpine town of Mürzzuschlag.

Even though Brahms was deeply self-critical, his fourth symphony is considered one of the greatest symphonies ever written. There are many recordings.

Genre: A **symphony** is a large-scale composition, which usually consists of strings, winds, brass, and percussion instruments. A full symphony is usually written in four movements and performed by eighty-five or more musicians.

YouTube: https://www.youtube.com/watch?v=ckuUq7im8H4

Bernstein conducting the Wiener Philharmoniker in 1988.

Birthday: 7 May 1833, Hamburg, Germany

Death Date: 3 April 1897, Vienna, Austria aged 63 (he is buried in the Vienna Central Cemetery in Vienna, Austria).

Fun: Facts:

1. He is considered one of the three "B's" of Classical music "Bach, Beethoven, and Brahms". This was first stated by 19th century conductor Hans von Bülow.

2. Brahms owned a trick rocking chair that when someone sat in it, the chair would tip all the way over backwards. He laughed out loud, especially if a proper lady came to call, and the chair tipped over!

3. He was part of the War of the Romantics in music. Brahms and Clara Schumann were on the side of the more traditional music composers. Liszt and Wagner were considered radicals who advocated for the "new path" of composition.

4. Even though Brahms started out in a family of modest means, he became so popular, that he was wealthy later in life. He gave money away to aspiring musicians, and often purchased candy, so he could give it away to children when he went on his walks.

CAMILLE SAINT-SAËNS (1835-1921)

amille Saint-Saëns – (1835-1921) was a brilliant **French** composer, pianist, organist, and conductor of the **Late Romantic** era. Camille was born 9 October 1835 in Paris, the only child of Jacques-Joseph-Victor Saint-Saëns, and Françoise-Clémence born Collin. His father Victor, who was an official in the French Ministry of the Interior, died of consumption two months after Camille was born. Camille was a sickly child, so he was sent to the country to live with a nurse for his health. When he came back to Paris, he lived with his mother and her Aunt Charlotte Masson. At the age of two, they realized that he had perfect pitch, and that he could pick out tunes on the piano. His great-aunt Charlotte was Camille's first piano teacher. Saint-Saëns composed his first piece at the age of three.

When his mother discovered that her son was a child prodigy, she did not want him to become famous too soon. He played his first concerts for small private audiences at the age of five, including a performance of the piano accompaniment to a Beethoven violin sonata. When he was seven, he began piano lessons with Camille-Marie Stamaty. But it was not until he was ten that his mother allowed him to start performing in public. Several critics have compared the young Camille Saint-Saëns to Mozart. Camille also distinguished himself in school in mathematics, French Literature, Greek and Latin, and divinity. He had a life-long passion for philosophy, archaeology and astronomy. At the age of thirteen, he was admitted into the Paris Conservatoire. There he studied organ with François Benoist, who was a better teacher than organist. He studied composition with Fromental Halévy, who was a student of Cherubini.

After leaving the Conservatoire in 1853, Saint-Saëns accepted the post of organist at the ancient Parisian church of Saint-Merri near the Hôtel de Ville. Since this parish had 26,000 parishioners, Saint-Saëns often performed two hundred weddings and several funerals. So, his organist's fees combined with his church stipend made him a comfortable income. This gave him extra time to compose. He was recognized for his talents as an organist and composer by composers Gioachino Rossini, Hector Berlioz and Franz Liszt, and the influential singer Pauline Viardot, who all encouraged him in his career. He moved to the high-profile post of organist of La Madeleine, the official church of the Empire. They had a much better organ there, and when Franz Liszt heard him perform there, he declared Camille Saint-Saëns to be the greatest organist in the world. In 1861, he accepted a post as an organ teacher at the École de Musique Classique et Religieuse, Paris. His most famous organ student was the composer Gabriel Fauré. Saint-Saëns introduced the music of J.S. Bach, and other composers to his students, who were little known at the time. He competed twice for the Prix de Rome prize in composition but lost both times (1852 and 1864). However, he won two first place prizes in composition from the Société Sainte-Cécile (1852 and 1853).

In 1870, during the Franco-Prussian War, Saint-Saëns served in the National Guard. In the brief but bloody Paris Commune that followed the superior at La Madeleine, where Saint-Saëns played organ, was murdered by rebels. Camille managed to escape to England and survived by performing recitals there. When he returned to Paris, he surprised everyone by marrying Marie Laure Emile Truffot in 1875. She was the sister of one of his pupils, and nineteen years younger than him. The marriage was not successful. His mother did not approve of the marriage, and she came to live with them. They had two children, both of whom died in infancy. The older boy, André aged two, fell out of the window of the upper story of their apartment. The younger boy, Jean-François aged six months, died of pneumonia six weeks later. Camille blamed his wife for the death of their older son. They continued to live together for three years, but during a vacation to La Bourboule, Saint-Saëns left her at the hotel, and they never saw each other again. She moved back in with her family.

In the 19th century, opera was one of the most important of the staged events. Saint-Saëns' first opera was not successful. In February of 1877 his lyric opera, *Le timbre d'argent* ("The Silver Bell"), was successfully staged. Unfortunately, the person he dedicated his opera to, Albert Libon, died three months after the premiere. Libon left money to Saint-Saëns "To free him from the slavery of the organ of the Madeleine and to enable him to devote himself entirely to composition" (Smith 1002 p. 108). Later in December of 1877, he completed and staged his most famous opera *Samson and Dalila*. Saint-Saëns was elected to the *Institut de France* in 1881. He had been passed over for Massenet the first attempt he made at becoming a member there in 1878. He soon became an international figure, who was sought after as a soloist and composer.

In December of 1888, Saint-Saëns got the news that his mother had died. Feeling her loss immensely, he went into a deep depression with insomnia, and even contemplated suicide. He left Paris for Algiers, where he recuperated by walking and reading, but he was unable to compose. Later, he went back to composing operas and other shorter pieces. He also traveled and performed extensively in his later years. In November of 1921, he gave one final recital at the Institute, which was well attended. In December of that year, he died of a heart attack, while vacationing in Algiers. His body was brought back to be buried in Paris. There in the crowd was his wife, Marie Truffot, who was heavily veiled. She had not seen him since 1881. His best-known works include: *The Carnival of the Animals* (1886), his *First Cello Concerto* (1872), *Danse macabre* (1874), *Introduction and Rondo Capriccioso* (1863), his *Second Piano Concerto* (1868), the opera *Samson and Delilah* (1877), his *Third Violin Concerto* (1880), and his *Third ("Organ") Symphony* (1886).

Dr. Carolyn Waters Broe

Title: *Carnival of the Animals* – Saint-Saëns wrote his best-known piece, *The Carnival of the Animals*, as incidental music for a one-act farce performed by his students at the Niedermeyer school where he taught. But he did not finish composing it until 1886, more than twenty years after leaving the school. It is scored for two pianos, two violins, viola, cello, double bass, flute (and piccolo), clarinet (C and B♭), glass harmonica, and xylophone. This piece is beloved by many children and chamber music lovers.

Genre: Incidental music is composed specifically to be performed as part of a play or other theater work.

YouTube: https://www.youtube.com/watch?v=eo2y23NVOg8

The Swan for Cello and Piano with the Brooklyn Duo.

YouTube: https://www.youtube.com/watch?v=O9P1LOBepcY

The complete **Carnival of the Animals** Cristina Ortiz, Piano Pascal Rogé, Piano with the London Sinfonietta.

Birthday: 9 October 1835, Paris, France

Death Date: 16 December 1921, Algiers, Algeria (aged 86).

Fun Facts:

1. Camille Saint-Saëns was the leading French composer of his generation, he was considered the "French Beethoven" during his lifetime, and he was often compared to Mozart.

2. Saint-Saëns was a serious musician, but he wrote his most famous piece, *The Carnival of the Animals*, as a joke for his friends and students.

3. Camille gave his first formal performance debut at the age of ten in 1846 at the Salle Pleyel in Paris. Near the end of the performance, the ten-year-old offered to play any of Mozart's piano concertos by memory. Mozart wrote twenty-one concertos, so we can get an idea of what a gifted prodigy Saint-Saëns was.

MODEST PETROVICH MUSSORGSKY (1839-1881)

Modest Petrovich Mussorgsky – (1839-1881) **Russian Romantic** composer and innovator, who sought to create a unique Russian style. He was a member of "The Five" who were all Russian composers, who worked together, often in opposition to traditional Western styles of music. He was born 21 March 1839 Karevo, Russia. The aristocratic land-owning Mussorgsky family traced their heritage back to the Boyers in the 17th century Velvet Book, and Rurik the 9th century founder of the Russian State. At the age of six, Modest began his piano lessons with his mother. After three years, he was able to play complex pieces like the John Field Concerto and works by Franz Liszt. Later, he and his brother Filaret were sent to St. Petersburg to study music. He studied piano with the noted Anton Gerke and published his first piece at the age of twelve.

His parents wanted him to continue in the family tradition of military service, so they entered him into the Cadet School of the Guards in St. Petersburg at the age of 13. However, the military school could be brutal, and may have been the cause of Modest going down the path to alcoholism. Modest continued his piano playing, by entertaining the other cadets with polkas and popular operatic songs. Upon his graduation, Modest received a commission in the elite regiment of the Russian Imperial Guard. At the age of 17 Modest met the composer Alexander Borodin at a military hospital in St. Petersburg, and they became good friends. Borodin remarked on how well-groomed Mussorgsky's appearance and uniform were. He said that the ladies made a fuss over him and his piano playing, and even said that Modest was a bit "foppish" (Gordeyva 1989: pp. 86-87). This means that he was overly concerned about his appearance in a vain and affected manner. Modest was invited to the best parties and met many important dignitaries. He was also influenced by the composer Mily Balakirev as to musical form and style. He gained theatrical style by assisting in the production of Glinka's opera *A Life for the Tsar*.

Within months of starting his music studies with Balakirev, Mussorgsky quit his position with the imperial regiment, so that he could focus on his music. He began to embrace "artistic realism" and identified with the lower strata of Russian life. He became very depressed with reality when his mother died in 1865. At the age of 26 he sank into an alcoholic fog. Yet this was the moment when he started to write some of his first songs based on "artistic realism". Rejecting his aristocratic heritage, he became a civil servant working for the forestry service. At age 29 he wrote his opera *Boris Godunov* after a play by Pushkin, which was later staged in 1874. His opera became immensely popular despite only twelve performances. He also started work on the choral version of his *Night on Bald Mountain*. Mussorgsky continued to associate with Bohemian thinkers, writers and artists. One of these men was the artist Viktor Hartmann. When Hartmann passed away in 1874, Mussorgsky composed the piano suite *Pictures at an Exhibition* in his memory. It is considered a virtuosic piano show piece. It was later orchestrated by the famous French composer Maurice Ravel.

Mussorgsky continued to decline due to his alcoholism. Because of frequent sickness and absences, he was transferred to another post in 1879. Fortunately, his new music loving boss was very lenient on him, and even allowed him to tour as a piano accompanist for a singer to twelve cities. After Mussorgsky's death in 1881, his friend the famous composer Nikolai Rimsky-Korsakov, published many of his compositions.

50 Famous Composers

Title: *Pictures at an Exhibition* for piano. After the death of Mussorgsky's artist friend, Viktor Hartmann, there was a show of over 400 of his paintings and artworks. They were displayed at the Academy of Fine Arts in Saint Petersburg, Russia. Mussorgsky lent several art works by Hartmann from his own collection to Stavov, who organized the show. Then he started working feverishly in June of 1874 on a piano piece, which was originally named "Hartmann". Mussorgsky states in a letter to Stasov that his physical appearance is depicted in the "Promenade". Mussorgsky was portly and tended to waddle when he walked. Each movement depicts various paintings in the show by Hartmann.

Genre: A **piano suite** in ten movements with interludes.

YouTube: https://www.youtube.com/watch?v=s8z1_A-Zlbw after the Genre.

Original piano version with the original Hartman paintings performed by four piano artists: Jean-Philippe Collard; Lilya Zilberstein; Wonny Song; and Kanon Matsuda.

Birthday: 21 March [O.S. 9 March] 1839 Karevo, Russia.

Death Date: 28 March [O.S. 16 March] 1881, Saint Petersburg, Russia (aged 42).

Fun Facts:

1. The Mussorgsky family spelled their name many ways. This may have been an attempt by Modest's elder brother Filaret to hide the name's similarity to the Russian word "músor" which means debris or rubbish.

2. In 1935 as part of reconstruction of the "so called" Necropolis of Masters Arts, the Soviet government moved only the tombstones in the graveyard where Mussorgsky is buried. They paved over the tombs with asphalt, so now his grave is under a bus stop.

3. "The Five," were also known as "The Mighty Handful," and "The New Russian School." They were all Russian composers, who were active in Saint Petersburg, composing in the Russian Romantic Nationalistic style. "The Five" were led by Mily Balakirev, and included Alexander Borodin, César Cui, Modest Mussorgsky, and Nikolai Rimsky-Korsakov. This group has also been called "The Russian Five".

4. Mussorgsky described his physical gait in the "Promenade" of the "Pictures at an Exhibition" as he imagined himself walking through the exhibition of Viktor Harmann's paintings. Mussorgsky was portly and tended to waddle when he walked.

Dr. Carolyn Waters Broe

PETER TCHAIKOVSKY (1840-1893)

Peter Ilyich Tchaikovsky – (1840-1893) was the first **Russian** composer and conductor to become internationally known and appreciated. His **Late-Romantic** music is some of the most popular classical music ever written. He was asked to make frequent appearances as a guest conductor in both Europe and the United States. Emperor Alexander III awarded Tchaikovsky a lifetime pension in 1884. He received many other awards during his life as well.

Tchaikovsky was originally educated as a civil servant; however, the opportunity arose for him to enter Saint Petersburg Conservatory, from which he graduated in 1865. His Western traditional training at the conservatory did not make him popular with other Russian composers, who were into the contemporary nationalistic movement. They even made jokes about his music. He did not have a solid relationship with The Five, who were the leading Russian composers of the 19th century. It was Tchaikovsky's desire to reconcile what he had learned about Western music, with the traditional Russian music that he grew up with as a child. This led to his development of a personal style that was unmistakably Russian. The folk music of Russia has many melodies and harmonies that are quite different from the rest of Europe. It is this fusion of the East and the West that makes Tchaikovsky's music so rich and exciting.

Peter Tchaikovsky was born 7 May 1840 in Votkinsk, Russia into a military family. His father, Ilya Petrovich Tchaikovsky, was a lieutenant colonel and engineer in the Department of Mines. Tchaikovsky's mother, Alexandra Andreyevna, was French on her father's side, and eighteen years younger than Ilya. Both Ilya and Alexandra were trained in the arts, and music, which was important living on a remote post. They hired a French governess to educate their children. Peter became overly attached to his governess and soon became fluent in French and German. Peter started learning piano at the age of five. He was so precocious, that he could outplay his teacher in three years. At first his parents were supportive of his musical talents and hired another piano teacher. They bought him an *orchestrion* (which is a type of barrel organ that could imitate fancy orchestral effects). However, in 1850 his parents decided to send Tchaikovsky (aged ten) to the Imperial School of Jurisprudence in Saint Petersburg, which was the city where they went to school. His parents wanted him to become a civil servant. Going to boarding school at such a young age was extremely hard on Peter. His emotional trauma was made even worse when his mother died of cholera in 1854 when he was fourteen. Eventually Peter became very depressed. He graduated and became an assistant counselor in the Ministry of Justice.

Fortunately, the Russian Musical Society (RMS) was founded in 1859 by the Grand Duchess Elena Pavlovna, (who was the German-born aunt of Tsar Alexander II) and her protégé, pianist and composer Anton Rubinstein. They were looking to foster native Russian talent instead of importing foreign artists (Maes 35). Rubinstein would become a close friend of Tchaikovsky. After taking classes with the RMS, he decided to enroll in the St. Petersburg Conservatory of Music. In 1865 Anton's brother Nikolai Rubinstein offered him the position of Professor of Music at the new Moscow Conservatory. He also received patronage from Nadezhda von Meck, the widow of a railway magnate.

Tchaikovsky's marriage in 1877 to his former student, Antonia Miliukova, at the age of 37, was a disaster. After only two and a half months, Tchaikovsky ended the marriage, and almost ended his life by jumping into the freezing cold waters of an icy river. Fortunately, he recovered. During his life Tchaikovsky composed many popular pieces including six symphonies, his *Romeo and Juliet*, the *1812 Overture*, three ballets (*The Nutcracker, Swan Lake and The Sleeping Beauty)*, his *Piano Concerto, Violin Concerto, March Slave, Serenade for Strings,* Manfred Symphony, *Cappricio Italien,* Francesca da Rimini, and his operas *The Queen of Spades* and *Eugene Onegin*. In 1892, Tchaikovsky was voted a member of the Académie des Beaux-Arts in France, and the following year he was awarded an honorary Doctorate of Music from Cambridge, England. Unfortunately, nine days after conducting the premiere of his Sixth Symphony (the *Pathetique*), Tchaikovsky died tragically at the age of 53, possibly from contracting cholera from dirty drinking water.

Title: *1812 Overture* . This piece is written for **Woodwinds:** 1 piccolo, 2 flutes, 2 oboes, 1 English horn or *cor anglais*, 2 clarinets in B♭ and 2 bassoons; **Brass:** 4 horns in F, 2 cornets in B♭, 2 trumpets in E♭, 3 trombones (2 tenor, 1 bass) and a tuba; **Percussion:** timpani, an orchestral bass drum, a snare drum, cymbals, a tambourine, a triangle, a carillon (chimes), and a battery of cannons; **Strings:** first and second violins, violas, violoncellos and double basses.

The *1812 Overture* begins with the plaintive Russian melody of the *Eastern Orthodox Troparion of the Holy Cross* (also known as "O Lord, Save Thy People") played by four cellos and two violas. He includes a fragment of the French *La Marseillaise* theme, after which he wrote a descending string passage where Tchaikovsky is depicting Napoleon's army running away from the Russian army. There is a total of sixteen cannon shots in this piece.

Genre: An **overture** is usually an introductory piece for orchestra, which precedes a lager work such as an opera or ballet.

YouTube: *The 1812 Overture* https://www.youtube.com/watch?v=0DFsF_0tfiM
Berliner Philharmonic with Seiji Ozawa conducting, without the cannons.

Title: Nutcracker Ballet – "The Dance of the Sugar Plum Fairy"

Genre: A **ballet** is a major orchestra work composed to accompany dancers.

YouTube: Royal Ballet https://www.youtube.com/watch?v=K65lcuHQn-E

Title: Swan Lake Ballet – "Waltz" and "Finale"

YouTube: "Waltz" with Bolshoi Theater https://www.youtube.com/ watch?v=vOp27I4rZ8g

YouTube: "Finale" with American Ballet https://www.youtube.com/ watch?v=JI7AsZGnyi4

Birthday: 7 May 1840 in Votkinsk, Russia.

Death Date: 6 November 1893 in St. Petersburg, Russia (aged 53).

Fun: Facts:

1. There are sixteen cannon shots in Tchaikovsky's 1812 Overture, although most orchestras use recorded cannon shots or a large drum today.
2. He never met his biggest fan. Madame Nadezhda von Meck sent Tchaikovsky money and corresponded with him frequently but insisted that they never meet.
3. The "Dance of the Sugar Plum Fairy" from *The Nutcracker Ballet* is famous for using an instrument that was very new at the time, called the *celesta*. It looks like a small piano and makes a high tinkling sound (this instrument also appears at the beginning of John Williams' *Harry Potter* film score).
4. Although the *1812 Overture* is exceedingly popular, Tchaikovsky did not really like it!
5. *Beauty*), his *Piano Concerto, Violin Concerto, March Slave, Serenade for Strings, Manfred Symphony, Cappricio Italien, Francesca da Rimini,* and his operas *The Queen of Spades* and *Eugene Onegin*. In 1892, Tchaikovsky was voted a member of the Académie des Beaux-Arts in France, and the following year he was awarded an honorary Doctor of Music from Cambridge, England. Unfortunately, nine days after conducting the premiere of his *Sixth Symphony* (the *Pathetique*), Tchaikovsky died tragically at the age of 53, possibly from contracting cholera from dirty drinking water.

JOHN PHILIP SOUSA (1854-1932)

ohn Philip Sousa – (1854-1932) **American** composer and conductor of the **Late Romantic** era. Sousa is so well known for his military and patriotic marches that he has been nick named "The March King" and the "American March King". Some of his most famous pieces are "The Stars and Stripes Forever" (National March of the United States of America), "*Semper Fidelis*" (Official March of the United States Marine Corps), "The Thunderer," "The Washington Post," and "The Liberty Bell" (used as the theme for Monty Python's Flying Circus). He achieved the rank of Sergeant Major in the United States Marine Corps, and Lieutenant Commander in the United States Navy. He is also famous for having developed the sousaphone with J. W. Pepper of Philadelphia, which is a large brass instrument, like the tuba and the helicon, and is most often used for marching bands.

John Philip Sousa was born 6 November 1854 in Washington, D.C. He was the third of ten children born to João António de Sousa (John Anthony Sousa), who was of Portuguese and Spanish ancestry, and his wife Maria Elisabeth Trinkhaus, who was of Hessian ancestry (part of Germany). Sousa started learning to play the violin at the age of six with John Esputa and took composition and harmony from Felix Benkert. They discovered that he had perfect pitch. During his childhood, Sousa learned voice, violin, piano, flute, alto horn, baritone horn, trombone, and cornet (a type of trumpet). In 1868, when Sousa turned thirteen, he wanted to join a circus band.

However, his father, who was a trombonist in the marine band, enlisted him in the U.S. Marine Corps Band as an apprentice instead. He served in this band until 1875, and then learned to conduct by working with a theater pit orchestra.

Starting in 1880 until his death, Sousa focused on composing and conducting. Later he rejoined the Marine Band, serving as their director for twelve years. After leaving the Marine Band, Sousa organized his own band, and toured Europe and Australia. At the outbreak of World-War I, Sousa was commissioned as a Lieutenant Commander and led the Naval Reserve Band in Illinois. Following his tenure, he returned to conduct the Sousa Band until his death in 1932. In the 1920's he was promoted to Lieutenant Commander in the naval reserve, but never saw active service again. He composed a total of 136 marches.

John Philip Sousa's band was famous in America and around the world. They toured from 1892 to 1931 performing a total of 15,623 concerts. Sousa's Band performed at the World Exposition in Paris, France and at the Royal Albert Hall in London. Sousa led "The President's Own" band under five presidents from Rutherford B. Hayes to Benjamin Harrison for important Whitehouse events in Washington D.C. Sousa's band also performed at the Inaugural Balls of James A. Garfield in 1881, and Benjamin Harrison in 1889.

On December 30, 1879, Sousa married Jane van Middlesworth Bellis (1862-1944). They had three children. He died of a heart attack after conducting a rehearsal of the "Stars and Stripes Forever" at the age of 77 in a hotel in Pennsylvania. Sousa received many honors during and after his life including: The Palms of Public Instruction from Portugal; the Royal Victorian Medal from King Edward VII of the United Kingdom; a star on the Hollywood Walk of Fame in California; and the World War II Liberty ship the U.S. John Philip Sousa was named after him. In 1976, he was inducted into the Hall of Fame for Great Americans and inducted into the American Classical Music Hall of Fame in Cincinnati, Ohio in 1998. The band hall used for the Marine band in Washington D.C. is dedicated as the "John Philip Sousa Band Hall". Most importantly, in 1987, an act of Congress was passed naming "The Stars and Stripes Forever" as the National March of the United States.

50 Famous Composers

Title: *Stars and Stripes Forever* – 1896. This piece was declared as our National March by the United States in 1987 by an act of Congress. Sousa wrote this piece while he was sailing back from a vacation abroad and became homesick. He based it on his memories of seeing our flag flying over the White House, and his time conducting the U.S. Marine Corp Band.

Genre: A **military march** is an instrumental piece, which is composed for and performed at parades, military events, and patriotic events.

YouTube: https://www.youtube.com/watch?v=a-7XWhyvIpE "The President's Own" U.S. Marine Band

Birthday: 6 November 1854 – Washington, D.C., U.S.

Death Date: March 6, 1932 (aged 77) – Reading, Pennsylvania, U.S

Fun Facts:

1. John Philip Sousa is nicknamed "The March King," as well as the "American March King" to distinguish him from Kenneth J. Alford, who is also known as "The March King" in Britain.
2. Sousa nearly died of pneumonia because he stayed out too long in the rain when he was five years old.
3. Sousa wanted to run away and join a circus band at the age of 13, but his father stopped him by enlisting him as an apprentice in the marine band.
4. Sousa did not always want to become a music composer and conductor. He wanted to become a baker instead.

CÉCILE CHAMINADE (1857-1944)

écile Chaminade (Louise Stéphanie) – (1857-1944) She was a French pianist and **Neo-Romantic composer**. Cécil was born 8 August 1857 Paris, France. She began her piano studies with her mother, who was a pianist and singer. Cécile started experimenting with composition at an early age. When she turned eight, she showed one of her wonderful compositions to the famous French composer Georges Bizet, who was extremely impressed. However, her father disapproved of her enrolling in the Paris Conservatoire. So, she studied privately with several members of their faculty including piano with Félix Le Couppey, Antoine Marmontel, and Marie Gabriel Augustin Savard, violin with Martin Pierre Marsick, and music composition with Benjamin Godard. She gave her first concert at the age of

eighteen. Cécile toured France as a pianist, and later made her debut in England in 1892. She was asked to perform in England many times, especially by singers.

Cécil Chaminade's music compositions gained in popularity. She wrote many character pieces for piano and solon songs. It is striking that nearly all 400 of her compositions have been published, when most women had difficulty getting published during this time. Chaminade married a music publisher from Marseilles, Louis-Mathieu Carbonel, in 1901. He was much older than her, so the marriage was rumored to be one of convenience. He died in 1907, but Chaminade never got married again.

In 1908 Chaminade toured to America, where she received a very warm welcome. Her music became immensely popular in the United States where her "Scarf Dance," and "Ballet No. 1," were frequently requested by audiences and pianists. She composed large pieces such as her *Konzertstück* for piano and orchestra, the ballet music to *Callirhoé*, and her *Concertino for Flute and Piano*, which was later arranged for orchestra. Her songs, such as "The Silver Ring" and "*Ritournelle*," were also great favorites. Ambroise Thomas once said of Chaminade: "This is not a woman who composes, but a composer who is a woman." (The Etude 2013). She was awarded the *Chevalier de la Légion d'Honneur* in 1913 (knighted) by the French government, a first for a female composer (Encyclopedia Britannica 2014) (Naxos 2014). She was asked to make recordings of seven of her compositions for the Gramophone and Typewriter Company of London in 1903. These early recordings are very sought after by collectors. Chaminade also made many piano roll recordings of her music between 1901 and 1914. After World War I started, Cecil's health got worse, so she composed less and less.

She passed away in April of 1944 in Monte Carlo. Chaminade was aware of the social difficulties facing women composers. Even at the height of her career, Chaminade often faced a brick wall with male critics. When she composed lighter genres such as small piano pieces and songs (which were often written by female composers), her work was thought to be trivial. But if she attempted to work in larger forms, she was criticized for her lack of femininity. She suggested in a Washington Post article from 1 November 1908, that perseverance and special circumstances are needed to overcome them. Chaminade is noteworthy among women composers for her quantity, and for the high percentage of her works that were published. She composed nearly 200 piano works and 125 *mélodies*, many of which she wrote at the request of her publisher Enoch for sales purposes. These two genres formed the basis for her popularity.

Dr. Carolyn Waters Broe

Title: *Concertino for Flute and Orchestra in D Major*, Op. 107 (1902)

Genre: A **flute concerto** is a concerto for solo flute with instrumental ensemble (usually orchestra). The solo flute concerto started in the Baroque era and has remained popular to the present. Chaminade's *Concertino for Flute and Piano* was commissioned by the Paris Conservatoire in 1902 (she later

arranged it for orchestra). It is likely that this piece was used as an examination piece for flute students at the Paris Conservatory. She dedicated her Concertino to the famous French flautist and teacher Paul Taffanel, who taught at the conservatory.

YouTube Video: https://www.youtube.com/watch?v=f5OTnlphaUI California Philharmonic Youth Orchestra, Senior Orchestra, directed by Prof B. Kim with Sonia Ruiz as soloist.

Instrumentation: Solo flute, a piccolo, two oboes, two clarinets, two bassoons, four horns, three trombones, tuba, timpani, harp, and strings.

Birthday: 8 August 1857 Paris, France.

Death Date: 13 April 1944 Monte Carlo (aged 86).

Fun Facts:

1. Chaminade's *Concertino for Flute* is so difficult, that it is legendary among flute players. There were even rumors that she made it fiendishly difficult to spurn a former flute playing lover, who had left her. However, she was already married to the French publisher when this piece was commissioned.

2. Her music was so popular in the United States, that a national group of music clubs was named after her.

3. In England, her *Prélude for Organ* was played at Queen Victoria's funeral in 1901.

CLAUDE DEBUSSY (1862-1918)

laude Debussy – (1862-1918) was a **French Impressionist** composer and pianist. He was one of the most influential composers of the late nineteen and early 20th centuries due to his use of symbolism, chromaticism, and non-traditional scales. Debussy's music was forward looking in his use of non-traditional harmonies and sensual motives. He was made a Chevalier of the Legion of Honor in 1903 (made a knight).

Debussy was born 22 August 1862 in Saint-Germain-en-Laye, France. Claude was the eldest of five children born to Manuel-Achille Debussy, who owned a china shop, and Victorine Manoury Debussy, who was a seamstress. They moved to Paris in 1867.

However, Claude's mother had to flee with him to his paternal aunt's house in Cannes in 1870 to escape the Franco-Prussian War. His aunt paid for Claude to start piano lessons at the age of seven with Jean Cerutti, who was an Italian violinist. In 1871, he took lessons with Marie Mauté de Fleurville, who claimed she had been a student of Frédéric Chopin. In 1872, at the age of ten, Claude Debussy was admitted into the Paris Conservatory of music. He stayed there for eleven years studying composition with Ernest Guiraud. He studied harmony with Émile Durand, and music history and theory with Louis-Albert Bourgault-Ducoudray. Debussy did not follow the traditional use of harmony at the academy, and he was very experimental in his use of dissonances. He was also a brilliant pianist, who could have been a solo artist if he had wanted that career.

Debussy was hired during the summers of 1880, 1881 and 1882 by patroness Nadezhda von Meck to travel with her family through Europe and teach her children the piano. She and Debussy played many piano pieces with four hands together during those summers. Madame Von Meck was also a patroness of Peter Tchaikovsky, but the Russian composer did not influence Debussy. Claude Debussy won the *Prix de Rome* with his composition "L'enfant prodigue" in 1884. He received a scholarship to the Académie des Beaux-Arts, which included a four-year residence at the Villa Medici, the French Academy in Rome. Unfortunately, Debussy could not stand the food or the accommodations at the monastery. He thought the people there were boring, and he was not into Italian opera. He became depressed and in 1885 he wrote of his desire to leave to follow his own dreams. Debussy wanted to follow the composer and pianist Franz Liszt, whom he admired. However, he fulfilled his promise to compose several pieces for the Academy including the symphonic ode *Zuleima* (based on a text by Heinrich Heine); the orchestral piece *Printemps;* and the cantata *La Damoiselle* élue (1887–1888).

Debussy did follow his dreams by composing music in the new Impressionist style. He decided to follow the French Impressionist painters, who were in fashion around the turn of the century, such as Claude Monet, Pierre-Auguste Renoir, Paul Cézanne, Edgar Degas, Édouard Manet and Camille Pissaro. Their art went against tradition by creating soft hazy effects like fog and landscapes with blurred lines rather than the bold clear portraits of the Romantic era that dominated the 19th century. Debussy was masterful at creating these same impressionistic effects in his music by avoiding clear downbeats, using chromatic scales, and painting programmatic musical landscapes and images in his music. His music has also been compared to the Bohemian artists of the late 19th and early 20th centuries because his music is unconventional, free flowing and roaming like a gypsy.

Debussy's music is full of symbolism, numerology, and hidden messages. He liked to dress up in a canary yellow suit and hat and discuss deep subjects with writers such as his friend Paul Verlaine. Debussy was influenced by the music of Liszt, Chopin, Bartok, Wagner, Messiaen, Benjamin, and jazz pianist Bill Evans. He was also influenced by the Russian composers Tchaikovsky, Balakirev, Rimsky-Korsakov, Borodin, and Mussorgsky. Like many of these composers, Debussy's music is full of themes, light motives and programmatic images that paint a picture in sound.

Debussy's personal life was often troubled. He made extremely poor choices in love. In 1899, he married a model named Rosalie ('Lilly') Texier. He found out later that she was not overly sensitive about music and could not carry an intelligent conversation well. So, he divorced Rosalie in favor of Emma Bardac, who was much more sophisticated. Bardac inspired Debussy to write his famous symphonic suite *La Mer*. However, Debussy's friends were very unhappy with his behavior and left him. Emma's family disowned her. This caused Debussy to become even more depressed. He married Bardac in 1908, and they had a daughter named Claude-Emma. She was a great inspiration to Debussy, who dedicated his *Children's Corner Suite* for piano to her.

Claude-Emma survived her father by only one year, dying of diphtheria. Debussy died of cancer on 25 March 1918 at his home in Paris at the age of fifty-five. Unfortunately, Paris was being bombed at the time by the Germans during their Spring Offensive during World War I. So, Debussy's body was rushed down the empty streets of Paris and buried without ceremony in the Père Lachaise Cemetery, but was reburied at the Passy Cemetery to be near the trees and birds later.

Claude Debussy composed many pieces which have become incredibly famous such as his *"Claire de Lune"* a movement from his *Suite Bergamasque*. Debussy's *Prelude to the Afternoon of a Faun* was premiered on 22 December 1894. His three *Nocturnes* of 1899 include the *"Nuages,"* *"Fêtes,"* and *"Sirènes"*. Debussy's only complete opera *Pelléas et Mélisande* was premiered in 1902 and was based on the play by Maurice Maeterlinck. His opera proved to be an immediate success, and it was immensely influential to younger French composers such as Maurice Ravel. His music brought a new flowing rhythm and color that was quite new and revolutionary to Western music.

Dr. Carolyn Waters Broe

Title: *Prelude to the Afternoon of a Faun* premiered 22 December 1894. This composition was inspired by Stéphane Mallarmé's poem *"L'après-midi d'un faune"*. Debussy wrote that "The music of this prelude is a very free illustration of Mallarmé's beautiful poem. By no means does it claim to be a synthesis of it. Rather there is a succession of scenes through which pass the desires and dreams of the faun in the heat of the afternoon. Then, tired of pursuing the timorous flight of nymphs and naiads, he succumbs to intoxicating sleep, in which he can finally realize his dreams of possession in universal Nature". It is thought that this piece was a turning point in music history. The flute represents the faun, who was a mythological half man half goat like Pan. Its unbridled chromaticism ushered in the modern era of music like a siren.

Genre: A **symphonic poem** for orchestra is usually a one movement piece that is programmatic. This means that there is a theme, poem or image depicted by the music.

YouTube: https://www.youtube.com/watch?v=EvnRC7tSX50

The Boston Symphony Orchestra with Leonard Bernstein conducting.

Birthday: 22 August 1862 in Saint-Germain-en-Laye, France.

Death Date: 25 March 1918 in Paris, France at age 55.

Fun Facts:

1. Debussy entered the Paris Conservatory at the age of ten to study music.
2. Debussy composed in the Bohemian style of music, which means unconventional and roaming free like a gypsy.
3. After winning the *Prix de Rome* for composition, Debussy moved from France to Italy. He found the people boorish, the food disgusting, the monastery appalling, and did not care for Italian opera. The only saving grace was hearing Franz Liszt.

AMY BEACH (1867-1944)

Amy Marcy Beach – **(1867-1944)** was an **American** composer and pianist of the late **Romantic** era. She had an amazing musical memory. Amy was a co-founder in 1925 of the Society of American Women Composers, and a leader of the Music Educators National Conference. She is considered the first successful American female composer of large-scale music works. Amy Beach is also the girl who loved birds. She was so good at musical dictation, that she was asked to write down most of the bird songs for the National Audubon Society.

Amy Beach was born 5 September 1867, in Henniker, New Hampshire in the United States. Her mother, Clara Imogene Marcy Cheney, was an excellent singer and pianist. Her father, Charles Abbott Cheney, was active in the anti-slavery and the women's rights movements in America. Amy was a child prodigy and an only child, who was born in New Hampshire. She could sing forty songs accurately by age one. By the age of two, Amy could improvise a counter melody to any song her mother sung. She taught herself to read at the age of three. By five Amy was composing simple waltzes. Her mother began to teach her piano at the age of six. Even though it was not considered proper for girls or women to perform on stage, Amy gave some recitals at the age of seven including works by Beethoven, Chopin, Handel, and even some of her own works. There were a couple of concert promoters who wanted to take her on tour, however, her parents declined. Amy was glad later that she was spared this life.

Dr. Carolyn Waters Broe

In 1875, the Cheney family moved to Chelsea, Massachusetts. They hired local pianists to teach Amy piano including Ernst Perabo and Carl Baermann. Baermann was a former student of the famous European pianist and composer Franz Liszt. At the age of fourteen, Amy received one year of formal training in composition from Junius W. Hill. Other than this, she was self-taught in composition. She learned a great deal about composition by studying the *Well-Tempered Clavier* of Johann Sebastian Bach, and orchestration from translating an orchestration book by the French composer Hector Berlioz. Amy published her first composition at the age of thirteen. She gave her concert debut as a pianist at age sixteen at the Boston Music Hall in 1883 performing Chopin's *Rondo in E flat*. Her performance was given high praise by critics. Amy was asked to perform concertos by Mozart, Beethoven, Mendelssohn, Chopin, Saint-Saens, and others.

In 1885, she married the Boston surgeon Dr. Henry Harris Aubrey Beach, who was twenty-four years older than her. She agreed to limit herself to two piano recitals a year, so that she could composer more. Due to her husband's name, she was later referred to as Mrs. H.H.A. Beach. He did not approve of her taking lessons in composition, so she taught herself by reading every book on composition she could find. She composed several major works including: her *Mass in E flat Major* in 1892, her *Gaelic Symphony* performed in 1896; and she premiered her *Piano Concerto in C Sharp Minor* with the Boston Symphony in 1900. She also composed many beautiful chamber music pieces including her *Piano Quintet in F Sharp Minor*, Op. 67, and her *Violin Sonata*. Amy Beach is considered part of the American composers called the Second New England School (unofficial title). This group includes George Whitefield Chadwick, Arthur Foote, Edward MacDowell, John Knowles Paine, Horatio Parker, and Amy Beach. They were also known as the Boston Six.

Her husband died in 1910 and her mother died seven months later. This left Amy Beach free to decide her own musical career after that. At first, she felt unable to work. So, she traveled to Europe for rest in 1912. She toured with soprano Marcella Craft, who sang many of Beach's songs. Audiences loved her music, and the critics were very enthusiastic. Soon a German publisher began publishing her music, because the demand for her songs was so great. Beach returned to America in 1914 due to the beginning of World War I. She had a trunk full of her music manuscripts confiscated at the Belgian border when she left Germany, however, the trunk and music was returned later.

After returning to America, she began teaching piano and composition privately. Beach was a member of the Counselors Board at the New England Conservatory of Music. She received an honorary master's degree from the University of New Hampshire in 1928. She started "Beach Clubs" to help young people learn music. She was the first president of the Society of American Women Composers. She traveled to Rome where she helped to raise money for an American Hospital there. She visited Leipzig, Germany to meet with her soprano friend Marcella Craft before returning to America. Amy Beach retired later due to heart disease. She died in New York City in 1944 at the age of 77.

Title: *Symphony in E Minor*, Op. 32 "*Gaelic*" 1896 – 1. Allegro con fuoco. Beach was inspired by the Native American and Czech songs that Antonin Dvorak wrote into his symphonic music, while he was in America. Therefore, she decided to put old English, Irish and Scottish songs into her symphony, hence the name "Gaelic".
Genre: A **symphony** is a large-scale music composition for orchestra. Symphonies are usually written in four movements.
YouTube: https://www.youtube.com/watch?v=nnYtZD3sldw&t=639s JoAnn Falletta conducting the Ulster Orchestra in Belfast.
Birthday: 5 September 1867, Henniker, NH in the United States.
Death Date: 27 December 1944, New York City, NY (aged 77).
Fun Facts:
1. Amy Beach had perfect pitch, and could sing forty songs accurately, and always in the same key, by the age of one.
2. She was most popular for her song writing, composing 150 songs.
3. Amy Beach memorized and wrote down the songs of most of the North American birds for the National Audubon Society.
4. Legend tells us that after hearing the *New World Symphony* by Antonin Dvorak, Amy Beach went home and wrote out the entire symphony by memory.
5. Amy Beach broke the gender barrier to become the first female composer of note in the United States (Library of Congress, Who Was She?).

Dr. Carolyn Waters Broe

MODERN COMPOSERS
(1910-Present)

IGOR STRAVINSKY (1882-1971)

Igor Stravinsky – (1882-1971) was a **Russian** composer, conductor, and pianist of the **Modern** era. Many other composers were influenced by Stravinsky's non-traditional music during the **twentieth century.** Stravinsky collaborated with the famous choreographer and impresario Sergei Diaghilev to compose music for his *Ballets Russes*. Stravinsky lived and worked in several countries including Russia, Ukraine, Switzerland, France and the USA. He developed groundbreaking innovations in his three most famous ballets which include: *The Firebird* (1910); *Petrushka* (1911); and *The Rite of Spring* (1913). He was a champion of nationalistic music during his "Russian Period" (1907-1919). Stravinsky also composed in a "Neo-Classical style" (1920-1954) with pieces such as *The Soldier's Tale*, Renard, and Les Noces. He experimented with twelve-tone music during his "Serial Period" (1954-1968). Stravinsky gave new dimensions to orchestration, rhythmic content and harmonic progressions in his ballets and symphonic music. He used primitive music and African drumming in his scores that was previously unheard of in classical music.

Igor Stravinsky was born 17 June 1882 in a suburb of Saint Petersburg, which was the Imperial capital of Russia then. His father, Fyodor Stravinsky, was a famous bass singer in the Kiev Opera House. His mother, Anna Kholodovsky, was one of the daughters of a high-ranking officer in the Kiev Ministry of Estates. They were both from Ukraine. Igor began studying piano and composition at a young age. He was very lonely as a schoolboy and remarked that no one really had any attraction to him. He was inspired by hearing a performance of Tchaikovsky's *The Sleeping Beauty Ballet* in 1890 at the Mariinsky Theater in St. Petersburg, where his father was a singer. His theory and composition teacher, the Russian composer Glazunov, considered Igor to be unmusical, and did not think that he would amount to anything.

Regardless of Igor's enthusiasm for music, his parents decided that he should study law. So, in 1901 he was enrolled for four years at the University of St. Petersburg in law. In the summer of 1902, Stravinsky stayed at the home of the most distinguished Russian composer Nikolai Rimsky-Korsakov, and his family, in the German city of Heidelberg. Rimsky-Korsakov suggested that Stravinsky should take private lessons in composition rather than try to enter the Saint Petersburg Conservatory at age twenty. Stravinsky received a half course diploma in law in 1905. He continued to study privately with Rimsky-Korsakov until the composer's death in 1908.

Stravinsky was a devout member of the Russian Orthodox Church. In 1905 Stravinsky was engaged to his cousin Katherine Gavrylivna Nosenko, whose nickname was "Katya". They had known each other since early childhood. Despite the Orthodox Church's opposition to marriage between first cousins, the couple married on 23 January 1906. They had two children, Fyodor (Theodore) and Ludmila, who were born in 1907 and 1908.

In February 1909, two of Stravinsky's orchestral works, the *Scherzo Fantastique* and *Feu d'artifice* (Fireworks) were performed at a concert in Saint Petersburg. This concert was heard by the ballet choreographer Serge Diaghilev, who was at that time planning to present Russian opera and ballet in Paris. Diaghilev was extremely impressed by Stravinsky's "Fireworks". He commissioned him to compose a full-length ballet score called *The Firebird*. This ballet was premiered in Paris in 1910. The family moved to Ukraine and spent their winters in Switzerland. They moved to Paris in 1920, with the aid of the French perfume manufacturer Coco Chanel. Later the Stravinsky's became naturalized citizens of France. In the 1920's Stravinsky traveled to New York to record Duo-Art Piano Rolls at the Aeolian recording studio where composer Louise Lincoln Kerr was working with pianists and composers as the proofreader of the piano rolls.

Unfortunately, Katya died from tuberculosis in March of 1939. Stravinsky already had ties with the United States composing his *Symphony in C* on commission for the Chicago Symphony Orchestra. He had also agreed to lecture at Harvard University in 1939. So, with a broken heart, the widowed Stravinsky sailed for New York in September of that year, despite the outbreak of World War II. Eventually, he settled in West Hollywood, California and spent the rest of his life there. Stravinsky became a US citizen in 1945. Los Angeles with its movie industry was a cultural hub for musicians, writers, composers and conductors. Stravinsky and the writer Aldous Huxley started a Saturday luncheon for luminaries. Some of the people Stravinsky met with included Otto Klemperer, Thomas Mann, George Balanchine and Arthur Rubinstein, Franz Werfel, and Bernard Holland.

In 1962, he accepted an invitation to visit Leningrad in the USSR, where he met with Soviet composers Dimitri Shostakovich and Aram Khachaturian. In 1969, he moved to the Essex Hotel in New York, and lived there until his death in 1971 at age 88 from a heart attack. He was buried at San Michele, France near the tomb of Sergei Diaghilev. He received many awards during his life. Stravinsky has a star on the Hollywood walk of fame, and he was also given a Grammy Lifetime Achievement Award posthumously in 1987. He was posthumously inducted into the National Museum of Dance's Mr. & Mrs. Cornelius Vanderbilt Whitney Hall of Fame in 2004.

50 Famous Composers

Title: *Le Sacre du Primtemps* "The Rite of Spring" Ballet – Premiered in Paris, 1913. The instrumentation includes:

Genre: Ballet music is written to accompany and enhance the staged choreography of dancers, and to tell a story with the combination of dance, sets and music.

YouTube: https://www.youtube.com/watch?v=jF1OQkHybEQ

The Joffrey Ballet with choreography by Vaslov Nijinsky and the Orchestra of the National Theater of Prague with Allan Lewis conducting.

Instrumentation:

Woodwinds: piccolo, 3 flutes, alto flute, 4 oboes, *cor anglais* (English horn), clarinet in E-flat and D, 3 clarinets in B-flat, A, bass clarinet, 4 bassoons, contrabassoon.

Brass: 8 horns in F (7th and 8th doubling Wagner tubas in B-flat), trumpet in D, 4 trumpets in C (4th doubling bass trumpet in E-flat), 3 trombones, 2 tubas

Percussion: timpani (2 players, with a minimum of 5 drums including a *piccolo timpano*), bass drum, cymbals, tam-tam, crotales (antique cymbals) in A-flat and B-flat, triangle, tambourine, guiro

Strings: violins I and II (16), (14), violas (12), violoncellos (10), double basses (8)

Birthday: 17 June [O.S. 5 June] 1882 – near St. Petersburg, Imperial Russia.

Death Date: 6 April 1971 – New York City, USA (aged 88).

Fun Facts:

1. At the 1913 premiere of Stravinsky's *Rite of Spring* in Paris, it was reported that there were fist fights that broke out, and the police had to be called in to control the audience during the second act. They feared it would become a riot.

2. In January of 1944, the Boston police threatened to fine Stravinsky 100 dollars for rearranging the "Star Spangled Banner" with a dominant seventh chord. It turned out that they could not fine him for rearranging our National Anthem, the law only forbade using it as a dance, an exit march, or any part was used in a melody.

3. Whenever composer George Gershwin met a famous composer, he claimed that he asked them for lessons. So, he sent a telegram off to Igor Stravinsky and waited for his response. Stravinsky told him that he charged for lessons on a sliding scale and needed to get Gershwin's annual salary. When Stravinsky found out how much money Gershwin made writing songs, Stravinsky replied "Then I should be taking lessons from you!" Stravinsky claimed later that this exchange never took place, and that he heard the money story for Ravel too. Gershwin may have made this story up to tell at fancy parties where he performed on piano.

REBECCA CLARKE (1886-1979)

Rebecca Clarke – (1886-1979) was an **English 20th Century composer** and an excellent viola player of German American descent. Clarke was one of the most distinguished British composers of the Victorian era and considered part of the New Independents. Conductor Sir Henry Wood selected her as one of the first six women to perform in the Queen's Hall Orchestra, which was a professional orchestra in London (1912-14). She originally tied for first place in the Elizabeth Sprague Coolidge 1919 composing competition in Massachusetts. She entered her *Sonata for Viola and Piano* under an assumed name (like everyone else). The judges said it was the work of a true philosopher. However, when the judges found out that she was a woman, they were shocked, and wanted to take the prize away from her. But Mrs. Coolidge said, "absolutely not". So, they compromised and gave her the second-place prize.

Rebecca born 27 August 1886 in Harrow to an American father, Joseph Thatcher Clarke, who came to England to work for Eastman Kodak. Her German mother, Agnes Paulina Marie Amalie Helferich, was the great-niece of the German historian Leopold von

Ranke. Rebecca began studying violin at the Royal Academy of Music (RAM) in 1903 with Hans Wessely at the age of seventeen. However, she was withdrawn from RAM by her father in 1905, when her harmony teacher, Percy Miles, proposed to her (he later bequeathed his Stradivari violin to her in his will). Rebecca then entered the Royal College of Music (RCM) in 1907 as Sir Charles Villiers Stanford's first female composition student. He recommended that she switch form violin to viola. Rebecca wrote a song called "Tears" based on Chinese poetry in 1910. She also sang under the direction of Ralph Vaughan Williams with a group that Clarke had organized that same year to study and sing the works of Palestrina.

Her father disapproved of her aspirations for a career in music, but she dared to disapprove of him. So, in 1910 after they had a fight, her father decided to turn her out of the house and cut her money off. She had no income and had to leave the Royal College of Music. But because of her excellent skills as a violist, she was able to make a living as a musician. Clarke later joined three female groups including the English Ensemble, the Norah Clench Quartet, and the d'Aranyi sisters. Rebecca Clarke also toured world-wide especially with cellist May Muklé.

Rebecca Clarke is best known for her chamber music compositions. She moved to the United States in 1916 to further her music career. She composed *Morpheus* for viola and piano in 1918. Clarke's *Sonata for Viola and Piano* was well received in America and was given a premiere in 1919 in the Berkshires. This work has recently been orchestrated. In 1921 Clarke entered the Coolidge's composition competition again with her piano trio but failed a second time to take the prize. In 1923 she presented her *Rhapsody* for cello and piano, which was sponsored by Coolidge, making Clarke the only female recipient of Coolidge's patronage at that time. These three pieces are considered Clarke's greatest works. She went on a world tour from 1922 to 1923. The next year she began her professional career as a soloist and chamber musician in London. In 1927, she helped to start the English Ensemble of Women Musicians including May Muklé, Marjorie Hayword, and Kathleen Long. She made a couple of recordings, and BBC broadcasts. Clarke also wrote several songs during this time.

At the outbreak of World War II in 1939, Rebecca Clarke was in the United States visiting her brothers. She was unable to get a visa to go back to England, so she stayed with her brothers' families. She had to take a job as a governess to make ends meet. During this war time, she wrote ten works between 1939 and 1942 including her *Passacaglia on an English Tune*. Rebecca first met her husband, James Frisken, when they were both students at the Royal College of Music. He was a concert pianist, composer, and a founding faculty member of the Juilliard School of Music in New York. They happened to meet again by chance on a street in Manhattan in 1944, and decided to get married the same year, both in their late 50's.

They had a good marriage, and Frisken helped her to achieve a greater sense of stability and happiness. Yet, her later output was sporadic as she suffered from a form of deep depression called dysthymia. This caused Rebecca to be conflicted about her life. Women were not often appreciated for their artistic abilities in the early part of the 20th century. At times, she received outright discouragement as a composer from a male dominated society, which made her depression worse. Yet Rebecca continued her love of music. She said about her composition "I can't do it unless it's the first thing I think of every morning when I wake and the last thing I think of every night before I go to sleep" (Ponder 2004).

Despite her husband's encouragement, Rebecca stopped composing and performing. However, she continued to arrange music after that. She sold the Stradivari violin she had been bequeathed and established the May Muklé prize at the Royal Academy of Music. This prize is still awarded every year to an outstanding cellist. After her husband's death in 1967, Clarke began writing her memoir, entitled *I Had a Father Too (or the Mustard Spoon)*. She completed her book in 1973 but never published. In it she describes her early life, marked by frequent beatings from her father and strained family relations, which affected her the rest of her life. Clarke died in 1979 at her home in New York City at the age of 93 and was cremated. She leaves us a legacy of beautiful chamber music.

50 Famous Composers

Title: *Sonata for Viola and Piano*, 1919. Clarke's viola sonata is in the Impressionistic style of Debussy, it opens with a pentatonic theme, has an emotionally intense nature, thick harmonies, and a rhythmically dense and complex texture. It was published in the same year as the Bloch Concerto and the Hindemith Viola Sonata. Her Sonata remains a part of standard repertoire for the viola.

Genre: A **sonata** is chamber music, which is usually performed with piano and another solo instrument. Sonatas are usually written with three to four movements.

YouTube audios: Sonata for Viola and Piano.

Sonata for Viola – I. Impetuoso – https://www.youtube.com/ watch?v=GsgFoLOid-g
Carolyn Waters Broe Violist with Miriam Hickman Pianist

Sonata for Viola – II. Vivace – https://www.youtube.com/ watch?v=J1Da4pOJwZc
Carolyn Waters Broe Violist with Miriam Hickman Pianist

Sonata for Viola – III. Adagio – Allegro – https://www.youtube.com/ watch?v=XOCaT7lDwkg
Carolyn Waters Broe Violist with Miriam Hickman Pianist

Birthday: 27 August 1886, Harrow, England.

Death Date: 13 October 1979, New York, USA (aged 93).

Fun Facts:

1. Rebecca Clarke tied for first place in the Elizabeth Sprague Coolidge composing competition of 1919, but when the judges found out she was a woman, they wanted to take her prize away. The founder of the competition, Mrs. Coolidge, said no. So, the judges gave her second place as a compromise.

2. She composed songs for voice and piano called "The Shiv and the Grasshopper," "Tiger, Tiger," "The Shy One," and "The Seal Man".

3. Conductor Sir Henry Wood selected her as one of the first six women to perform in the Queen's Hall Orchestra, which was a professional orchestra in London (1912-14).

FLORENCE PRICE (1887-1953)

Florence Price – (1887-1953) was the first **African American** woman to gain recognition as a symphonic composer, and the first to have her composition performed by a major orchestra. Florence Beatrice Smith was born 9 April 1887 in Little Rock, Arkansas to a mixed-racial family. Her father, James H. Smith, was a dentist, and her mother, Florence Gulliver was a music teacher. They were well respected in the community. She was one of three children. Her mother taught her how to play music at an early age. Florence gave her first piano performance at the age of four and published her first piece at the age of eleven. She attended the same elementary school as William Grant Still, another future classical music great. Both composers studied under educator Charlotte Andrews Stephens. Florence graduated early from high school at the age of fourteen, as the valedictorian of her class.

Florence enrolled in the New England Conservatory of Music. She was a piano and organ major, but also studied composition and counterpoint with composers George Chadwick and Frederick Converse. She pretended to be Mexican to avoid the prejudice that was common at the time with African Americans. Florence graduated with honors in 1906, and she was awarded both an artist diploma in organ, and a teaching certificate. She composed her first string trio and symphony at the conservatory.

After graduating college, Florence taught in Little Rock briefly before moving to Atlanta, Georgia in 1910 to take another teaching job. Eventually she became the head of the music department at Clark Atlanta University. Florence married Thomas J. Price, who was a lawyer in 1912, and they moved back to Little Rock, Arkansas. Unfortunately, racial violence was escalating there, so after a lynching in 1927 they moved to Chicago. She studied composition there with some of the leading composers including Leo Sowerby, Arthur Olaf Anderson, Carl Busch, and Wesley La Violette. Price studied at several colleges in Chicago including the University of Chicago, Chicago Musical College, Chicago Teacher's College, and American Conservatory of Music. Due to financial troubles, she divorced and became the single parent of her two daughters in 1931. To make ends meet, she worked as an organist in movie theaters for silent movies. She also composed jingles for radio ads under a pen name. Due to her dire financial situation, Price moved in with her former student Margaret Bonds, who was also a black composer and pianist. Bonds helped to connect Price with writer Langston Hughes and contralto Marian Anderson.

Florence Price won the Wanamaker Foundation First Place Award for her *Symphony in E minor*, and third for her *Piano Sonata*, which earned her a $500 prize. The Chicago Symphony Orchestra, conducted by Frederick Stock, premiered her symphony on June 15, 1933. Price's symphony was the first composition by an African American woman to be performed by a major orchestra. Her music was also performed by the WPA Symphony Orchestra of Detroit, and the Chicago Women's Symphony. Price composed over three hundred pieces including works for symphony, piano, organ, violin, chamber music, vocal works, and arrangements of spirituals. She was inducted into the American Society of Composers, Authors and Publishers in 1940.

She died of a stroke on June 3rd of 1953 in Chicago. After she passed away some of her works were lost. Her music was nearly forgotten due to the changing tastes in modern music. Then in 2001 the Women's Philharmonic recorded an album of her music. As black and women composers have gained more interest in recent years, Florence Price's music is being rediscovered, and performed by an increasing number of music ensembles and musicians. Her symphonic music has been recognized for its rich orchestration, driving rhythmic interest, and beautiful blues inspired thematic melodies. Price's classical music is infused with spirituals and American folk music. Many of Florence Price's works have helped to define the meaning of American music.

Title: *Mississippi Suite for Orchestra*

Genre: A **Suite for orchestra** is a large-scale instrumental work for symphony orchestra, which usually has several movements. Price's Suite incorporates gospel songs such as "Nobody Knows the Trouble I've Seen," and American folk songs into her classical music.

YouTube: https://www.youtube.com/watch?v=wfdvCrqzTm0 The Women's Philharmonic

Birthday: April 9, 1887 in Little Rock, Arkansas.

Death Date: June 3, 1953 in Chicago, Illinois at age 66.

Fun Facts:

1. When Florence Price broke her foot, she found enough undisturbed time to write her *Symphony No. 1 in E Minor*. As a result, she won the First Place Award in the Wanamaker Foundation contest and was given a much needed 500-dollar prize.

2. To make ends meet Florence Price played organ in a movie theater for screenings of silent movies.

3. Marian Anderson sang Price's arrangement of the spiritual "My Soul's Been Anchored in de Lord" during the famous Easter Sunday recital at the Lincoln Memorial in 1939.

THE BOULANGER SISTERS

NADIA BOULANGER (1887-1979)

Nadia Boulanger – (1887-1979) **French** teacher and **20th Century composer**, and sister of composer Lili Boulanger. Her father, pianist, and composer Ernest Boulanger (1815-1900), and her grandfather both taught at the Paris Conser-vatoire. Her mother, Raissa Myshetskaya (1856-1935), a Russian princess, had been one of her father's piano students. Nadia Boulanger taught many of our most famous American and European composers of the 20th century. Some of her students at the Paris Conservatory include Aaron Copland, Leonard Bernstein, Roy Harris, Thea Musgrave, Elliot Carter, and Walter Piston. She was deeply affected by the premature death of her sister Lili Boulanger, who was also a composer.

Nadia Boulanger was born 16 September 1887 in Paris, France. When Nadia was a small child, she would become upset whenever she heard music, and run and hide. After her sister, Lili was born, when Nadia was six, she changed and took her singing lessons with her father more seriously. At the age of seven, Nadia began to study at the Paris Conservatory for her entrance exams by sitting in on classes and studying with their teachers. Lili was often brought along as an infant, listening to the piano music. At the age of nine, Nadia officially entered the conservatory. She won third place in the *solfége* competition in 1897. When their father died in 1900, their mother Raissa did not have enough money to continue her extravagant lifestyle. So, Nadia studied hard to become a teacher.

Nadia won the first prize in harmony in 1903. She studied with the famous French composer Gabriel Fauré. She also met many famous composers such as Igor Stravinsky and Paul Valéry.

Dr. Carolyn Waters Broe

In 1904, she won competitions in organ, piano accompaniment, and fugue (composition). She was appointed to teach elementary piano and piano accompaniment at the newly created *Conservatoire Femina-Musica* in 1907. Nadia was also appointed as assistant to Henri Dallier, who was the professor of harmony at the Conservatoire. In 1908, after causing a stir in the media for submitting an instrumental fugue instead of the required vocal fugue, Nadia Boulanger won the Second Grand Prix for her cantata, *La Sirène*. Nadia debuted as a conductor in 1912. When the First World War broke out in 1914, Nadia and Lili formed a charity to help the soldiers. Lili became ill from her work on the war effort and died in March of 1918.

After her sister died, Nadia performed twenty piano concerts of music by herself and her sister. Nadia lost herself in work teaching harmony and organ at the École *Normale de Music de Paris* (teaching school) with composer Alfred Cortot. Nadia did not compose again until 1920, when she composed her series of songs to words by Camille Mauclair. In the summer of 1921, Boulanger joined the French Music School for Americans in Fontainebleau as their professor of harmony. She was the first woman to conduct the London Philharmonic. When World War II broke out in 1940, she helped many of her students escape France for New York. She taught at the Peabody Conservatory for Music in Baltimore in 1942, and toured teaching and performing in the US.

She returned to France in 1946 at the end of the war and accepted a position teaching piano accompaniment at the Paris Conservatory. In 1953 Boulanger was appointed the overall Director at the Fountainbleau Music School for Americans. Her list of famous American students is extensive. She was friends with the Prince Rainier of Monaco and American actress Grace Kelly. She was also invited to the White House to meet then President John F. Kennedy and First Lady Jacqueline. She was also invited to the Moscow Tchaikovsky Competition. Boulanger worked almost up to the time of her death in October of 1979. She composed many vocal works, as well as chamber music, and a couple of orchestral pieces including her *Fantaisie for Piano and Orchestra*. She was buried in the Montmartre Cemetery with her sister Lili.

Title: *Fantaisie Variée pour piano et orchestra* (1912).

Genre: A **fantasy** is a one movement work, which is through composed, and usually performed on a solo instrument like the piano.

YouTube Audio: https://www.youtube.com/watch?v=_TVON0HwRCI

Birthday: 16 September 1887 in Paris, France.

Death Date: 22 October 1979 in Paris, France (aged 92).

Fun Facts:

1. In Nadia's early years, even though both of her parents were active musically, she used to run crying and hide when she heard music, until it stopped. When her mother got pregnant with her sister Lili, this all changed. Nadia heard a fire bell and rushed to the piano to try and imitate this sound.

2. When American composer Georges Gershwin came to Paris to study with Nadia Boulanger in 1927, she said "I can teach you nothing." Taking this as a compliment, Gershwin repeated the story many times.

3. Nadia Boulanger taught over 600 American composers and musicians. Many of them became the leading lights of the twentieth century (Who Was She? Library of Congress).

LILI BOULANGER (1893-1918)

Lili Boulanger (born Marie-Juliette Olga) (1893-1918) was a **French 20th Century** composer and child prodigy, who was the sister of composer and teacher Nadia Boulanger. Marie-Juliette (nicknamed Lili) was born 21 August 1893 in Paris, France. Her father was Ernest Boulanger, an opera composer, who won the *Prix de Rome* in 1835. Unfortunately, Marie-Juliette became ill with pneumonia in 1895 at the age of two and suffered from Crone's disease the rest of her life. So, her ability to study and compose was limited. Her mother was very protective of Lili after that. Her older sister Nadia often helped Lili with her studies to develop a strong career in music. She studied at the Paris Conservatory with Paul Vidal in 1912. Lili wanted very much to follow in the footsteps of her father and older sister. In July of 1913, Lili became the first woman to win the *Prix de Rome* competition for her cantata *Faust e Hélène* (Sadie 1995). After

this everything she did became headline news. She also signed a contract to compose for Ricordi.

Lili's musical talent was discovered when she was two years old by the famous composer Gabriel Fauré, who was a friend of the Boulanger family. He realized that she had perfect pitch. Later, Faure became Lili's composition teacher. Both of Lili's parents were musicians, who encouraged their daughter in music. Her father was 77 years old when she was born, so she became very fond of him. Her mother, Raissa, was a Russian princess, who married her Paris Conservatory teacher Ernest Boulanger. Before she was five years old, Lili went to classes at the Paris Conservatory with her sister Nadia, who was only ten. Later she studied the organ with Louis Vierne, and learned to play piano, violin, cello and harp.

Nadia had attempted to win the *Prix de Rome* competition four times and failed. This was the biggest prize in Europe for music composition. She decided to concentrate on helping Lili learn to compose and became her first teacher. Lili also studied with Paul Vidal, Georges Caussade, and Gabriel Fauré. Her health was never good, so she was only able to study when she felt well enough. Lili was deeply affected by the death of her father in 1900. After that, her music always had a touch of sadness. In 1911 she composed *Les Sirens*, which is written for solo soprano and three-part choir. This song is about mermaids and uses a text by Charles Grandmougin.

In 1912 Lili competed in the *Prix de Rome* but collapsed from illness during the performance. In 1913 she tried again, and this time Lili became the first women ever to win the *Prix de Rome* for her cantata "Faust e Hélène" at the age of nineteen. She was given a recording contract with the music publisher Ricordi after that. She only spent six months at the Villa Medici during 1914 and 1916 due to World War I. Lili decided to help the war effort by founding the Comité Franco-Americain du Conservatorie National. This organization helped keep musicians in touch with their families during the war. Unfortunately, her work weakened her already fragile immune system.

In February of 1916, Lili was given permission from Maurice Maeterlink to set *La Princesse Maleine* to music. Her contract with Ricordi included the composition of two full-length operas. She identified closely with the isolation of the fragile and tragic heroine in Maeterlink's story. Lili nearly finished this opera, but only one scene survives. She also worked on her settings of three Psalms: 24, 129 and 130, while she was studying in Rome. *Du fond de l'abîme* (Psalm 130: *De Profundis* "Out of the depths"), is composed for voice & orchestra, and dedicated to the memory of her father. In July of 1917, she had surgery to remove her appendix. But this only brought her temporary relief. She became so weak, that she had to dictate her *Pie Jesu* from her bed. She dedicated this piece to her sister Nadia. Tragically, Lili died on 15 March of 1918 of "intestinal tuberculosis" (Crohn's disease) at the age of 24. She was buried in Paris, in a tomb located in the Cimetière de Montmartre. In 1979, when Nadia passed away, she was buried with her sister in the same tomb.

Title: *Cantata Faust e Hélène* (1913). Scored for mezzo-soprano, tenor, baritone, and orchestra. You can hear the influences of Debussy and Fauré in her music.

Genre: A **cantata** (to sing) is a vocal composition with instrumental accompaniment, which is often in several movements, and often includes a choir and vocal soloists.

YouTube: https://www.youtube.com/watch?v=3BQgfSfMG4E The BBC Philharmonic directed by Yan Pascal Tortelier. Lynn Dawson, soprano, Ann Murray, mezzo-soprano, Bonaventura Bottone, tenor and Jason Howard, baritone.

Birthday: 21 August 1893 in Paris, France.

Death Date: 15 March 1918 in Mézy-sur-Seine, France (aged 24).

Fun Facts:

1. Lili Boulanger had perfect pitch, which is the ability to identify music notes by name just by listening to them.
2. As a child, Lili would accompany her sister Nadia, while she was taking music lessons at the Paris Conservatory of music.
3. Many scholars consider Lili Boulanger to have been a music genius.

SERGEI PROKOFIEV (1891-1953)

ergei Prokofiev – (1891-1953) was a **20th century Ukrainian** (and Soviet) composer, who wrote symphonies, concerti, film scores, and operas. His best-known works include the *March from The Love for Three Oranges*, *Lieutenant Kijé Suite*, the *Ballet Romeo and Juliet* (from which "Dance of the Knights" is taken), *Cinderella*, and *Peter and the Wolf*. He completed seven operas, seven symphonies, eight ballets, five piano concertos, two violin concertos, a cello concerto, a *Symphony-Concerto for Cello and Orchestra*, and nine completed piano sonatas.

Sergei was born 23 April 1891, Sontsovka in a remote rural part of the Ukraine, which was part of the old Russian empire in 1891. His father was Alexeyevich Prokofiev, who was an agronomist (someone who produces more food through genetics, herbology, and taking soil samples). His mother was Maria (née Zhitkova), who came from a family of former serfs, who had been owned by the Sheremetev family. Under their patronage, the serf-children were taught theatre and arts from an early age. His mother was a devoted pianist, who went to Moscow and St. Petersburg to study. Sergei was inspired by his mother practicing music by Chopin and Beethoven. He wrote his first composition at the age of five called "Indian Gallop". Sergei learned to play chess at age seven and won a major championship in 1914 against another chess master José Raúl Capablanca. At the age of nine, Sergei completed his first opera *The Giant*.

In 1902 Sergei's mother met with the director of the Moscow Conservatory, Sergei Taneyev.

He arranged for composer and pianist Reinhold Glière to spend the summer in Sontsovka, teaching Prokofiev piano and composition. The eleven-year-old Prokovief insisted on writing his first symphony during these lessons. Later, his mother took him to the Saint Petersburg Conservatory, where he was introduced to composer Alexander Glazunov, who was a professor there. Glazunov was so impressed with Prokofiev's early operas, that he urged his mother to have him apply for the conservatory. He passed the introductory tests and enrolled that year. Unfortunately, since he was younger than most of the other students, they felt that he was arrogant and annoying, especially when he kept a tally of their errors. During this time, he studied with many excellent professors including orchestration with Nikolai Rimsky-Korsakov (although he was part of a large class of students rather than individual lessons). He experimented with dissonance and harmonic progressions and was considered a musical rebel.

Prokofiev finished at the conservatory by entering the "battle of the pianos" where the prize was a Schroeder grand piano. He won the competition by performing his own *Piano Concerto No. 1* (Nice 2003). Soon afterwards, Sergie made a trip to London in 1914, where he heard Sergei Diaghilev's *Ballets Russes*. Diaghilev commissioned Prokofiev's first ballet, *Ala and Lolli*; but rejected it in 1915 when Prokofiev brought the work in progress. Diaghilev then commissioned the ballet *Chout* or "The Fool" (the original Russian meaning is "The Tale of the Buffoon who Outwits Seven Other Buffoons"). Diaghilev helped Prokofiev to make extensive revisions on this work. The ballet's premiere in Paris on 17 May 1921 was a huge success. Prokofiev was greeted with great admiration by an audience that included Jean Cocteau, Igor Stravinsky and Maurice Ravel. Stravinsky called the ballet "the single piece of modern music he could listen to with pleasure," while Ravel called it "a work of genius (Wakin 2009).

During the first world war and revolution, Prokofiev returned to the St. Petersburg Conservatory. He wrote several works including his *"Classical" Symphony*. He decided to go to America to try his luck there. He arrived in San Francisco, California and was released by the immigration officials on 11 August 1918. Later he worked with the Chicago Opera Association to produce his opera *The Love of Three Oranges*. The premiere was delayed, which meant that the opera became a failure.

This also destroyed his solo career in America as a pianist. So, he decided to go to Paris and work with Diaghilev and the *Ballet Russes* again. In 1922 Stravinsky got into a fight with Prokofiev over a reading of his opera *The Love of Three Oranges* for Diaghilev, telling him he was wasting his time writing operas. Prokofiev replied that Stravinsky "was in no position to lay down a general artistic direction, since he is himself not immune to error"! According to Prokofiev, Stravinsky "became incandescent with rage" (Prokofiev 2008, p. 680). Prokofiev decided to move to the town of Ettal in the Bavarian Alps with his mother, where he wrote the opera *The Fiery Angel*. In 1923, Prokofiev married the Spanish singer Carolina Codina (1897–1989), her stage name was Lina Llubera). They moved back to Paris and had two sons. He and Stravinsky mended their relationship, and Prokofiev premiered several more of his works in Pairs including his second piano concerto.

In 1927, Prokofiev made his first concert tour in the Soviet Union, where he enjoyed an extraordinarily successful staging of *The Love for Three Oranges*. In 1928, Prokofiev completed his *Third Symphony*, which was based on his unperformed opera *The Fiery Angel*. The conductor Serge Koussevitzky characterized Prokofiev's Third as "the greatest symphony since Tchaikovsky's Sixth." (Prokofiev 2012, p. 826). After traveling back and forth between Paris and Moscow, Prokofiev and his family settled permanently in Moscow in 1936. That year he composed one of his most famous works, *Peter and the Wolf* for chamber orchestra and narrator, for Natalya Sats who ran the Central Children's Theatre. His symphonic fairy tale has become one of the most beloved pieces ever written for children. She also persuaded Prokofiev to write two songs for children, "Sweet Song", and "Chatterbox". Later he wrote "The Little Pigs" and published them as *Three Children's Songs*, Op. 68.

Unfortunately, his wife Lina was arrested in 1948 for "espionage," when she tried to send money to her mother in Spain. She was sentenced to twenty years hard labor. After that, Prokofiev was in ill health for five years. Unfortunately, Prokofiev died on 5 March of 1953 near Red Square, which was the same day that the Communist leader Joseph Stalin died. There were so many people in the streets of Moscow, that no one could carry Prokofiev's body out for a funeral service at the Composer's Union while Stalin was mourned. After Stalin's death, Lina was released from prison. She left the Soviet Union for London in 1974 and lived on a modest income from the sales of Prokofiev's music.

Dr. Carolyn Waters Broe

Title: *Peter and the Wolf,* Op. 67, 1936

Genre: A **symphonic fairy tale** for children with narration. This piece is one of the most frequently performed pieces by Prokofiev. It is also one of the most popular pieces in all classical literature. It was commissioned by Natalya Sats, who ran the Central Children's Theatre in Moscow. She asked him to compose a children's symphony. The first draft was about a Young Pioneer (the Soviet equivalent of a Boy Scout) named Peter, who rights a wrong by challenging an adult (a popular theme in Soviet propaganda). Prokofiev did not like the original libretto, so he rewrote it by having Peter capture a wolf. Each instrument in the orchestra is introduced by the narrator, who tells the story of Peter.

YouTube: https://www.youtube.com/watch?v=Ot7m9i70JDg The Disney animated version of *Peter and the Wolf*

Birthday: 23 April 1891, Sontsovka, Ukraine, Russian Empire.

Death Date: 5 March 1953, Moscow, Russia, U.S.S.R (age 61).

Fun Facts:

1. Prokofiev composed his first piece at the age of five, and his first opera at the age of nine.
2. Prokofiev was several years younger than the other students at the Saint Petersburg Conservatory. They considered him to be an eccentric, who was arrogant, and annoying for keeping track of their mistakes.
3. At the premiere of Prokofiev's second piano concerto, the audience walked out saying "The cats on the roof make better music"! This piano concerto is now considered a great work of art and is performed by leading piano soloists.

LOUISE LINCOLN KERR (1892-1977)

ouise Lincoln Kerr – (1892-1977) was a **20th century American** composer, violist, and patroness of the arts. Louise Kerr studied composition and theory at Columbia University through Barnard College for women in New York from 1910 to 1913. She won two awards at Barnard for her choral pieces. She studied violin at the pre-Juilliard School of Music in New York. Louise was one of the first two women to join the early Cleveland Municipal Orchestra in 1913.

Kerr wrote over one hundred music compositions including her *Ballet Tableau Vivant, Enchanted Mesa* for soprano and orchestra, *Arizona Profiles* for orchestra, *String Quartet in A Major, Five Character Pieces for Viola and Piano*, and her *Trio for Piano, Clarinet, and Cello*. Kerr helped to co-found the Phoenix Symphony, the Phoenix Chamber Music Society, and other arts organizations.

Louise Lincoln was born 24 April 1892 in Cleveland, Ohio in the United States, and died 10 December 1977 in Cottonwood, Arizona at her ranch. She was the daughter of John C. Lincoln, who was an engineer and real estate tycoon, who founded Lincoln Electric in Ohio. Her mother Myrtie taught her to play the piano at age six, violin at seven, and later Louise learned to play viola. She studied violin in Cleveland with Sol Marcosson, concertmaster and soloist with the early Cleveland Municipal Orchestra. She attended Barnard College for women in New York in 1910 where she studied music composition with two prominent Columbia University professors: Cornelius Rubnor and Daniel Gregory Mason. She left New York around 1913 to join the early Cleveland Municipal Orchestra as a violinist under the direction of her violin teacher the famous Dutch violinist Christiaan Timmner. She was one of the first two women to join that orchestra as a violinist. The other lady played the harp.

By 1920 she had returned to New York where she met and married Peter Kjer, a business partner of her father, and started her family. They had eight children and the last two were identical twins. She did not play her violin or compose for many years while she was raising her family. Later Louise changed the spelling of their name to match the actress Deborah Kerr, but she pronounced her last name "Care" (JoAnn Cleland 2020). While in New York, she got a job working for the Aeolian Recording Company proofing piano rolls for player pianos. There Louise Kerr met with noted pianists and composers who were recording their music, including Sergei Prokofiev, Alfred Cortot, and George Gershwin. She was also a friend of the renowned conductor Dimitri Mitropoulos and the violinist virtuoso Isaac Stern. Later, when Kerr worked in the sound booth studio of Duo Arts Records (at Aeolian), she assisted conductors by correcting mistakes on early disk recordings of modern pieces. It was her job to sit in the glass booth, follow the score, and tell the conductors when a mistake happened, so they could re-record it.

In 1936 the Kerrs moved west to Arizona for the health of one of their daughters. The family lived in Phoenix and later built homes in Cottonwood and Scottsdale. Her husband died in 1939. Two of her daughters died in the 1940's, one of a tragic accident in Flagstaff and the other of tuberculosis. Louise Kerr's nephew, John G. Lincoln Jr., said "They were both teenagers at the time. Can you imagine how hard that must have been? … We always saw her as a strong person who didn't let the pain show." (Broe 2001 p.12). It was after that when she started composing again to relieve her grief.

Louise Kerr's violin was stolen on 7 December 1941, the day that Pearl Harbor was attacked. So, she decided to perform on the viola as her main instrument with the Pasadena, Phoenix and Flagstaff Symphonies. Mrs. Kerr owned many valuable instruments but performed in the Phoenix Symphony on a 1781 viola labeled Michele Deconte. It is thought that Deconte

(1713-1799), who was a German born traveling violinist, brokered instruments for Venetian luthiers in other Italian cities during the latter part of the 18th century. The Michele Deconet viola is part of the string collection that was donated to ASU Herberger School of Music by Louise Kerr and two other families.

In Arizona, Louise Kerr became known as the "Grand Lady of Music" (Taylor c. 1991). In 1959 she used an inheritance from her father (who had owned most of the mining rights in Arizona) to build her home, studio, and an artist's colony in Scottsdale. Her studio included a music theater and was the original site of the Phoenix Chamber Music Society performances. Many famous musicians from around the world performed there, and she played chamber music at her studio with Isaac Stern, inviting professors and local musicians to join in. In addition, she helped co-found and/or develop The Phoenix Symphony, Phoenix Chamber Music Society, The Scottsdale Center for the Arts, The National Society of Arts and Letters (Arizona Chapter), Monday Morning Musicals, The Bach and Madrigal Society, Young Audiences, The Musicians Club, and the Phoenix Cello Society (now the Arizona Cello Society) (Taylor 1991). She was extremely generous with both her time and money.

As a composer, Kerr wrote more than one hundred works including fifteen symphonic tone poems, twenty works for chamber or string orchestra, a violin concerto, five ballets and incidental music, numerous piano pieces, and about forty pieces of chamber music. Kerr's chamber music includes a rich selection of Impressionistic and Neo-Romantic music including her *String Quartet in A Major*; her *Five Character Pieces for Viola and Piano*; and her *Trio for Clarinet, Cello and Piano*. In the latter part of her life, Kerr composed many string quartet movements; piano quartets and quintets; numerous duos for piano and other instruments; and a couple of vocal pieces. According to her son, William Kerr who was one of her twins, she composed mostly at night, no doubt a necessity with eight children to care for (William Kerr 2001).

The Phoenix Symphony performed her tone poem *Enchanted Mesa* for soprano and orchestra, written in 1948, as well as her other symphonic works. Most of her symphonic compositions were written for and premiered by the Arizona State University Symphony. Other local groups such as the Mesa and Sun City Symphonies also performed her music.

Dr. Carolyn Waters Broe

Kerr's symphonic piece *Arizona Profiles* was commissioned for the groundbreaking dedication ceremonies of the Scottsdale Center for the Performing Arts in 1968 and premiered by the Phoenix Symphony. Her *Ballet Tableau Vivant* was performed for the dedication of John Waddell's sculptures entitled *Dance* at Phoenix Symphony Hall in 1974. It was choreographed by a woman professor at Arizona State University.

Kerr excelled at composing short character pieces, infusing them with colorful harmonic passages and exciting rhythmic motives. Most of her chamber music pieces were written for friends to play at the many music gatherings held in her Scottsdale home and studio. She also composed during the summers at her ranch in Cottonwood, near Flagstaff. She won several awards in composition during her life and was a member of the Phoenix Composer's Society. Unfortunately, almost none of these amazing pieces has ever been edited or published.

Kerr's overall compositional style may be characterized as tonal and inspired by Classical and Romantic genres and forms. Her music is often enhanced by the local color of the American Southwest. Louise Kerr and other members of the Phoenix Composer's Society developed a concept of Southwest Impressionism in music inspired by Ferde Grofé, who composed the *Grand Canyon Suite* in 1931. Kerr studied the works of the Southwest Impressionist painters who lived in California, New Mexico, and Arizona during the 1940s (she and her eldest daughter, Tammara, were both painters). The region was populated by Native Americans and Hispanics, so Kerr used elements of their music in her own compositions as well as the music of local cowboys. One can also hear the influence of the many famous pianists that she worked with in New York in the early 1920s and some jazz influence inspired by pianist Charles Lewis and others.

Even though she had the means and connections to publish her music in New York, Louise Kerr was a very modest woman who did not seek fame. Nearly all her music remains unedited and unpublished. Unfortunately, very few of her works are dated and premiere dates and names of compositions were lost after her death. Reel-to-reel recordings of most of the premieres of her music have also been lost, so it is difficult to get a full picture of how her music is to be performed. Five of Kerr's piano and viola works, edited by Carolyn Waters Broe, were the first of her music compositions to be published as the *Five Character Pieces for Viola and Piano* in

2001. Chris Bynog edited Kerr's *Etude for Violin and Viola* which was published by the American Viola Society in 2012.

When Louise Kerr died in 1977, she left a great legacy to the College of Fine Arts at Arizona State University (ASU). She was a major benefactor of the Herberger School of Music at Arizona State University by establishing the Kerr Memorial Scholarship Fund. Kerr presented her private music library to the ASU School of Music. Most importantly, she also donated her extensive collection of orchestral and chamber music manuscripts (labeled MSS-90) to the ASU Archives and Manuscripts at Haydn Library. In addition, she donated her Scottsdale home and studio to ASU to be used as a chamber music venue, now the ASU Kerr Cultural Center. She received a gold medal for distinguished contribution to the arts from the National Society of the Arts and Letters. Shortly before her death, Louise Kerr was awarded an honorary Doctorate from ASU, however she was unable to receive this award in person. Kerr was posthumously inducted into the Arizona Women's Hall of Fame on 21 October 2004. Her music is our national treasure. Louise Lincoln Kerr will be remembered as one of the most prolific American Southwest composers of the 20th century.

Dr. Carolyn Waters Broe

Title: *Enchanted Mesa* for orchestra and soprano

Genre: A **symphonic tone poem** is a one movement work on a theme for orchestra.

Title: *String Quartet in A Major* – movement No. 2 Andante.

Genre: A **string quartet** is chamber music composed for two violins, viola and cello. It is usually written in four movements and features each of the instruments in an ensemble.

YouTube: Four Seasons String Quartet of Scottsdale, Arizona https://www.youtube. com/watch?v=TV_C44vKWyI

Title: "Habanera" from the *Five Character Pieces for Viola and Piano*. The five viola and piano duos were not originally grouped together but written as separate character pieces. These viola solos are perfect for the solo artist as well as advanced students. The *"Habanera," "Las Fatigas Del Querer,"* and *"Berceuse"* were all inspired by Spanish and French Impressionists. The "Lament" is more German in harmonic language. The "Toccata" is a brilliant through composed fantasy. Each one is a gem that pleases both audiences and musicians alike.

Genre: Character pieces are short one movement pieces that are usually written for piano or piano with one other instrument.

YouTube: Carolyn Broe violist with Miriam Yutzi Hickman pianist https://www. youtube.com/watch?v=yR24R4hviPU

Birthday: 24 April 1892 in Cleveland, Ohio.

Death Date: 10 December 1977 in Cottonwood, Arizona, aged 85.

Fun Facts:

1. Louise Kerr was one of the first two women in the early Cleveland Symphony Orchestra as a violinist.

2. Louise Kerr snuck out of her college dorm to go into New York City, and broke her leg getting out of a trolley car.

3. Louise Kerr got her first job proofreading piano rolls performed by famous pianists for the Aeolian Recording Company in New York City in the 1920's. She was later the person who corrected early disk recordings.

4. Louise Kerr liked to play chamber music with her friends all night until dawn.

5. Louise Kerr liked to BBQ entire cows, fix cars, garden, and make her famous red cabbage dish.

6. According to a cellist who played at Louise's summer home, when they were performing the Flagstaff Festival, "One day we struggled through a tough Dvorak quartet. After the first several movements she got up, left the room, and came back with a broom. She swept around us vigorously and murmured, 'Got to get rid of all those bad notes!'"

7. Louise Kerr had a wonderful relationship with the Hopi Indians of Arizona, who called her "Mother". She would drive out to the Hopi Reservation in her chauffer driven limousine with all her children in the back. There she and violin virtuoso Sydney Tretick would record the Hopi ceremonial chanting on a reel-to-reel recorder. They were early ethnomusicologists, as non-Native Americans and women were rarely allowed to see these ceremonies in the 1940's.

GEORGE GERSHWIN (1898-1937)

George Gershwin – (1898-1937) was a **20th century American** composer and pianist, whose music spanned both the Classical and popular genres. He was born September 26, 1898, Brooklyn, New York City as Jacob Gershwine, who was the second son of Jewish Russian immigrants Rose and Morris Gershwine. Rose was the daughter of a Russian fur maker, who left for America due to increasing violence against Jews. Morris was a Russian leather cutter, who left due to compulsory Russian military service. His older brother Ira became a lyricist, who collaborated with George on many famous songs. They grew up in a second-floor apartment of the Russian and Yiddish immigrant community in Brooklyn, New York. They also had another brother and sister, Arthur, and Frances. Jacob soon became known as George and changed his last name to Gershwin. Later, many of his family members changed their name to Gershwin as well.

George grew up like most kids in Brooklyn, playing in the streets, roller skating and getting into mischief. He and his brother Ira liked to frequent the Yiddish Theater shows, and George even got to be an extra on stage a few times. George did not care all that much about music until 1908 when he heard a violin recital by his friend Maxie Rosenzweig. His parents bought a piano for Ira to practice, but to their surprise, George was the one who ended up playing it most of the time. His sister Frances was the first to become a professional musician. However, she married young, had kids, and gave up her music career for her family. Arthur followed in his two older brother's footsteps, becoming a song writer and composer of musicals and piano pieces. George tried several piano teachers before he found Charles Hambitzer and Jack Miller. Hambitzer, who was the pianist with the Beethoven Symphony Orchestra, was to become his mentor and teacher for many years. He gave George his classical training in music and encouraged him to attend symphony concerts. George would come home from each concert and try to recreate the music from memory on his piano. He also studied with classical composer Rubin Goldmark, and avant-garde composer Henry Cowell.

George Gershwin left school by age fifteen to work as a "song plugger" at a publishing firm in "Tin Pan Alley". In 1916, he got a job at Aeolian Recording Company in New York City doing recording and arranging. He produced hundreds of piano rolls that were used in player pianos. He used his own name and assumed names like Fred Murtha and Bert Wynn. It was at Aeolian studios that Gershwin met composer Louise Lincoln Kerr, who started working at Aeolian studies in 1920. Kerr worked with George Gershwin on some of his piano rolls. He also recorded rolls of his own compositions for the Duo-Art and Welte-Mignon player pianos. Gershwin made a brief foray into vaudeville, accompanying both Nora Bayes and Louise Dresser on the piano. His first hit song was "Swanee" with lyrics by Irving Caesar. The famous Broadway singer, Al Jolson, heard Gershwin performing "Swanee" and decided to sing it in one of his shows.

Gershwin met songwriter and music director William Daly in the late 1910's. They collaborated on the Broadway musicals *Piccadilly to Broadway* (1920) and *For Goodness' Sake* (1922). Daly and Gershwin composed the score for *Our Nell* (1923) together. This was the beginning of a long friendship. Daly was a frequent arranger, orchestrator, and conductor of Gershwin's music. Gershwin turned to him for musical advice. He worked with Buddy De Sylva on the opera *Blue Monday*, and musical *Lady Be Good* that included hit songs like "Fascinating Rhythm" and "Oh, Lady Be Good!". He also wrote the song "Strike up the Band," which he later gave to UCLA in 1930 as their football fighting song. Gershwin composed his first classical work for piano and orchestra *Rhapsody in Blue* in 1924, which was orchestrated by the composer and arranger Ferde Grofé. This was a ground-breaking fusion of classical and jazz genres. This piano concerto was premiered by the Paul Whiteman Concert Band in New York City. This became Gershwin's most popular work.

Gershwin traveled to Paris, France in the mid-1920's. He wanted to study composing with Nadia Boulanger and Maurice Ravel but was rejected by both. Ravel wrote in a letter "Why become a second-rate Ravel, when you are already a first-rate Gershwin?" They thought that formal classical training would ruin his jazz influenced style. During this time, he composed another famous orchestral work *An American in Paris*. It received a mixed review at Carnegie Hall in New York but became standard repertoire with European and American orchestras. He grew tired of Paris and returned to the United States where he was hired by Fox Film Corporation to write the film score to *Delicious*. They only used two of his songs, so Gershwin became furious and refused to work for Hollywood again for seven years. George and his brother Ira collaborated on two musicals *Show Girl* in 1929, and *Crazy Girl* in 1930, which included the hit songs "Embraceable You," "I Got Rhythm." They produced *Of Thee I Sing* in 1931, which was the first musical comedy to win a Pulitzer prize for drama, with Ira Gershwin as one of the winners. George Gershwin became famous for his opera *Porgy and Bess* in 1935. It is now considered one of the most important American operas due to the dramatic story of an African American couple and based on a novel by DuBose Hayward. Unfortunately, *Porgy and Bess* was a failure during the middle of the Great Depression, and the public has only realized its genius more recently. "Summertime" is a famous song from that opera.

Gershwin moved to Hollywood, California in 1936 to compose the film score to *Shall We Dance*, for RKO Pictures starring Fred Astaire and Ginger Rogers. This was another ground-breaking score that fused jazz with dance. It took him several months to write this music and orchestrate it. He met the composer Kay Swift and often asked her advice on composing. They had a ten-year relationship, but never got married. In 1937 Gershwin began to have burning headaches. He complained of smelling burning rubber. During a performance of his *Piano Concerto in F* with the San Francisco Symphony with Pierre Monteux conducting, Gershwin had several black outs. He was living with his brother Ira and Ira's wife Leonore in Hollywood. She became upset that he kept spilling food at the table and kicked him out, fearing that he was becoming mentally ill. He moved into lyricist Yip Harburg's empty quarters nearby and was taken care of by his valet Paul Mueller. His headaches and hallucinations continued. After trying to push Mueller out of the car, Gershwin was admitted to Cedars of Lebanon Hospital in Los Angeles. The tests claimed that he had hysteria, and he was released. He got worse.

Unfortunately, on the night of 9 July 1937 Gershwin collapsed at Harburg's house, while he was working on the score for *The Goldwyn Follies*. He was rushed back to the Cedars of Lebanon Hospital, but he fell into a coma. It was only then that his doctors suspected that he had a brain tumor. Leonore called George's close friend Emile Mosbacher who sent for a neurosurgeon. Dr. Walter Dandy was recommended, but he was on a fishing trip on the Governor of Maryland's yacht in the Chesapeake Bay. Mosbacher called the White House, who called the coast guard to alert the Governor of Maryland to bring the boat in to shore. Mosbacher got on a private plane and took Dr. Dandy to the airport, so they could fly back to Los Angeles. Meanwhile Gershwin's conditions became worse, and he needed surgery immediately. The doctors performed surgery on him and removed a large tumor. However, Gershwin died on 11 July 1937 at the age of 38.

Gershwin's friends and fans were shocked and could not believe that he had died so young. The memorial service was held at the Hollywood Bowl with conductor Otto Klemperer conducting his own arrangement of the second of Gershwin's *Three Preludes*. He was interred at Westchester Hills Cemetery in New York. More current doctors feel that the fact that Gershwin collapsed after standing up indicates that he had a brain herniation. It is hard to imagine how many songs, concertos, and musicals he might have composed if he had lived longer. Gershwin's early death is a terrible loss to modern music, but his music will live on the concert stage for as long as people have a song in their hearts.

50 Famous Composers

Title: *Rhapsody in Blue* for piano and orchestra.

Genre: Piano concerto with orchestra. This piece is an early fusion of both jazz and classical music for orchestra and piano.

YouTube: Arizona State University Symphony with Walter Cosand piano soloist, and Timothy Russell conductor. https://www.youtube.com/watch?v=RJLM3W5NK18

Birthday: Born Jacob Gershwine, 26 September 1898, Brooklyn, New York City, New York, U.S.

Death Date: 11 July 1937, Los Angeles, California, U.S., aged 38.

Fun Facts:

1. At the age of 15, Gershwin quit school and went to work as a "song plugger" in Tin Pan Alley, which was a collection of music publishers and song writers in New York City.

2. Gershwin liked to go to lots of parties and dated many glamorous women, but never married any of them.

3. It was reported that Gershwin asked Stravinsky for orchestration lessons, but the Russian/French composer asked, "How much money do you make a year?" Upon hearing the answer Stravinsky replied, "Perhaps I should study with you, Mr. Gershwin."

AARON COPLAND (1900-1990)

Aaron Copland – (1900-1990) was a **20th century American** composer, conductor, writer, and composition teacher. Many of his most famous works were written about American themes including his ballets *Appalachian Spring, Billy the Kid, Rodeo,* his *Symphony No. 3,* and *Fanfare for the Common Man.* Because of his "Populist" music, Copland has been called "The Dean of American Music".

Aaron Copland was born on 14 November 1900 Brooklyn, New York in the United States. Aaron was the youngest of five children born to a Russian Jewish immigrant family. They lived in an apartment above his father Morris Copland's store, which was like a miniature Macy's. Most of the Copland children helped with running the store. Aaron had his Bar Mitzvah at the Congregation Baith Israel Anshei

Emes. He was not very athletic, so he became an excellent reader. His favorite activity was reading Horatio Alger stories on the front steps of the store. The heroes of Alger's books rise from "rags to riches" in these classic American success stories. They defeat evil people, or mischievous children, and triumph for good.

Even though Aaron's father was not interested in music, his mother, Sarah Mittenthal Copland, sang and played the piano. She arranged music lessons for her children. His oldest brother Ralph was an excellent violinist. His sister Laurine was a student at the Metropolitan Opera School. She was Aaron's first piano teacher, and later helped him get started in his music career. When Laurine frequented opera productions, she brought a copy of the libretto home for Aaron to study. He went to the Boys High School and attended camps in the summer. He began composing songs at the age of eight and notated a few bars of an opera scene he called "Zenatello" at the age of eleven. Aaron took piano lessons with Leopold Wolfsohn, who taught him the classical literature. His first public recital was at Wanamaker's.

At fifteen he decided to become a composer after attending a concert by the composer and pianist Ignacy Jan Paderewski. Between 1917 and 1921 Aaron studied composition with Rubin Goldmark, who also taught Gershwin three lessons. It was through Goldmark that Aaron learned the German tradition in music composition. His graduation piece was a three-movement piano sonata in the Romantic style, however, he wrote other more daring pieces that he never showed his old-fashioned teacher. He attended the Metropolitan Opera and New York Symphony performances. After graduating high school, Aaron played piano in dance bands. Despite a serious rebuke by his father and uncles, Aaron was fascinated as a young adult with the Russian Revolution and made friendships with people who had Socialist and Communist leanings.

Aaron Copland decided to further his musical studies in Paris at the Fontainebleau School of Music. The French government offered a program of study for Americans. His father wanted him to stay in America and go to college, but his mother's vote allowed him to give Paris a try. At Fontainebleau, he studied piano with Isidor Philipp, and composition with Paul Vidal. However, he felt that Vidal was too much like Goldmark, so he started studying with Nadia Boulanger. At first, Copland had reservations about studying with a woman. However, he later wrote to his brother Ralph "This intellectual Amazon is not only professor at the Conservatoire, is not only familiar with all music from Bach to Stravinsky but is prepared for anything worse in the way of dissonance. But make no mistake... A more charming womanly woman never lived." (Pollack 1999, pg.41). He also said of Boulanger that she "could always find the weak spot in a place you suspected was weak. She could also tell you why it was weak." (Copland & Perlis 1984, p. 63) He liked the strict regimen that she insisted on for her composition students, and she immediately recognized Copland's talents in music. He spent three years studying with Boulanger.

While in Paris, Copland frequented the English language bookstore Shakespeare and Co.

— **168** —

where he met many of the greatest writers and artists of the day. These included Sinclair Lewis, Ernest Hemmingway, Gertrude Stein, Ezra Pound, Pablo Picasso, Marc Chagall, Jean-Paul Sartre, Marcel Proust, Paul Valéry, and André Gide. He began writing critiques of music concerts starting with Gabriel Fauré. This helped to spread his fame and increase his stature in the music community.

Upon his return to America, Copland was extremely optimistic. He rented a studio apartment at the Empire Hotel in New York City, which was close to Carnegie Hall and publishers. He managed to survive with two Guggenheim Fellowships of $2,500 given to him in 1925 and 1926. He got several small commissions to compose music. He also gave lecture-recitals, wrote articles, and taught music. Copland made friends with the conductor Serge Koussevitzky, who was the music director of the Boston Symphony Orchestra and known as a champion of "new music." Koussevitzky performed more of Copland's music than any other conductor starting with his *Symphony for Organ and Orchestra* in 1924. Copland followed the careers of several jazz musicians, such as George Gershwin, Benny Goodman, Louis Armstrong, Glenn Miller, and Bessie Smith, but decided that his music was going in a more abstract direction by the end of 1929.

During the Great Depression, Copland found that composing large symphonic works was not financially productive. So, he turned towards smaller useful pieces. He traveled to Mexico, Europe, and Africa. During a trip to Mexico, he met the composer Carlos Chavez, and was inspired to write *El Salón México* in 1936. He taught at the New School of Social Research in New York City. Based on these lectures, he wrote two books *What to Listen for in Music* (1937, revised 1957), and *Our New Music* (1940, revised 1968 and retitled *The New Music: 1900-1960*). He developed a new simpler style, which he called American *Gebrauchsmusik*, which was based on the German "useful" music. Copland began to write music for young audiences such as his piano pieces *The Young Pioneers* and his opera *The Second Hurricane*. His goal was to create music that had a wider appeal to more people.

Aaron Copland and Leonard Bernstein started their life-long friendship in 1937 after a chance meeting at a modern-dance concert in New York. Bernstein was a young unknown nineteen-year-old student at Harvard. Copland was a 36-year-old well respected composer. Copland helped Bernstein to get into the Curtis School of Music in Philadelphia, and a place at the Tanglewood Music Center in Massachusetts in conducting. Later Bernstein became the conductor of the New York Philharmonic, and conducted and recorded Copland's music.

Copland wanted to make music that expressed American themes and inspired by American melodies and folk songs. As part of a commission from the Columbia Broadcast System, Copland composed *Prairie Journal* for radio broadcast. This was the start of his music about the American West. He composed his *Billy the Kid Ballet* in 1939, which along with *El Salón México* became his first popular pieces. That same year, Copland completed two Hollywood film scores, for *Of Mice and Men* and *Our Town*. He also composed the radio score *John Henry*, which is based on the folk ballad. During the 1940's Copland composed some of his most important works including his ballet scores for Rodeo (1942), *Appalachian Spring* (1944), which were huge successes. His pieces *Fanfare for the Common Man* and the *Lincoln Portrait* have become patriotic standards. His *Third Symphony* has also become a favorite. He composed two film scores, *The Red Pony* based on a novel by John Steinbeck, and one for William Wyler's *The Heiress* at the end of the 1940's.

Copland received a US-Italian Fulbright Scholarship to study in Rome in 1950. He was also investigated by the FBI in the 1950's during the Red Scare, because of his left leanings towards communism, his support of the Communist Party USA, and voting for the Progressive Party candidate Henry A. Wallace. Copland had to testify in front of Congress that he was never a Communist. During this time, he started experimenting with the twelve-tone series of composition after Schoenberg, and composed his *Piano Quintet*, and his *Old American Songs*.

Copland also gave a series of lectures at Harvard University under the Charles Eliot Norton Professorship. He traveled extensively around the world, and listened to music by Soviet, Polish, and Japanese composers that was unfamiliar to the West. He felt that much of the modern music, such as electronic and aleatoric music was dull and unimaginative. He felt that getting the right note was much better than just throwing it out there to chance as other modern composers were doing at the time. He became the Music Director of the Ojai Music Festival for several years, which performed new music.

In his later years, Copland was asked to conduct many orchestras in the United States and United Kingdom. He recorded mostly on Columbia Records, and on RCA Victor with the Boston Symphony performing his *Appalachian Spring* and *The Tender Land* in 1960. The New York Philharmonic also recorded many of Copland's works under the direction of his long-time friend and conductor Leonard Bernstein starting in the 1950's. His health started deteriorating in the 1980's. He died of Alzheimer's disease and respiratory failure on 2 December 1990 in Tarrytown, New York (which is now Sleepy Hollow). His ashes were scattered around Tanglewood Music Center, Massachusetts. Copland never married nor had any children. So, he bequeathed most of his wealth to the creation of the Aaron Copland Foundation for Composers, which gives over $600,000 a year to music groups to perform new music. During his long life of ninety years, Copland left a monumental legacy of music, which has helped to define what American music is.

Title: "Hoedown" from *Rodeo Ballet* (1942). This work was written for dancers, who were dressed as cowboys, with Western hats, and wielding six shooters. No one had ever written a ballet like this before with an American Southwest theme.

Genre: Ballet music is written for an orchestra to accompany a story choreographed for dancers.

YouTube: Leonard Bernstein conducting Copland's "Hoedown" with the New York Philharmonic in 1961, Young Person's Guide to the Orchestra series. https://www. youtube.com/watch?v=Qhw3PYXmOLE

Birthday: 14 November 1900, Brooklyn, New York, United States

Death Date: December 2, 1990 (aged 90), Sleepy Hollow, New York, United States

Fun Facts:

1. Copland notated his first melody, which was seven bars long, for an opera he called "Zenatello," at the age of eleven.

2. Copland returned to the U.S. in 1925 after studying music in Paris, France. He and his younger music contemporaries formed a group called the "commando unit." The members included Roger Sessions, Roy Harris, Virgil Thomson, and Walter Piston. They performed joint concerts of their modern music.

3. Some of Copland's many awards include: the Pulitzer Prize in composition for *Appalachian Spring*; as a film composer, his scores for *Of Mice and Men* (1939), *Our Town* (1940), and *The North Star* (1943) received Academy Award nominations; *The Heiress* won the Oscar for Best Music in 1950. He was also awarded the Presidential Medal of Freedom by President Lyndon Johnson in 1964. In 1986. Copland received the National Medal of Arts in 1987, and the United States Congress presented him with a special Congressional Gold Medal.

BENJAMIN BRITTEN (1913-1976)

Benjamin Britten – **(1913-1976)** was an **English** composer, pianist, and conductor. Britten was one of the most influential British composers of the twentieth century. He composed in a variety of genres including vocal works, fifteen operas, orchestral music, and chamber music. Some of his most famous works include the *War Requiem* (1962); his opera *Peter Grimes* (1945); and *The Young Person's Guide to the Orchestra* (1945).

Edward Benjamin Britten was born on 22 November 1913 in the fishing port Lowestoft in Suffolk, England. He was the youngest of four children of Robert Britten, and Edith Hockey Britten. His father became a dentist but did not enjoy his work. He was a loving father, but often stern and distant with his children. His mother was a talented amateur musician, and the secretary of the Lowestoft Musical Society. She often invited friends to musical soirées at their house. Unfortunately, when Benjamin was only three months old, he contracted pneumonia, and nearly died. His heart was damaged, and the doctors told his parents that he might not lead a very full life. Surprisingly, Benjamin made a better recovery than expected. When he was older, he loved to play tennis and cricket (a British game with a ball and bat). His sisters seemed to have no interest in music like their father. His brother liked music but was only interested in ragtime. To his mother's joy, Benjamin turned out to be musically talented. She taught him how to play piano and notate music at an early age, and he made his first attempts at composition at age five. He started piano lessons at age seven and started the viola at age ten. Benjamin's father would not allow a radio or a gramophone (early record player) in their house, so he became one of the last composers to be brought up entirely on live music.

Benjamin went to a fee-paying elementary school growing up in Lowestoft. In 1928, he went to Gresham's School in Norfolk for two years, which was a boarding school, that he absolutely hated. Benjamin despised the music master there, did not like being separated from his family, especially his mother, and was shocked by the bullying (even though he was not the target). He even contemplated suicide while he was there. Fortunately, he won a scholarship to the Royal College of Music in London in 1930, his examiners were John Ireland and Ralph Vaughan Williams. Britten studied composition with Ireland, and piano with Arthur Benjamin. He won the Ernest Farrar Prize twice for composition, the Sullivan Prize for composition, and the Cobbett Prize for chamber music. Britten's *Sinfonietta No. 1* (1932), and his choral variations *A Boy Was Born* (1933), were his first compositions to attract attention at the RCM. He was not inspired by Ireland, so he studied privately with Bridge.

Britten got an incredible break in 1935 when Bridge convinced him to interview for a job at the British Broadcasting Corporation's music department. The BBC's Music Director, Adrian Boult, did not give him the job, but to Britten's delight he was asked to write the score for a documentary film, *The King's Stamp*, which was directed by Alberto Cavalcanti for the GPO Film Unit. He collaborated with W. H. Auden, and together they worked on several other documentary films. Auden influenced Britten to expand his world view and broaden his horizon. Britten wrote nearly forty scores for cinema, theater, and radio between 1935 to 1937. During this time, he composed his *Variations on a Theme of Frank Bridge*, which became a popular favorite.

Britten was devastated when his mother died in 1937. Fortunately, he met tenor Paul Pears at about the same time. They were helping to clear out the cottage of a friend, who had died in a plane crash, and soon become lifelong friends. Pear's excellent voice inspired Britten to compose many of his best song cycles including *The Seven Sonnets for Michelangelo* (1940). He and Pears toured to America where Britten heard Aaron Copland's *Billy the Kid Ballet* and *An Outdoor Overture*. His own music was influenced by Copland's. When World War II broke out, Pears and Britten were advised by the British embassy to remain in the US as artistic ambassadors. During

50 Famous Composers

this period, Britten composed his *Violin Concerto* and *Sinfonia da Requiem*.

In 1942 Britten read the work of poet George Crabbe called "The Borough," which made him so homesick, that he knew he had to return to England. He decided that he wanted to write an opera based on Crabbe's poem about the fisherman Peter Grimes. It happened that before Britten left the US, he met the conductor Koussevitzky, who offered him a generous $1,000 commission to write an opera. During his long journey by boat across the Atlantic, Britten wrote his choral pieces *A Ceremony of Carols* and *Hymn to St. Cecilia*. After writing this last large-scale work, he no longer collaborated with Auden, who was offended, and never spoke to him again. Britten used the money he inherited from his mother to purchase the Old Mill in Snape, Suffolk as a country home. He spent much of his time there in 1944 writing his opera *Peter Grimes*. Pears joined Sadler's Wells Opera Company. Their Artistic Director, singer Joan Cross, decided to move the company's home base to London, and open with Britten's opera. She cast herself and Pears in the leading roles. *Peter Grimes* opened in June of 1945 and the ticket sales matched those of *Madame Butterfly*, and *La Bohème*. Both the public and the critics loved this opera. It was hailed as the first successful British opera since Purcell (Blyth 1981, p. 79). Britten and his associates set up their own English Opera Group.

Britten helped to set up the Aldeburgh Festival in 1948 with Pears and Crozier directing. He also worked with Imogen Holst, the daughter of composer Gustav Holst, at Aldeburgh. His operas *A Midsummer Night's Dream* (1960), and *Death in Venice* (1973) were premiered there. *Billy Budd* was premiered at Coven Garden in 1951. He composed *Gloriana* in 1953 for the coronation of Queen Elizabeth II, but it was not well received. He composed his *Cello Suites*, *Cello Symphony*, and *Cello Sonata* for the famous cellist Mstislav Rostropovich. Britten's famous *War Requiem* was premiered in 1962. It is a large-scale work for soloists, chorus, chamber ensemble and orchestra that was written to commemorate the victims of both World Wars at the consecration of the new Coventry Cathedral, that had been destroyed in and air-raid. Shostakovich told Rostrapovich that he believed this to be "the greatest work of the twentieth century." (Blyth 1981, p. 15).

Benjamin Britten was given the honor of a life peerage in 1976, becoming Baron Britten.

He was the first composer to receive this title. After finishing his opera *Death in Venice* in 1973, Britten's health began to fail. On his 63rd birthday, 22 November, his friend Rita Thomas gave a champagne party and invited all his friends and his two sisters to say their goodbyes to the dying composer. Rostropovich came by a few days later, and Britten gave him what he had written of *Praise We Great Men*. Britten died of congestive heart failure on 4 December 1976. His funeral service was held at the Aldeburgh Parish church where he is buried.

Title: *The Young Person's Guide to the Orchestra* (1945) Subtitled "Variations and Fugue on a Theme by Purcell". This large-scale orchestral work was based on the second movement, "Rondeau", of the *Abdelazer Suite* by Henry Purcell. It was originally commissioned for an educational documentary film called *Instruments of the Orchestra*. This documentary was directed by Muir Mathieson and featuring the London Symphony Orchestra conducted by Malcolm Sargent.

Genre: Large-scale orchestra theme and variations.

YouTube: EMS Music Department. https://www.youtube.com/watch?v=– WrlwY-Kjp4

INSTRUMENTATION:

Woodwinds: piccolo, 2 flutes, 2 oboes, 2 clarinets in B flat and A and 2 bassoons

Brass: 4 horns in F, 2 trumpets in C, 3 trombones (2 tenors and 1 bass) and bass tuba

Percussion: timpani, bass drum, cymbals, tambourine, triangle, snare drum, cowbell, xylophone, castanets, tam-tam, and whip

Strings: harp, first and second violins, violas, cellos, and double basses

Birthday: 22 November 1913, Lowestoft, United Kingdom.

Death Date: 4 December 1976, Aldeburgh, United Kingdom (aged 63).

Fun Facts:

1. Benjamin Britten is the only composer to have the same name as the country of his birth Britain, but it is spelled differently!
2. He lived in a little red house in Aldeburgh, that has now become the foundation for a charity promoting Britain's works.
3. On the 100th anniversary of his birth in 2013, a stamp with Britten's image was issued commemorating "Great Britons" and a new 50 pence piece with his image was made.
4. Britten was the first composer ever to be honored with a "life peerage" and became Baron Britten of Aldeburgh, in the county of Suffolk in 1976.

VÍTEZLAVA KAPRÁLOVÁ (1915-1940)

Vítězlava Kaprálová – **(1915-1940)** is the most important **Czech** woman composer and conductor of the twentieth century. Vítězslava was born on 24 January 1915 in Brno, which was part of the Austro-Hungarian Empire and now in the Czech Republic. She was the daughter of composer and pianist Václav Kaprál and singer Viktorie Uhlirova. Her father studied with composer Leoš Janáček. It was soon discovered that she was a music prodigy. With help from her father, Vítězlava composed her first piano work *In the Realm of Legend* at the age of nine. She entered the Brno Conservatory at fifteen and studied composition with Vilém Petrželka and conducting with Zdeněk Chalabala from 1930 to 1935. Her graduation work was her *Piano Concerto in D Minor* that she conducted herself at the age of twenty. She graduated at the top of her class. For the next two years, she continued her

musical education with Vítězslav Novák and Václav Talich in Prague. A French government scholarship allowed Vítězlava to move to Paris in 1937. It was there that Vítězslava studied with composer Bohuslav Martinů and conductor Charles Munch (1937–39). There are also some unverified accounts that Vítězslava studied with the composer Nadia Boulanger (1940) in Paris. It was in Paris that she achieved her mature mastery of the contemporary music language. In 1937 Kaprálová conducted the Czech Philharmonic. A year later she conducted her *Military Sinfonietta* with the BBC Symphony Orchestra to great acclaim. Kaprálová's *Suite Rustica* has also been given great praise.

Vítězlava Kaprálová married the Czech writer Jiří Mucha in April of 1940, who was the son of a great Art Nouveau painter. With the threat of war in Europe, she planned to join the theater of the comic playwrights Jan Werich and Jiří Voskovec in New York. She was going to replace Jaroslav Ježek. Unfortunately, two weeks after her marriage she was misdiagnosed with miliary tuberculosis, during the evacuation of Paris. She died 16 June of 1940, the day that the Nazis invaded Paris, at the age of 25 in Montpellier, France. It is more likely that she died of typhoid fever or peritonitis from a bacterial infection.

During her short life, Kaprálová created an impressive body of work including: two piano concertos, two orchestral suites, a sinfonietta, an orchestral cantata, a concertino for clarinet, violin, and orchestra, her remarkable art songs, music for piano solo, a string quartet, a reed trio, music for cello, and music for violin and piano. Her music was admired by conductor Rafael Kubelík, who premiered her orchestral song *Waving Farewell* and conducted her other orchestral works. Kaprálová composed her best-known piano work *Dubnová preludia* (April Preludes) for the pianist Rudolf Firkušný, who performed many of her works. Her compositions were published by various music publishing houses including Bärenreiter Verlag. Many of her compositions have been released on compact disc recordings on a variety of labels, including Naxos, Koch Records and Supraphon. Her life and works were featured in the television series *Mozart in the Jungle* in two episodes of season three. The BBC Radio featured Kaprálová as the "Composer of the Week" in a set of five one-hour programs playing her music and discussing her life during October of 2015.

After World War II her ashes were sent home to Moravia. In 1946 the Czech Academy of Sciences and the Arts awarded Kaprálová membership in memoriam, in appreciation of her contributions to music. Only ten women, out of 648 members of the Academy, were given this honor by 1948. A complete list of her works is included in the only English biography of Kaprálová, which was published by Lexington Books in the United States (Hartl and Entwistle 2011). Many of her works and letters are preserved at the Moravian Museum in Brno.

The Kapralova Society is a Canadian non-profit arts organization, founded by Karla Hartl in Toronto in 1998. The Society's mission is to promote the music of Czech composer Vitezslava Kapralova (1915-1940) and to build awareness of women's contributions to musical life. The Kapralova Society has worked towards getting more of her music published, made compact disc recordings of her music, as well as helped to publish many books and articles about her life and works.

Title: *Piano Concerto in D Minor* (1935). Kaprálová's concerto includes: 1– *Allegro entusiastico* (9.25). 2– Largo (3.06), and 3– Allegro (7.45)

Genre: A **piano concerto** is a major solo work for piano with symphony orchestra. Piano concertos are typically in three movements.

YouTube: https://www.youtube.com/watch?v=2k-tIEBV_rM

Piano Concerto in D Minor with Pianist Alice Rajnohova and Conductor Thomas Hanus.

Birthday: 24 January 1915 Brno, Austria-Hungary (now Czech Republic).

Death Date: 16 June 1940 Montpellier, France (aged 25).

Fun Facts:

1. Kaprálová was a child prodigy who started composing at the age of nine.
2. Vítězslava Kaprálová saw her homeland for the last time at the end of 1939, after the Germans invaded the Sudetenland.
3. Kaprálová died of a fever at the young age of twenty-five, while escaping the Nazi occupation of Paris on 16 June 1940.

LEONARD BERNSTEIN (1918-1990)

Leonard Bernstein – (1918-1990) American composer, conductor, pianist, author, and lecturer. He is one of the most well-known and respected of the **twentieth century** composers. He is best known for his extremely popular musical *West Side Story*. He also composed other theater works such as *Candide, On the Town, On the Water-front, Wonderful Town,* and *Peter Pan.* He wrote in many styles including his *Mass,* vocal works, orchestral works, ballet, chamber music, and opera. He was the first conductor to give a tele-vised lecture series on classical music. He started his fifty-three concert lecture series known as the *Young People's Concerts* for CBS in 1954. He continued this style of lecture concerts the rest of his life. Bernstein was the conductor of the New York Philharmonic from 1958 to 1969. He also

made many recordings and often performed as both piano soloist and conductor.

He was born Louis Bernstein on 25 August 1918 in Lawrence, Massachusetts. He was the son of Ukrainian-Jewish parents. His father was a hairdressing supply whole-salesman, and his mother was Jennie Resnick Bernstein. His grandmother had insisted on calling him Louis, but his parents preferred Leonard. He officially changed his name to Leonard when he turned fifteen, which was shortly after his grandmother passed away. To his friends he was simply known as "Lenny". At first his father was opposed to Leonard learning music. However, he took him to orchestra concerts. Leonard heard a piano concert at a young age and started to learn piano after his family got his cousin Lillian's unwanted piano. Leonard was close to his younger sister Shirley. He loved to play entire Beethoven symphonies and operas together with her at the piano. He had many piano teachers including Helen Coates, who later became his secretary.

After graduating from the Boston Latin School in 1935, Leonard attended Harvard University where he studied music. His professors included Edward Burlingame and the theorist Walter Piston. His life was changed by his aesthetics teacher David Prall, who had a multi-disciplinary approach to the arts and music. Bernstein met the famous conductor Dimitri Mitropoulos, whose power and charisma as a musician convinced Bernstein to become a symphonic conductor. Although Mitropoulos did not teach Bernstein, he did influence his love of Mahler, and conducting without the baton. The other important influence on his life and work was meeting Aaron Copland during his Harvard years. They met by chance at a dance concert. Bernstein later performed one of Copland's "Piano Variations" at Copland's birthday party in 1938. Bernstein often sought advice from the older composer, but never formally took lessons from him.

After graduating from Harvard with a Bachelor of Arts *cum laude* in 1939, Bernstein enrolled at the Curtis Institute of Music in Philadelphia. He studied conducting with Fritz Reiner, piano with Isabelle Vengerova, orchestration with Randall Thompson, and counterpoint with Richard Stöhr. At the suggestion of Aaron Copland, Bernstein began his studies at the Boston Symphony Orchestra's summer institute, at Tanglewood, near Lenox, Massachusetts in 1940. Bernstein's friendships with Copland and Mitropoulos helped him to get a place in the conducting class of Serge Koussevitzky at Tanglewood. Lukas Foss was also in this class, and they became lifelong friends. Leonard Bernstein became Koussevitsky's assistant conductor, and later dedicated his *Symphony No. 2* "The Age of Anxiety" to him. Bernstein gained his emotional way of interpreting music from Koussevitsky and considered him to be a father figure.

Bernstein had a very conversational style of conducting. He would move around the podium almost shaking hands with the cellos, then the violas and the violins. Bernstein was appointed the assistant conductor to Artur Rodzinki of the New York Philharmonic Orchestra in 1943. On 14 November of that year Bernstein made his major conducting debut on short notice, and without a rehearsal, after their guest conductor Bruno Walter came down sick with the flu. CBS Radio carried the concert nationally, and Bernstein became an instant success story. Afterwards he was asked to conduct many symphonies.

Bernstein became the Music Director of the New York City Symphony from 1945 to 1947 (which was founded by Leopold Stokowski). This organization performed more modern pieces than the New York Philharmonic. He conducted the premiere of his *Jeremiah Symphony* in 1944 in Pittsburgh. His ballet *Fancy Free*, which was choreographed by Jerome Robbins, opened in New York in April of 1944. This work was later used by Bernstein as the basis for his musical *On the Town*. After the end of World War II, Bernstein's career went international with his debut with the Czech Philharmonic in Prague. He conducted the World premiere of *Fancy Free* with the Ballet Theater at the Royal Opera House in London. He also conducted the American premiere of Benjamin Britten's opera *Peter Grimes* at Tanglewood, which had been Koussevitzky's commission. That same year Bernstein conducted two concerts with the NBC Symphony at the invitation of their conductor Arturo Toscanini. He was the piano soloist and conductor for Ravel's concerto. He also conducted in Tel Aviv, Israel, and later recorded with the Israel Philharmonic on *Deutches Grammophone* recordings.

Bernstein married the Chilean-born American actress Felicia Cohn Montealegre on 10 September 1951. They had three children. His *Young People's Concerts* for CBS made Bernstein famous for his educational work. However, due to his Left-wing (Communist) sympathies, Bernstein was Blacklisted by the US State Department and CBS in the early 1950's, but he did not have to testify. Shortly after that he began his tenure as the principal conductor of the New York Philharmonic. The original 1957 Broadway production of Bernstein's *West Side Story*, directed and choreographed by Jerome Robbins and produced by Robert E. Griffith and Harold Prince, marked Sondheim's Broadway debut as the author of the lyrics. It ran for 732 performances before going on tour. The production was nominated for six Tony Awards including Best Musical in 1957. The film version of Bernstein's *West Side Story* came out in 1961. The film was nominated for eleven Academy Awards and won ten, including George Chakiris for Supporting Actor, Rita Moreno for Supporting Actress, and Best Picture.

In 1959 he toured with the New York Philharmonic to Europe and the Soviet Union. He recorded all nine of Mahler's Symphonies with them. He also conducted Mahler's symphonies with the Vienna Philharmonic after he retired from the New York Philharmonic. His lecture on "Humor in Music" received a Grammy Award in 1961 for Best Spoken Word Recording. He won a Grammy award in 1972 for his recording of Bizet's opera *Carmen* with Marilyn Horne and James McCracken in the title roles after he had conducted several live performances with the Metropolitan Opera.

Bernstein was elected to the Charles Eliot Norton Chair as Professor of Poetry at his *alma mater* Harvard in 1973. He went to the Paris Conservatory to study with Nadia Boulanger in 1976. Bernstein was already fifty-eight, but she made him feel like he was a twenty-one-year-old beginner again. He later invited her to become the first woman to conduct the New York Philharmonic. He began a turbulent time in his life when his wife Felicia was diagnosed with lung cancer and died in 1978. Afterwards, he conducted Beethoven's *9th Symphony* and Bernstein's *Chichester Psalms* with the Israel Philharmonic and the Choral Arts Society of Washington at the Kennedy Center in Washington D.C., and at Carnegie Hall in New York. In 1979 Bernstein conducted two charity concerts with the Berlin Philharmonic for Amnesty International, one of Mahler's *Ninth Symphony*. He received the Kennedy Center Honors Award in 1980. In 1982, he and Ernest Fleischmann founded the Los Angeles Philharmonic Institute as a summer training academy along the lines of Tanglewood. Bernstein taught conducting there as the Artistic Director until 1984. He also performed and recorded several of his own works with the Los Angeles Philharmonic for *Deutsche Grammophon* around the same time. He premiered his opera *A Quiet Place* in 1983. Bernstein was a committed supporter of nuclear disarmament. In 1985 he took the European Community Youth Orchestra in a "Journey for Peace" tour around Europe and to Japan.

Bernstein conducted Beethoven's *Symphony No. 9* on December 25, 1989, in East Berlin's *Schauspielhaus* as part of a celebration of the fall of the Berlin Wall. He had conducted the same work in West Berlin the previous day. This monumental concert was broadcast live in more than twenty countries to an estimated audience of 100 million people.

Dr. Carolyn Waters Broe

Bernstein made his final performance as a conductor at Tanglewood on August 19, 1990, with the Boston Symphony. They performed Benjamin Britten's "Four Sea Interludes" from *Peter Grimes*, and Beethoven's *Seventh Symphony*. Unfortunately, he started coughing violently during the Third Movement of the Beethoven symphony. Even though he was exhausted and in pain, maestro Bernstein continued to conduct the piece until its conclusion. This concert was later released by *Duetsche Grammophon* as *Leonard Bernstein – The Final Concert*. He announced his retirement from conducting on October 9, 1990. He died of a heart attack five days later from mesothelioma. He had been a heavy smoker for fifty years of his life, and battled emphysema, which is a disease of the lungs. During his funeral procession in Manhattan, people removed their hats and said, "Goodbye Lenny" (PBS Documentary 2006). Bernstein will be remembered for his amazing wit, brilliant conducting style, and moving music.

Title: *West Side Story* (September 26, 1957 in New York City). Based on Shakespeare's play *Romeo and Juliette*. Lyrics by Stephen Sondheim and music by Leonard Bernstein.

Genre: A **musical** is a play which is performed with spoken words, song, and dance, that is accompanied by an orchestra. The musical is an American genre.

YouTube: https://www.youtube.com/watch?v=JKXKkgQf51A

INSTRUMENTATION:

Winds:

   Reed I: Piccolo, Flute, Alto Saxophone, Clarinet in Bb, Bass Clarinet

   Reed II: Clarinet in Eb, Clarinet in Bb, Bass Clarinet

   Reed III: Piccolo, Flute, Oboe, English Horn, Tenor Saxophone, Baritone Saxophone, Clarinet in Bb, Bass Clarinet

   Reed IV: Piccolo, Flute, Soprano Saxophone, Bass Saxophone, Clarinet in Bb, Bass Clarinet

   Reed V: Bassoon

Brass:

   2 Horns in F, 3 Trumpets in Bb (2nd doubling Trumpet in D), 2 Trombones

Percussion:

   Timpani. Percussion (four players), Piano / Celesta

   Traps, Vibraphone, 4 Pitched Drums, Xylophone, 3 Bongos, 3 Cowbells, Conga, Timbales, Snare Drum, Police Whistle, Gourd, 2 Suspended Cymbals, Castanets, Maracas, Finger Cymbals, Tambourines, Small Maracas, Glockenspiel, Woodblock, Claves, Triangle, Temple Blocks, Chimes, Tam-tam, Ratchet, Slide Whistle

Strings:

   Electric Guitar, Spanish Guitar, Mandolin, and strings.

Birthday: Louis Bernstein, 25 August 1918 in Lawrence, Massachusetts, U.S.

Death Date: 14 October 1990 (aged 72) in New York City, New York, U.S.

50 Famous Composers

Fun Facts:

1. Leonard Bernstein said, "I can't live one day without hearing music, playing it, studying it, or thinking about it."
2. Leonard Bernstein was the first conductor to appear on TV. He started giving lectures about classical music from 1954 until his death in 1990.
3. Bernstein was remarkably close to the Kennedy family, and conducted the funeral mass for President John F. Kennedy after he was assassinated.
4. While at the Curtis Institute, Bernstein was awarded the only "A" grade in conducting that his teacher Fritz Reiner ever gave.

Dr. Carolyn Waters Broe

THEA MUSGRAVE (1928-)

Thea Musgrave – (1928-   ) is a **Scottish – American 20th Century** composer, and conductor, who wrote operas, choral music, orchestral and classical chamber music. She is one of the most important British composers. Thea was born on 27 May 1928 in Barnton, Edinburgh in Scotland. She started learning music at the age of five and studied the piano. Thea was educated at Moreton Hall School, which was an independent boarding school for girls near the market town of Oswestry in Shropshire.

Thea started at the University of Edinburgh as a medical student. However, the music school was next to the medical school, so Thea kept dropping in to hear what was going on. Eventually she decided to switch her major to music at the university. She studied harmony and analysis with Mary Grierson and counterpoint and history privately with Hans Gál. Her mother wanted her to be a doctor, so she was not happy about this. Thea went to the Paris Conservatory in 1952 to study composition. She studied privately with the famous French composer and music professor Nadia Boulanger from 1950-54. Boulanger warned her that she could not get married and be a composer. She won the Lili Boulanger Memorial prize while she was a student, and Donald Francis Tovey prize.

Thea composed *Suite O'Bairnsangs* for her first commission by the Scottish Festival at Braemar in 1953. The following year she composed her *Cantata for a Summer's Day* on commission from the BBC. During this time, she also composed two major stage works, a ballet *A Tale for Thieves* and the chamber opera *The Abbot of Drimock*. In 1958 Thea traveled to the United States to attend the Tanglewood Festival in Massachusetts and studied with Aaron Copland. In 1967 she composed her *Concerto for Orchestra*. She did not grow up thinking that women didn't compose, because her colleagues in England were Dame Ethel Smyth, who was her grandmother's generation, and Elizabeth Lutyens– "Twelve-tone Lizzie" as she was called –who was her mother's generation. Sir William Glock featured Musgrave's music with these other two composers on several concerts. (Gena Raps 2009)

In 1970 Thea Musgrave became a Guest Professor at the University of California, Santa Barbara, which gave her an excellent platform to compose in the United States. Musgrave married American violist and opera conductor Peter Mark in 1971, and she moved to the United States in 1972. Her fascination with 'dramatic-abstract' musical ideas is evident in her *Concerto for Horn* of 1971. Her *Viola Concerto* was written in 1973. She has achieved international renowned as a conductor of operas. In 1976 she became the first woman to conduct her own composition with the Philadelphia Orchestra with her *Concerto for Orchestra*. Some of her work is serial or twelve-tone music, but much of it may be described as abstract. This means that the music may not follow a set form or have reoccurring themes.

She became the Distinguished Professor at Queens College, City University of New York from 1987 to 2002. Some of her more recent works include Musgrave's oboe concerto *Helios* of 1994. This composition is programmatic as the oboe represents the Sun God Helios. Musgrave's orchestral work *Phoenix Rising* of 1997 is also programmatic. The visual arts inspired her to composer her *Seasons* after a visit to the Metropolitan Museum of Art in New York. *Turbulent Landscapes* depicts a series of paintings by J. M. W. Turner. This work was commissioned by the Boston Symphony Orchestra and premiered by them in 2003.

Thea Musgrave has composed twelve operas, which often feature a strong central character, many of whom are female. They include her operas *The Voice of Ariadne* (1973), *Mary Queen of Scots* (1977), *Harriet Tubman* (*Harriet, the Woman called Moses*, 1984), *Simón Bolívar* (1993; premiere 1995 at the Virginia Opera), and *Pontalba* (2003). Her operas have been performed by major opera companies all over the world. Musgrave's *Song of the Enchanter* for orchestra

Dr. Carolyn Waters Broe

(1990) was commissioned to honor the 125th anniversary of the birth of Jean Sibelius. Musgrave has been given many prestigious awards including: the Koussevitzky Award (1974); and two Guggenheim Fellowships (1974/5 and 1982/3). She holds honorary degrees from Old Dominion University (Virginia), Glasgow University, Smith College, and the New England Conservatory in Boston. In 2002 she was appointed a Commander of the Order of the British Empire (CBE) in the Queen's New Year Honors List.

Title: *Song of the Enchanter* for orchestra (1990) written for the 125th birthday of composer Jean Sibelius.
Genre: Abstract for orchestra. Abstract compositions do not follow a set form of music. They are
  through-composed pieces that express random ideas, and generally do not have reoccurring themes.
YouTube: https://www.youtube.com/watch?v=Ee3mf9E-n_Q Song of the Enchanter for orchestra.
Birthday: 27 May 1928 in Barnton, Edinburgh in Scotland
Death Date: Still living at the printing of this book (aged 92).
Fun Facts:
1. Musgrave commented in an interview that "Yes, I am a woman; and I am a composer. But rarely at the same time." (Gena Raps 2009)
2. Disregarding a warning not to get married by her composition teacher Nadia Boulanger, Thea Musgrave married the opera conductor Peter Mark and enjoyed a fulfilling marriage and social life.
3. Musgrave said about composing "I guess it's like being a doctor practicing. You can learn a lot of stuff, but until you actually work with patients you don't know your trade. And it's the same with composing. Nowadays, young composers work with computers. I am glad they can, but it's not like working with an orchestra and learning what goes well, what might be difficult, and why". (Gena Raps 2009).

JOAN TOWER (1938-   )

oan Tower – (1938-   ) is an **American Contemporary** composer and pianist. Joan was born on 6 September 1938 in New Rochelle, New York. She moved with her family to La Paz, Bolivia in South American when she was nine, which she feels was a major influence in how she uses rhythms in her music. Joan's father was a mineralogist, who insisted that she get a thorough education in music. She became very advanced as a pianist. Due to his career, Joan wrote several pieces about gems and minerals including *Black Topaz* and *Silver Ladders*. After ten years in South America, she returned to the United States to study at Bennington College, in Vermont, and then at Columbia University. Joan studied with Otto Luening, Jack Beeson, and Vladimir Ussachevsky. She was awarded her doctorate in composition in 1968.

She co-founded the Da Capo Chamber Players in New York with violinist Joel Lester and flautist Patricia Spencer, as the group's pianist. This group specialized in performing contemporary music. They commissioned and performed many of her early works including *Platinum Spirals* (1976), *Amazon I* (1977), *Petroushskates* (1980), and *Wings* (1981). This ensemble won several awards including the Naumburg award in 1973. In 1972 Joan Tower accepted a faculty position at Bard College in composition, a post she continues to hold today. She received a Guggenheim fellowship in 1976. Joan Tower's first orchestral work *Sequoia* (1981) was a great success. This tone poem depicts the structure of a giant tree starting with the trunk and going all the way up to the needles. She left the Da Capo Chamber Players in 1984. Tower accepted a position at the St. Louis Symphony Orchestra in 1985, where she was a composer-in-residence from 1988-1991. During this period Tower produced *Amazon,* which is one of her most significant works. Tower became the first woman recipient of the Grawemeyer Award for Music for her composition *Silver Ladders* (1990). In 1993 she received a commission from the Milwaukee Ballet to compose *Stepping Stones.* Tower conducted a selection from this work at the White House. She wrote some of her most famous compositions in the 1990s including the third *Fanfare for the Uncommon Woman*, her *Piano Concerto No. 2*, and *Tambor* (1998), which was written for the Pittsburgh Symphony Orchestra. She won the Delaware Symphony's prestigious Alfred I. DuPont Award for Distinguished American Composer in 1998. Tower accepted a position as composer-in-residence with the Orchestra of St. Luke's in 1999.

Joan Tower won the Annual Composer's Award from the Lancaster (Pennsylvania) Symphony in 2002. She debuted her *DNA* for percussion quintet, which was commissioned by Frank Epstein. In 2004 the Pittsburgh Symphony's recording of *Tambor*, *Made in America*, and her *Concerto for Orchestra* earned a Grammy nomination. In 2004 Carnegie Hall's "Making Music" series featured Tower's music performed by artists including the Tokyo String Quartet and pianists Melvin Chen and Ursula Oppens. She composed her work *Purple Rhapsody* for viola and chamber orchestra in 2005. The same year Tower became the first composer commissioned for the "Ford Made in America" program. As part of this program Tower's 15-minute work *Made in America* was performed in every state of the union during the 2005-2007 season by sixty-five smaller budget orchestras. In 2008 Tower's *Made in America*, and the recording of it by the Nashville Symphony conducted by Leonard Slatkin, won three Grammy Awards: in the categories Best Orchestral Performance, Best Classical Album and Best Classical Contemporary Composition.

Joan Tower is currently the Asher B. Edelman Professor of Music at Bard College in New York. She is a member of the American Academy of Arts and Letters. Her early music reflects the influences of her mentors at Columbia University, and is rooted in *serialism. Serialism* is the practice of writing tone rows of twelve notes, which are not repeated until the entire row has been played. The sparse texture of her music comes from her love of chamber music. Tower later began to move away from strict serialism, and towards the works of Oliver Messiaen and George Crumb. Her music became more colorful and is often described as *Impressionistic*. Tower's five-part *Fanfare for the Uncommon Woman* is one of her most important works. Each section is dedicated to "women who are adventurous and take risks". This work was inspired by Aaron Copland's *Fanfare for the Common Man* as a form of commentary by Tower.

Joan Tower's compositions include works for solo instruments such as the piano and viola, numerous chamber music works for string quartet and other combinations of instruments, major orchestral works, her ballet *Stepping Stones*, and her vocal work *Can I*. Her orchestral music has been premiered by many orchestras. She has become one of the leading women composers in America.

Title: *Made in America* for chamber orchestra (2004) is scored for an orchestra comprising two flutes (doubling piccolo), two oboes, two clarinets, two bassoons, two horns, two trumpets, trombone, timpani, percussion, and strings. Commissioned by the League of American Orchestras and Meet the Composer.
Genre: A one movement **through-composed** orchestra piece.
YouTube: https://www .youtube .com/watch?v=bVocAdx5eKE
Joan Tower – *Made in America* with Nashville Symphony Orchestra conducted by Leonard Slatkin.
Birthday: born 6 September 1938 New Rochelle, New York, USA
Death Date: She is still alive at the publishing of this book (aged 82).
Fun Facts:
1. The recording of Joan Tower's work *Made in America* by the Nashville Symphony won three Grammy Awards.
2. Tower conducted music from her ballet *Stepping Stones* at the White House.
3. Joan Tower was born in New York but grew up in Bolivia in South America.

GWYNETH WALKER (1947-   )

Gwyneth Walker – (1947-   ) is an **American 20th Century** composer who was born on 22 March 1947 in New York, but grew up in Canaan, Connecticut. Gwyneth began composing at the age of two. Her father was a physicist and inventor. Both parents had excellent musical ears, however it was her mother, Adele Van Anden Frank Walker who guided her musical talents at a young age. Her mother was related to seven generations of Quakers who lived on Long Island, and her grandfather was Dr. John Walker, a surgeon, who was the President of the New York Medical

Society. So, she has a definite New York connection in her life.

Gwyneth developed a love for folk music and rock and roll before starting her formal music training. In high school she sang in an octet for which she composed most of their arrangements. Gwyneth studied both physics and music at Brown University. Gwyneth Walker graduated from Brown University in 1968 with a Bachelor of Arts from Hartt School of Music. She earned her Master of Music in 1970 and her Doctor of Musical Arts in 1976 from the University of Hartford in 1976, where her chief composition teacher was Arnold Franchetti. After teaching at Oberlin (1976-80), she worked part-time at Hartford Conservatory and Hartt School of Music but left teaching to pursue composition full-time in 1982. For almost thirty years, Gwyneth has lived on a dairy farm in Braintree, Vermont. Now she is living back in her hometown of

Canaan, Connecticut again.

In 1988, Dr. Walker formed the Consortium of Vermont Composers of which she later was the director. She used a grass roots form of writing music, often composing for local groups. Melodic textures are the main sources of organization and movement in Walker's compositions. Her harmonies are often based on simple two and three note chords in thirds with some harmonies based on fourths. She has composed over 300 works for professional orchestras, choruses, concert soloists, chamber ensembles, individual instrumentalists, and the Women's Philharmonic.

Walker's choral works include "Cheek to Cheek" for mixed chorus and piano (1978); "White Horses" (E. E. Cummings) for mixed chorus and piano (1979); and *A Heart in Hiding* (The Passionate Love Poems of Emily Dickinson), which was commissioned and performed by the Thomas Circle Singers in Washington DC, in 2008. Her orchestra works include *Fanfare for the Washington Festival Orchestra* (1978); *Match Point* (1985); the *Light of 3 Mornings* (1987); and her *Bassoon Concerto* for bassoon and strings (2000).

Gwyneth Walker was also a Nationally ranked junior tennis player. Several of her works have themes associated with athletics such as *Match Point*. Walker invited the famous tennis player Billie Jean King to perform as the soloist at Lincoln Center, where she bounced tennis balls on the percussion instruments, and mimed a tennis rally between her and the conductor. Walker also composed *Holding the Towel*, which is a comic song cycle for Super Bowl Sunday in 1992. She has received several commissions and awards including: The Brock Commission from the American Choral Directors Association in 1999; Lifetime Achievement Award from the Vermont Arts Council in 2000; The "Athenaeum Award for Achievement in the Arts and Humanities" from the St. Johnsbury (VT) Athenaeum in 2008; and she was elected as a Fellow of the Vermont Academy of Arts and Sciences in 2012.

Dr. Carolyn Waters Broe

Title: "How Can I Keep from Singing" for SATB Chorus

Genre: Choral music is vocal music for a mixed group of voices. It is often scored for SATB Chorus, which means that there are four parts for soprano, alto, tenor and bass voices. Most choral pieces are arranged with piano accompaniment. In this case, the song has also been arranged to include a brass quintet. They usually double the vocal parts.

YouTube: "How Can I Keep from Singing" https://www.youtube.com/ watch?v=pBsE2WB9lT0

The Choral Project and the Canadian Brass

Birthday: 22 March 1947 in New York

Death Date: Alive at the publication of this book (aged 73).

Fun Facts:

1. Gwyneth Walker lived on a dairy farm for almost 30 years.
2. Gwyneth Walker started composing at the age of two.
3. In her choral work *Three Songs in Celebration of the Family Farm* the chorus imitates the sounds of farm machinery and cows. The conductor uses milking gestures. This piece has been performed in non-traditional places such as a dairy barn.
4. Gwyneth Walker invited celebrity tennis star Billie Jean King to perform as the soloist at Lincoln Center for her piece *Match Point*, where King bounced tennis balls on the percussion instruments and mimed a tennis rally between her and the conductor.

ALMA DEUTSCHER (2005-   )

lma Deutscher – (2005-   ) **English 21st Century** composer, pianist, violinist, and child prodigy. Alma was born in February 2005 in Basingstoke, England to Israeli linguist Guy Deutscher, and Janie Deutscher (née Steen). They are both professors. Her father began to teach her how to read music and play the piano at the age of two. Alma could name the notes on the piano at this early age. She could read music before she learned to read words. Her father gave her a violin at age three, as a toy, but she started playing so well that he decided to get her a violin teacher. In under one year, she was playing Handel's violin sonatas. Alma began composing and

improvising at the piano at the age of four. She started to write down her compositions at five. Her first attempts at composing were unclear, but by the age of six her compositions became clear, and she wrote her first piano sonata. Alma Deutscher has shown an astonishing ability to compose melodies. They seem to just play in her mind all the time. Alma composed her first short opera at the age of seven, which is based on Neil Gaiman's story "The Sweeper of Dreams." The text to this opera was adapted from a libretto by Elizabeth Adlington. Parts of this opera came to her in a dream. She entered this work in the English National Opera Competition, but it just missed making it into the final round. Alma prefers writing about girls who overcome adversity. The main character of "The Sweeper of Dreams" commits two crimes, being a child and being a girl. Yet her character overcomes this and triumphs.

By nine Alma Deutscher had written her first violin concerto, and by the age of ten Alma had written a full-length opera. Her second opera is based on the fairy-tale "*Cinderella*". She began work on this opera in 2013, and a chamber version was performed in July of 2015. The German newspaper *Die Zeit* interviewed her. Deutscher finished composing the overture to *Cinderella* just a few days before the first performance. She has also been interviewed by *60 Minutes*. Alma decided to make Cinderella a composer, and the Prince a poet. The story is set in an opera company run by the Evil Stepmother. She decided that Cinderella is not just a pretty face but has a mind of her own and a spirit like hers. In December of 2016, a fuller version of *Cinderella* was premiered in Vienna with conductor Zubin Mehta as the patron of this production. He and other noted musicians are astonished by her ability to compose as well as her ability as a virtuoso pianist and violinist. She has performed as the pianist or violinist with many noted orchestras.

It seems that Alma's role models come straight out of the Viennese classical and 19th century eras. She adores Mozart but does not want to be compared with him. In her interview with Scott Pelley on *60 Minutes* Alma said, "I think I would prefer to be the first Alma than to be the second Mozart." (Deutscher 2019) She has several imaginary composers who help her out with her compositions and give her ideas. Alma composes in the classical style, and her music sounds very Viennese. She was discovered at the age of seven when her father's friend comedian Stephen Fry publicized her YouTube channel on Twitter. She became an instant success with millions of followers. These videos were meant to be viewed privately by family members, but the world has wanted to share Alma Deutscher's amazing talent and beautiful music. During an interview with the BBC in 2012, her mother said that Alma heard a lullaby by Richard Strauss when she was three, and asked how any music could be that beautiful? (Brian 2012). It was this moment that inspired Alma to learn music.

A production of Deutscher's opera *Cinderella* in English was performed in December of 2017 in California by the Opera San Jose through the Packard Humanities Institute. Alma expanded her Viennese version to 44 musicians and added new songs. This production was conducted by British conductor Jane Glover. Alma performed during the opera on both piano and violin. Alma's parents decided to move to the country to Dorking, Surrey, England, so that Alma could be near a major music school. She takes piano and violin lessons at the Yehudi

Menuhin School in Surry. As far as academics, Alma is home schooled. She composes about five hours a day, then goes outside to play with her younger sister, who is also musical.

Alma says that melodies come to her when she is relaxing, rather than when she wants them to come. She says that melodies just burst out of her fingertips. She also uses her purple skipping rope to help her to compose. She gets many ideas about music while she is skipping. She is working with renowned Swiss Improvisor Rudolf Lutz, as well as Professor Robert Gjerdingen, who has done a lot of work on how prodigies were taught in eighteenth century Italy. She has had lessons in improvisation, harmony, and counterpoint from Swish musician Tobias Cramm via Skype.

Alma was the subject of some of her father's linguistic experiments when she was a toddler. He was careful never to tell her that "the sky is blue". He wrote about his results in 2010 in his book *Through the Language Glass: Why the World Looks Different in Other Languages*. Music is of course known as The Universal Language. During her concert preview on "Why Music Should Be Beautiful" Alma explains that some people have told her that she should not compose beautiful melodies in the twenty-first century, because music must reflect the complexity and ugliness of the modern world. "But I think that these people just got a little bit confused. If the world is so ugly, then what's the point of making it even uglier with ugly music?" (Deutscher 2017). Alma Deutscher has given us so many beautiful music works with many more to come.

Title: The *Opera Cinderella*. The original chamber version premiered in Israel in 2015. The Austrian premiere was in December of 2016, and the American premiere in 2017.

Genre: An **opera** is a major musical work written for singers and accompanied by an orchestra with staging.

YouTube: https://www.youtube.com/watch?v=Q77Mv3bgqjE

Cinderella's Ballade "When the Day Falls Into Darkness" from her opera *Cinderella*. https://www.youtube.com/watch?v=7yf_pbVvIWk

Alma Deutscher concert preview video on her YouTube channel.

Birthday: February 2005, Basingstoke, England.

Fun Facts:

1. Alma Deutscher composed her first piano sonata at the age of six.
2. Alma Deutscher composed her first opera at that age of seven.
3. She gets musical ideas while skipping rope.
4. She has imaginary composer friends, who help her to compose.

ILLUSTRATIONS

50 Famous Composers

PRINCESS COMPOSERS – Wilhelmina and Anna Amalia of Prussia

HUSBAND AND WIFE COMPOSERS − Clara and Robert Schumann

50 Famous Composers

FUN FACTS QUIZ ILLUSTRATIONS

About the Author
CAROLYN WATERS BROE

GLOSSARY

A cappella – (Italian, ăh căhp-pel'lăh) is a type of vocal music that was sung without instrumental accompaniment. It was typically sung in "a chapel" hence the name. It is also known as "church style" music.

Ballet music – is written to accompany and enhance the staged choreography of dancers, and to tell a story with the combination of dance, sets, and music.

Baroque music – is a contrapuntal music developed during the period 1600 – 1750. Bach and Handel composed this music. The original meaning may have come from a misshapen pearl but has come to mean music that is precise and dignified. The concerto and the opera were new and important genres during the Baroque.

Choreographer – cho·re·og·ra·pher/kôrēˈägrəfər/noun a person who composes the sequence of steps and moves for a performance of dance.

Classical music – is a European style music that developed during the period 1770 – 1830. It was very symmetrical like a Classical Greek temple, hence the name. If you use a small "c" in classical music, it refers to any serious rather than popular music and includes Romantic music and other non-popular music.

Clavichord – a keyboard instrument that was a precursor to the pianoforte. The clavichord had upright wedges instead of hammers like a piano has. When a key was struck the wedges hit the back of the string and held it until the pressure is let go. Only one string vibrates.

Concerto – (Italian – kohn-chair-toe) Is an extended composition for a solo instrument, usually with orchestral accompaniment, often in sonata form.

Concerto grosso – (Italian – kohn-chair-toe gro soh) Is an instrumental composition employing a small group of solo instruments against a larger group or full orchestra.

Conductor – The director of an orchestra, band, ensemble, or chorus. It is the conductor's job to not only keep the time and tempo, but to lead the group of musicians in the style and expression designated by the composer of the music.

Conservatory of music – is a school where music instruction takes place. Students learn about music history, theory, and performance of an instrument or voice. Conservatories prepare students to become professional musicians and solo artists. Music students are also trained by professors to become composers, pianists, conductors, and music teachers.

Contrapuntal – means that the composer used the art and practice of counterpoint in the composition of the music. This may include imitation, fugues and/or canons.

Counterpoint – 1. refers to the art of polyphonic composition. 2. Music that contains two or more melodies that are performed at the same time.

Fugue – (fewg) is a highly developed form of contrapuntal imitation, based on the principal of equality of parts. A theme is presented by one part and then followed by each part in the music successively one after the other. The elements needed for a fugue are (1) the Subject, (2) the Answer, (3) Countersubject, (4) Stretto. It is common to add (5) Episodes, (6) an Organ point, (7) a Coda. In a Real Fugue the answer is a transposition of the subject. In a Tonal Fugue the subject is modified so it will go back to the same key that it started in. There are many kinds of fugues.

Harpsicord – A keyboard stringed instrument where the strings are plucked by quills or bits of hard leather. This instrument was popular before the piano was invented.

Impresario – im·pre·sa·ri·o/ˌimprəˈsärēˌō,ˌimprˈserəˌō/ noun. A person who organizes and often finances concerts, plays, or operas. Also, a manager of a theater, symphony, music group, ballet company or operatic company.

Impressionism – in music was a movement among various composers in Western classical music, during the late 19th and early 20th centuries, whose music focuses on mood and atmosphere. They were inspired by the Impressionist painters who painted out of focus, often foggy landscapes that gave the impression of the scene rather than a detailed painting. The Impressionist composers wrote music in a similar fashion that evaded strong downbeats, avoided tonal centers, often used modes rather than major and minor scales, included unusual rhythms and explored alternate uses of instruments in non-traditional ranges such as the darker alto flute rather than the higher flute.

Kapellmeister – (German, kăh-pel-mīs-ter) the conductor of an orchestra or the choirmaster. The kapellmeister leads the orchestra or choir by waving a baton or their hands in time to the music.

Libretto – is the script for the spoken, sung and staged part of the opera. A librettist is the person who writes the script for an opera.

Lyric – comes from the Greek word for the stringed instrument known as the lyre. Lyric poetry was sung with the lyre and featured emotion, brief stanzas in a recognizable form. In music a lyric aria is also emotional and has a recognizable form. In general, lyric music is flowing and beautiful.

Medieval music – is a Western music consisting of songs, instrumental pieces, and sacred music from about 500 A.D. to 1400. Sacred music (also called liturgical) was used for the church while secular music was used for non-religious purposes. Medieval music included Gregorian chant, which was entirely vocal. It also included music, which was for singers alone, instruments alone, and music that was for both singers and instruments. Vocal music was the most common form of Medieval music though.

Melody – the word melody comes from the Greek word "melos". To the Greeks it referred to both poetry and music together. Today a melody is a single line of notes. Melody is also the principal line in harmonized music.

Military March – is an instrumental piece, which is composed for and performed at parades, military events, and patriotic events.

Modern music – refers to music that developed at the turn of the 20th century. Modulation from one key to the next was given complete freedom. Dissonances carried equal weight with harmonies. Several keys could be combined in a style known as "dodecaphony". Melodies could move away from tonality and some modern music was completely atonal (not based on tonal relationships). For a while rock and jazz music was also labeled modern music to make it different from serious classical music.

Modulation – the passage of one key or mode to another. There are different kinds of modulation including chromatic, diatonic, enharmonic, and final modulation. Composers used these different types of modulation to change their music from the original key, such as C major, to a new key such as A minor. Then they might explore more keys before coming back to the home key.

Music – Comes from the Greek word "muse". The muses were nine goddesses who each specialized in teaching an artform such as poetry, music, dance, sculpture and even history. Music is the combination of vocal and/or instrumental sounds in such a way to produce beauty, harmony, rhythm, and expression of emotions. Music is also the written notation that symbolizes those sounds and rhythms.

Opera – a form of drama, of Italian origin, where the vocal and instrumental music are the most important elements. Operas are usually performed in several acts, and consist of vocal scenes, songs, recitatives, arias, duets, trios, choruses, and other movements that are accompanied by the orchestra.

Orchestra – (or'kĕs'trăh) a company of musicians performing on instruments that are usually employed in a symphony, concerto, opera, chorus, or oratorio.

Overture – is an instrumental piece which is usually performed at the beginning of a larger work such as an opera. The overture often introduces many or all the themes or melodies of that work and is performed by the orchestra or an instrumental ensemble. However, a concert overture may be composed as a stand-alone piece that was never performed as part of another work.

Polyphonic – 1. consists of two or more independently treated melodies that are contrapuntal. 2. An instrument that can produce two or more tones at the same time such as the piano, guitar, harp, and organ.

Programmatic music – This means that the music follows a theme, poem or image which is depicted by the music.

Renaissance music – in music history is the period between 1400 to 1600. This music is polyphonic with several melodies performed at once with imitation between the parts. Renaissance music emphasized humanistic principals such as those of the ancient Greeks. The growing middle class wanted more music for entertainment.

Ritornello form – was a Baroque form of composition where the music theme repeats many times. The Italians called it the "little return". Vivaldi was a master of the ritornello style. There are different music episodes in between each return of the main theme or melody. The music would start and end with the ritornello passage.

Romantic music – is an emotional and melodic music composed from around 1815 to c. 1910. This period of music overlaps with late Classical music in the beginning of the 19th century and with Impressionism and Expressionism at the beginning of the 20th century. Romantics idealized death and transfiguration in their music. They expanded the orchestra and the harmonic language in symphonic music.

Serialism – is the practice of writing tone rows of twelve notes, which are not repeated until the entire row has been played or sung.

Sonata – is chamber music, which is usually performed with piano and another solo instrument. Sonatas are usually written with three to four movements.

Sonata form – Is a type of composing style that presents two or more themes and then develops them. The sonata form was used for first movements of Classical symphonies, sonatas, and chamber music works. It can be used for other movements as well.

Stretto – (Italian, stret'tōh) is a division of a fugue (usually in the final section) where the subject and answer come so close together as to overlap. Stretto means pressed together.

Symphony – (sim-fō-nē) 1. A large group of instrumentalists who perform together. 2. An orchestra composition with three to five distinct movements (or divisions). Each movement has its own theme or themes and its own development. The usual plan of a symphony is I. Allegro (sonata form), II. Adagio, III. Minuet or Scherzo, IV. Allegro or Presto.

Symphonic poem – Is a work for orchestra that is usually a one movement piece that is programmatic. This means that there is a theme, poem or image depicted by the music.

FUN FACT QUIZ

LUDWIG VAN BEETHOVEN

At what age did Beethoven begin his hearing loss, and at
what age was he completely deaf by?

A. He ate macaroni and cheese almost every day of his life, and a soup with twelve
drowned eggs to settle his stomach.

B. Beethoven sawed the legs off his piano, so that he could put it on the wood floor and
feel the vibrations from the music.

C. Beethoven was paid to walk by his patrons because he did his best
composing then.

D. Beethoven was kicked out of twenty-seven apartments for banging on his piano.

Which of the above statements are true? _____

ÉLISABETH CLAUDE-JACQUET DE LA GUERRE

She was called "the marvel of our century," and singled out for
special favor by Louis XIV (the fourteenth). What honor did the
king bestow on Élisabeth after her death?

A. Élisabeth Jacquet was a child prodigy and virtuoso harpsichordist (a keyboard
    instrument that came before the piano).

B. Élisabeth Jacquet said NO to the king when he decided to move his court to Versailles,
    outside of Paris. She wanted to stay in Paris.

C. Élisabeth Jacquet was allowed to wear the famous necklace with the Hope Diamond to
    a ball.

D. Élisabeth Jacquet invented the keyboard concerto.

Which of the above statements are true? _____

FRANZ JOSEPH HAYDN

Haydn's contributions have earned him the epithet of "Father of the Symphony" and "Father of the String Quartet". How many symphonies and string quartets did he compose?

A. The young Beethoven took composition lessons from Haydn and nicknamed him "Papa Haydn".

B. The slow movement of Haydn's "Surprise Symphony" was written to wake up British patrons, who were snoring at his concerts.

C. Haydn is famous for having invented the saxophone concerto.

D. After Haydn died, his body was dug up and the skull was removed for "scientific purposes" by a misguided secretary. His skull was not reunited with his skeleton for 145 years.

Which of the above statements are true? _____

FANNY MENDELSSOHN HENSEL

Her husband, the court painter Wilhelm Hensel, encouraged Fanny to publish, while her brother Felix opposed it. It was because of Felix's negative attitude that very few of Fanny's compositions were ever published during her brief lifetime. How many pieces did she compose?

A. Fanny Mendelssohn was the younger sister of composer Felix Mendelssohn.

B. Felix got in trouble with Queen Victoria for signing his name to Fanny's pieces, when the queen said she wanted to sing her favorite piece by him, and he had to admit to her that it was really written by Fanny.

C. Each of her pieces was written on colored paper, illustrated by her husband Wilhelm Hensel, and accompanied by a poem.

D. Her composition teacher, Carl Friedrich Zelter favored Fanny over Felix, and praised her piano skills in a letter to Goethe by saying "She plays like a man".

Which of the above statements are true? _____

LOUISE LINCOLN KERR

She left New York in 1913 to join the early Cleveland Symphony
Orchestra as a violinist, and she was one of their first two female musicians.
What instrument did the other lady play?

A. Louise Kerr worked at the Aeolian player piano company in New York City in 1920
where she proofed the piano rolls. She later worked in the recording booth editing the
earliest disc recordings.

B. Louise Kerr composed fifteen symphonic works, five ballets, numerous chamber
music pieces, piano solos, and one violin concerto.

C. Louise Kerr co-founded the Phoenix Symphony and the Phoenix Chamber Music
Society.

D. Louise Kerr's violin was stolen the day Pearl Harbor was attacked 7 December 1941, so
she switched to viola.

Which of the above statements are true? _____

GEORG F. HÄNDEL

When Händel was rehearsing a new piece in a public park, there was a three-hour traffic jam of carriages on London Bridge caused by twelve thousand patrons coming to hear the performance. Name this piece.

A. Händel was the boy who sang in the streets.

B. The "Water Music Suite" was performed by musicians on a boat floating down the Thames River as part of King George II's coronation celebrations.

C. When the "Music for the Royal Fireworks" was first performed, the stage caught fire.

D. Händel got into a duel with Johann Mattheson, a friend and composer. When the large button on Händel's coat broke the nearly fatal blow from Mattheson's sword, Händel's life was spared.

Which of the above statements are true? _____

HILDEGARD VON BINGEN

Hildegard has become famous for her work as the earliest German Scientist of botanical and herbal medicine. She was also an artist, composer, visionary, religious leader, and author. In what year was Hildegard Sainted?

A. Hildegard was the first Western composer ever to have their name attached to their music composition.

B. Hildegard composed *Ordo Virtutum* which is the earliest surviving morality play.

C. Hildegard's music is highly melismatic, which means that it had soaring melodies that were beautifully ornamented by stretching out each syllable with various notes.

D. Sixty-nine of Hildegard's many music compositions survived, each with its own poetic text.

Which of the above statements are true? _____

ANTONIO VIVALDI

Vivaldi established the three-movement concerto form.

How many concertos did Vivaldi compose?

A. Vivaldi composed for a virtuoso orchestra of girls and women at an orphanage in Venice.

B. Vivaldi Influenced many other Baroque composers, including J. S. Bach.

C. Vivaldi was an Ambassador to France from Venice, and liaison to the Pope in Rome.

D. Vivaldi was friends with Charles VI of Bavaria and may have been murdered for this connection.

Which of the above statements are true? _____

JOHANN SEBASTIAN BACH

Bach composed cantatas, twenty concertos, two passions, keyboard pieces, art of the fugue, the Magnificat, and chamber music. How many cantatas did he compose?

A. Bach was more famous during his life as a composer than as an organist.

B. Bach was the inventor of the keyboard concerto.

C. Bach developed the art of the fugue, invention, canon, and counterpoint.

D. Bach influenced many famous composers including his sons, both Fanny and Felix Mendelssohn, and countless others.

Which of the above statements are true? _____

Dr. Carolyn Waters Broe

Answers to the Fun Facts Quiz

Ludwig van Beethoven – Beethoven started becoming deaf at age fifteen and was completely deaf by age forty-six.

A. B. C. and D. are all True.

Élisabeth Claude-Jacquet de la Guerre – After her death he struck a commemorative medal in her honor in 1729. It was stamped with her portrait and the words, "I contended with the greatest of musicians."

A. True B. True C. False D. False

Franz Joseph Haydn – He composed 106 symphonies and 68 string quartets.

A. False (Beethoven was Haydn student, but Mozart nicknamed him Papa Haydn). B. True C. False D. True

Fanny Mendelssohn Hensel – She composed over 460 pieces of music.

A. False (she is Felix's older sister) B. True C. True D. True

Louise Lincoln Kerr – The other female Cleveland Symphony member played harp.

B. C. and D. are all True.

Georg F. Händel – "Music for the Royal Fireworks."

A. False B. False C. True D. True

Hildegard von Bingen – She was canonized a Saint on 10 May 2012 by Pope Benedict XVI.

A. B. C. and D. are all True.

Antonio Vivaldi – Composed over 700 concertos.

A. B. C. and D. are all True.

Johann Sebastian Bach – Composed over 200 cantatas.

A. False B. True C. True D. True.

MUSICAL TIMELINE

Major Events and Dates

Ancient Music (3500 B.C.E to 475 A.D.)

ca. 3500-3000 B.C.E. The rise of Sumerian cities in Mesopotamia.

ca. 3100 B.C.E. Cuneiform writing is established.

ca. 2500 B.C.E. Royal tombs are built at Ur.

ca. 2300 B.C.E. The Akkadian high priestess Enheduanna of Ur in Mesopotamia composers her hymns to the Moon God Nanna and the Moon Goddess Inanna. She is the earliest composer known to us by name. Only the text of her hymns survives, not the music.

ca. 1800 B.C.E. The Babylonians write about music in cuneiform on clay tablets.

ca. 1400-1250 B.C.E. The oldest nearly complete work of music is composed in Ugarit near the Syrian coast and has survived on a clay cuneiform tablet. This hymn to Nikkal, a wife of the Moon God, is the earliest known example of music notation. It has both text and music.

ca. 475 B.C.E. The Greek philosopher **Pythagoras** discovers the overtone series. He worked out the mathematical ratios of dividing the strings of the lyre into different lengths which produce the ratio of 2:1 for the octave, 3:2 for a fifth, and 4:3 for a fourth. He is known as the father of music theory.

ca. 500 B.C.E. Pythagoras dies.

ca. 500 B.C.E. The Roman Republic begins.

480 B.C.E. The Greek philosopher **Euripides** writes his play *Orestes* which includes a chorus of singers. Greek plays were accompanied by the aulos (a wind instrument) and kithara (a stringed instrument).

ca. 380 B.C.E. The Greek philosopher **Plato** writes his *Republic* and *Timaeus* including discussions about the power of music and the proper usage of music.

ca. 330 B.C.E. The Greek philosopher **Aristotle** writes about music in his *Politics*.

ca. 330 B.C.E. The Greek philosopher **Aristoxenus** writes the first books of music theory called *Harmonic Elements* and *Rhythmic Elements*. He was a pupil of Aristotle.

146 B.C.E. Greece becomes a province of Rome.

128-127 B.C.E. The second *Delphic Hymn* to Apollo is composed.

27 B.C.E. Rome becomes and empire under **Augustus**.

1st cent. C.E. The *Epithaph of Seikilos* is written.

98-117 C.E. The Roman Empire reaches its peak.

ca. 127-148 C.E. Ptolemy writes his doctrine on *Harmonics.*

2nd century Cleonides writes his doctrine on *Harmonic Introduction.*

4th century Aristides Quintilianus writes his doctrine *On Music.*

392 C.E. Christianity is declared the official Roman religion by **Emperor Constantine.**

The Dark Ages (476-800 A.D.)

476 The end of the Western **Roman Empire**. Northern European armies invade Rome and sack it, thus ending the Western Roman Empire centered in Italy.

590-604 – Reign of **Pope Gregory I** (The Great). Gregorian chant is named after him because he reorganized the Catholic liturgy during his reign.

711 The Moors of Western Africa invade Spain bringing with them their music, poetry, mathematics, religion, and higher learning. This knowledge helps to end the Dark Ages of Europe, and usher in the Medieval Era later. They also bring their string instruments.

Pepin The Short (reign 751-768) of the Franks becomes King with the help of the pope. He decides that he wants to import the Roman liturgy and chant to his domain, which is now part of France. His son Charlemagne expands his kingdom to an empire.

Medieval Era (approximately 800-1450 A.D.)

800 Charlemagne (reign 768-814) is crowned Emperor and Pope. He unified Europe by establishing the Empire of Francia. His father was Pepin The Short.

1025 Guido of Arezzo (991-92 to after 1033) was the Italian music theorist who invented modern music staff notation. He held up five fingers and pointed up or down, so the monks in his choir could learn to sing various chants. Eventually he just drew five lines on the page and put notes on the lines to symbolize music. He also invented the solfege system (do re mi fa so la) representing the first six half lines of the hymn "*Ut Quiant laxis*". His book on music the "*Micrologus*" was the second most widely distributed treatise on music in Europe.

Hildegard von Bingen – **(1098-1179) German.** She was the first western composer ever to have their name attached to their music. She publishes several books of her art, music, and botanical science discoveries. She also travels around Germany speaking to crowds.

1099 Jerusalem falls to the Crusaders, who slaughter the city's Jewish and Muslim inhabitants. The Crusaders bring back knowledge of poetry and chivalry as well as valuable spices to Europe. These spices change the course of European history and World travel.

1100 A Persian, **Omar Khayyam** (Ghiyath al-Din Abu'l-Fath Umar ibn Ibrahim Al-Nisaburi al-Khayyami), writes his poem the *Rubaiyat*.

1101 Towns are becoming an important part of life in Europe, even though only ten percent of people live in towns and ninety percent live in rural areas (farms and country areas). It is the beginning of a new century. Some enlightened feudal lords and kings have granted the town charters, but other big landowners resist the rise of towns. Towns are the new center of commerce. The towns people fight back to preserve their new independence.

1149 The Second Crusade to the Middle East causes many changes to Europe. Crusaders who have returned alive bring back sugar and spices, which increases trade. Many of the people who joined the Second Crusade have died from starvation and disease as well as injuries from battle. Edessa remains under Muslim control.

1150 Troubadours were musicians who traveled from town to town singing and giving news to the people of Southern France. They started a secret religion and put secret messages into their poetry and music, so the Pope will not discover their worship places.

1150 The **University of Paris** is founded.

1163 The first stone of the **Cathedral of Notre Dame in Paris**, France is laid with Pope Alexander III in attendance. The cathedral was not finished until 1345. The outside was built of stone including the two towers. The roof was made from an entire forest. A great deal of early music was written for this church and for various ceremonies.

1215 The Magna Carta was signed by King John of England on 15 June in Runnymede, Surrey in England. The Magna Carta was meant as a peace treaty between King John and his subjects. The lords demanded that every person had to obey the law, including the king. King John later went back on his word.

1347-1352 The Black plague in Europe started in the fortress at Caffa near the Black Sea when the Mogul army threw their dead plague-ridden soldiers into the fortress during a siege. Genoese and Venetian sailors escaping this event spread the Black plague to Italy, and many ports in Europe, on their return home by bringing the disease and infected black rats with them. It is estimated that this plague killed between 25 million and 200 million people. Oddly, this changed the dynamics of class structure in Europe and helped to usher in the Renaissance through the rise of the middle class.

1337-1453 The Hundred Years War was a series of conflicts fought between the English ruling House of Plantagenet and the French ruling House of Valois over who would rule the Kingdom of France. The end of this war helped to usher in the Renaissance as there was more money for universities and education.

Renaissance Era (1450-1600)

1397-1494 The Bank of the powerful **Medici family** is created and falls in Florence, Italy. These wealthy bankers produce four Popes and two queens. They patronize the arts bankrolling the first surviving opera in 1600 and later the invention of the piano.

1440 German goldsmith **Johannes Guttenburg (c. 1398-1468) invents the printing press** in Strasburg, Germany around 1440. This revolutionary technology enables the mass printing of books which were distributed across Europe and allowed people to gain knowledge rapidly. The Guttenburg bible becomes the first bestselling book.

Josquin des Prez – (c. 1450/1455-27 August 1521) is a Franco Flemish composer who writes polyphonic masses and motets. His music became very popular due to new printing techniques for music. The earliest printed music was around 1465.

1492 Italian ship captain **Christopher Columbus** gains the funding from King Ferdinand and Queen Isabella of Spain to search for a Western sea passage to Asia for the spice trade. He discovers the Canary Islands first, off the Western coast of Africa near Morocco, and the Guanche Indians. He writes a letter to the Spanish king and queen telling them of how peaceful and innocent these extremely tall white Indians were. Later they sent the Spanish army to the Canary Islands and killed most of the Guanche people. They capture 500 of them and send them back to Spain as slaves. That same year Columbus manages to stumble onto an island inhabited by the Carib Indians in what later becomes known as the Caribbean Sea in what is later called the Americas, instead of finding a passage to the spice islands in Asia. The Spanish king and queen and their armies repeat the same brutality to the Indians across the Americas in search of gold.

1498 Italian printer **Ottaviano Petrucci** convinces the Doge in Venice to give him an exclusive twenty-year monopoly on printing music in Venice. He publishes mostly music by Flemish composers such as Josquin des Prez and Heinrich Isaac, instead of Italian composers, because Flemish music was popular during the Renaissance in Europe. Petrucci is considered the father of modern music printing. His first collection of music was entitled *Harmonice Musices Odhecaton* and contained 96 polyphonic compositions. His printing shop used the triple-impression method, in which a sheet of paper was pressed three times. The first impression was the staff lines, the second the words, and the third the notes. This method took a long time, but it produced very clean music books.

1517 Martin Luther (1483-1546) was a German Augustinian monk and university lecturer in Wittenberg, Germany when he composed his famous "95 Theses" that started **The Reformation** and the Lutheran Protestant religion. His theses, which he nailed to the door of the castle church, protested the pope's sale of reprieves from penance, called "indulgences". He felt that penance could only come from faith and not by purchasing them.

c. 1520 The Counter Reformation establishes a new order to the Catholic Church which preserves its Medieval structure. Many of the newer modern music compositions are prohibited by this order. The older Latin chants are brought back to the church in the church modes. Nuns are prohibited from learning music theory and composition. **Pope Paul III (1534-1549)** initiates the **Council of Trent (1545–1563)**. This council reaffirms the traditional seven sacraments of the Catholic Church.

c. 1525 The Violin Family develops in Italy from the *lira da braccia*, which was an instrument like the viola, and other stringed instruments. The name "viola" means a bowed stringed instrument in Italian. "Violino" means a small viola. "Violoncello" means a large viola.

1585 The Gregorian Calendar is introduced in October 1585 by **Pope Gregory VIII**. He spaces out leap years, so there are approximately 365.2425 days in those years. This helps to make the year correspond to one rotation of the Earth around the Sun or 365.2422. Pope Gregory also codifies the Latin chants into several volumes of liturgical books. These are later called Gregorian chants.

Claudio Monteverdi – (1567-1643) is the Italian composer who introduces the "*Secunda Pratica*" or Second Practice in music, which modernizes melody and harmony, and helps to usher in the Baroque era in music.

Baroque Era (1600-1750)

Francesca Caccini – (1587-c. 1638) She was an **Italian composer** who was the first to have their opera performed outside of Italy.

1597 Italian composer **Jacopo Peri invents the opera** in collaboration with poet Ottavio Rinuccini. Peri is best known for composing what was probably the first opera, "*La Dafne*" (1598). Jacopo Corsi was the patron in Florence, Italy who sponsored this first opera. His *"L'Euridice"* (1600), also, in collaboration with Rinuccini, was the first opera for which complete music still exists.

1618-1648 The Thirty Years War in Europe took place between the Protestant states and allies and the Catholic states and allies.

1626 King Louis XIII of France founds the **Twenty-four Violins of the King** (*Les Vingt-quatre Violons du Roy*) as part of his *Musique de la Chambre*. This famous five-part string orchestra performed at the French royal court from 1626 to 1761. When the French court moved to Versailles by the command of Louis XIV, then the orchestra moved with them to perform at festivals and celebrations.

Elisabeth-Claude Jacquet de la Guerre – (1665-1729) She was a French composer and harpsichordist who composed in every style of music for the Court of Louis the XIV. Jacquet and her family help to establish the harpsichord as a major Baroque instrument.

1661 King Louis XIV, who ruled France from 1638 – 1715, starts work on building his famous **palace of Versailles** outside of Paris. He filled his palace with brilliant artwork, lavish gardens, and beautiful music. He adds a smaller elite group of sixteen strings.

Antonio Vivaldi – (1678-1741) Italian composer who wrote over 700 concertos, mostly for the violin, making the three-movement form of the concerto standardized in Europe. Vivaldi also composed over forty-five operas which were staged in the Republic of Venice.

Georg Friedrich Händel – (1685-1759) was a famous German/English opera composer who worked for the King of England George I. He also composed twenty-four oratorios including "The Messiah".

Johann Sebastian Bach – (1685-1750) was the German composer who invented the keyboard concerto with his Brandenburg Concerto No. 5.

The Age of Enlightenment (1685-1815) – was a time during the eighteenth century of great advances in both science and philosophy, but also brought about revolutions against Imperialism in both the Americas and Europe. The American Revolution and the French Revolution were both a direct result of Age of Enlightenment thinking. There were also revolutions in the Caribbean and in Latin America.

1698 -1712 The Steam Engine was developed by Thomas Newcomen and others. James Watt made important improvements to the steam engine by diverting spent steam to another vessel for condensation.

1701-1714 The War of Spanish Succession was started when Charles II of Spain died childless in 1700. His closest heirs were either the French Bourbon family or members of the Austrian Hapsburg family. If either family won this conflict, it would destabilize Europe. The winners would divide up the Spanish Empire which now included vast territories in the Americas as well as in Spain and Europe. The results of the treaties were extremely complicated.

1709 The invention of the piano is credited to Bartolomeo Cristofori, in full Bartolomeo di Francesco Cristofori, (born May 4, 1655, Padua, Republic of Venice [Italy]—died January 27, 1732, Florence). Cristofori was a well-known Italian harpsichord maker who was hired by Prince Ferdinando de 'Medici in 1690. The piano was called the gravicembalo col piano e forte, or "harpsichord that plays soft and loud" at the time. This was later shortened to piano when the instrument went through further developments later. The Medici family ordered many piano fortes to be built for their court including the first 1709 Cristofori instrument.

Wilhelm Friedemann Bach – (1710-1784) German composer of chamber music, symphonies, and harpsichord concertos.

1740-1748 The War of Austrian Succession started over the right of the Archduchess Maria Theresa to succeed to her father Charles VI's various crowns including the Hapsburg monarchy in Austria. Salic law forbade a woman to become queen. This war took place in Northern Europe, North America, and the Indian subcontinent. The treaty of Aix-la-Chapelle declared that Maria Theresa kept her monarchy in Austria, Bohemia and Hungary. Her husband became the Holy Roman Emperor. Prussia maintained control of Silesia, and the Spanish Bourbons regained their lands that had been taken. The treaty was fragile and soon lead to the Seven Years War.

Classical Era (1750-1820)

Carl Philipp Emanuel Bach – (1714-1788) is a German composer and son of the famous Johann Sebastian Bach.

Johann Christoph Friedrich Bach – (1732-1795) was a German Classical composer and harpsichordist. He was the sixteenth child of J. S. Bach and is referred to as the "Bückeburg Bach".

Johann Christian Bach – (1735-1782) is a German/English composer and son of the famous Johann Sebastian Bach.

Wilhelmina Princess of Prussia (Sophie Friederike Wilhelmine) – (1709-1758) Prussian composer and patroness of music.

Leopold Mozart – (1719-1789) was a German conductor, violinist, author, teacher and composer of symphonic music, piano pieces, and chamber music. He writes the first treatise on the violin asking the question of whether musical genius is nurture or nature. He was also the father of two incredibly famous musicians including Wolfgang A. Mozart and Maria Anna "Nannerl" Mozart.

Anna Amalia – (1723-1787) Princess of Prussia and Abbess of Quedlingburg and composer.

Maria Antonia Walpurgis – (1724-1780) Bavarian composer and Duchess of Bavaria. She composed two operas, in the style of Hasse, and was a patroness of opera.

Franz Joseph Haydn – (1732 -1809) is an Austrian composer who develops the symphony and the string quartet.

Marianne von Martínez – (1744-1812) is an Austrian composer, pianist and singer who was a student of Joseph Haydn and premiered some of Mozart's piano concertos.

Henriette de Beaumesnil – (1748-1813) is a French opera singer and composer.

Maria Anna Mozart – (nick-named "Nannerl") (1751-1829) She was an Austrian pianist, teacher and composer of piano pieces and chamber music.

Wolfgang Amadeus Mozart – (1756-1791) He was an Austrian composer of symphonies, quartets, piano concertos, violin concertos, a requiem, chamber music, songs, and many operas.

1756-1763 The Seven Years War was a global conflict that spanned five continents including Europe, the Americas, West Africa, India, and the Philippines. European combatants were split into two groups. One was led by the Kingdom of Great Britain and included Prussia, Portugal, the Electorate of Brunswick-Lüneburg, and other smaller German states. The other faction was led by the Kingdom of France and included Austrian-led Holy Roman Empire, the Russian Empire, the Kingdom of Spain, and the Swedish Empire. The British coalition won. France cedes the Louisiana territory west of the Mississippi River to Spain. France cedes its colonial territories east of the Mississippi, Canada, and colonies in India to Great Britain. Spain cedes Florida to Great Britain.

Maria von Paradis – (1759-1824) She was an Austrian pianist, teacher and composer of a symphony, piano concerto, piano music, songs, and chamber music.

50 Famous Composers

Ludwig van Beethoven – (1770-1827) He was a German pianist, organist, and composer of nine symphonies, five piano concertos, a violin concerto, piano music, chamber music and an opera.

1763-1787 The timeline of the **American Revolution** starts with the signing of the **Treaty of Paris** in 1763 (ending the French and Indian War), and continues through the **Revolutionary War**, until the ratification of the **Constitution** at the Constitutional Convention in 1787.

1789-1799 The French Revolution was inspired by the American Revolution. This was a very violent time in France, which lead to the death of French royal family, and the reorganization of France. The French Revolutionary Government was formed.

1800 The first steam ships come into practical use. The first sea-going steam ship was built by Richard Wright which sailed from Leeds to Yarmouth in July of 1813. Soon steam ships were crossing the Atlantic and other oceans. This led to the first wave of global trade between 1870 to 1913.

Romantic Era (1820-1910)

Gioachino Rossini – (1792-1868) He was an Italian opera composer and of chamber music. He was also a singer and performer in theater groups.

Franz Schubert – (1797-1828) He was a German composer of symphonies, chamber music and beautiful lieder (songs).

1801-1829 The Napoleonic Wars continued the French Revolution when Napoleon Bonaparte seized power from the French Revolutionary Government in 1799. In 1802 Napoleon ends ten years of war with Great Britain under the Peace Amiens. Napoleon crowns himself Emperor of France in 1804 at the Cathedral de Notre Dame in Paris. Napoleon is defeated at the Battle of Waterloo by the British on June 18, 1815. He was exiled to the Isle of Elba in Italy.

(Jeanne-) Louise Farrenc – (1804-1875) She was a French composer, pianist, and teacher. She wrote piano music, two overtures, chamber music, and three symphonies

Fanny Mendelssohn – (1805-1847) She was a German composer of chamber music and songs. She was also the older sister of Felix Mendelssohn.

Felix Mendelssohn – (1809-1847) He was a German composer of symphonies, quartets, songs, and a famous violin concerto.

1812-1815 The War of 1812 was fought between the United States and Britain over British violations of American maritime rights. Tensions between Britain and France during the Napoleonic Wars caused the British to attack U.S. ships. The British marched on Washington DC and burned the White House down in 1813. This war was resolved by the Battle of New Orleans and the Treaty of Ghent.

Clara Wieck Schumann – (1819 -1896) She was a German piano solo artist and composer of a piano concerto, piano music, three Romances for Violin, and chamber music. She toured around Europe performing 1,000 piano recitals.

Robert Schumann – (1810-1856) He was a German pianist and composer of four symphonies, a piano concerto, quartets, and piano music.

Johannes Brahms – (1833-1897) He was a German composer of four symphonies, quartets, two piano concertos, piano music, and songs.

Saint-Saëns – (1835-1921) He was a French composer of symphonies, piano music, an organ concerto, a cello concerto, and chamber music such as the "Carnival of the Animals".

Modest Mussorgsky – (1839-1881) He was a Russian composer of piano music such as the "Pictures at an Exhibition". His symphonic music such as "Night on Bald Mountain" and his opera "Boris Godunov" include Russian stories and folklore.

Peter I. Tchaikovsky – (1840-1893) He was a Russian composer of symphonies, piano music, concertos, ballet music, and chamber music.

1846 Adolf Sax patented the saxophone. Sax was a Belgian-French instrument maker, who made improvements and invented many instruments during the 19th century. He made significant improvements to the French horn and the bass clarinet. Hector Berlioz liked his set of valved bugles called saxhorns so well, that he arranged to have some of his music performed on them. These instruments developed into other band instruments.

John Philip Sousa – (1854-1932) He was an American composer of band music and marches. He invented the Sousaphone which is like a marching tuba.

Cécile Chaminade (Louise Stéphanie) – (1857-1944) She was a French composer and pianist who wrote a flute concerto, the Dramatic Symphony of the Amazons, chamber music and many songs.

1861-1865 The American Civil War was fought between the Northern United States Union Army and the Southern Confederate Army over slavery. The South wanted to secede from the United States over slavery rights. The North wanted to free the slaves and maintain the territory of the United States.

Claude Debussy – **(1862-1918)** was a French composer who helped to develop French Impressionism in music after the French Impressionist painters. His music blurs the bar lines so that regular down beats are obscured. He includes secret symbolism in his music.

Amy Marcy Beach – **(1867-1944)** was an American composer, who wrote a symphony, chamber music, and helped the Audubon Society by taking music dictation of bird songs.

1872 Impressionism was a genre in painting which was first used to describe a painting by Claude Monet for his painting Sunrise, which was painted outdoors in France. The Impressionist movement gained popularity through a series of art exhibitions held by various artists including Nadar in 1874 in Paris. The style includes small thin brush strokes or dots which produce a hazy effect.

Modern Period (1910-Present)

Igor Stravinsky – **(1882 -1971)** Russian composer and conductor who wrote music for the Rite of Spring and the Firebird ballets, which were produced in Paris.

Rebecca Clarke – **(1886-1979)** British/American composer and violist.

1895 Early Motion Pictures – On 28 December 1895, the Lumière brothers held a commercial public showing of ten short films in Paris. This was the start of cinematographic motion pictures. There had been earlier films, but not of this quality.

Florence Price – **(1887-1953)** was an American composer who was the first black woman to have her symphonic music performed by a major orchestra. She performed in movie theaters.

Nadia Boulanger – **(1887-1979)** was a French composer and professor at the Paris Conservatory of music. Boulanger taught many important 20th century composers.

Lili Boulanger – **(1893-1918)** was a French composer who won the Prix de Rome composing competition and she was the younger sister of Nadia Boulanger.

Sergie Prokofiev – **(1891-1953)** Ukrainian composer who wrote symphonies, ballet music, and major piano concertos.

Louise Lincoln Kerr – **(1892-1977)** American composer who wrote in the **Southwest Impressionist** style of music, along with Ferde Grofé and other composers, in Arizona. She composed symphonies, chamber music, ballets, and a violin concerto.

1895-1927 New Orleans Jazz develops in the French Quarter of this city in Louisiana. The music of black African American musicians combines with European instruments and African/Caribbean rhythms to form American and New Orleans jazz.

George Gershwin – **(1898-1937)** American composer who fuses jazz music with classical and symphonic music. He wrote the Rhapsody in Blue Piano Concerto and American in Paris.

Aaron Copland – **(1900-1990)** American composer who helps to establish the American sound in music with his "Appalachian Spring" and "Rodeo Ballet" music.

1903 The Wright Brothers built the first successful manned, powered, and piloted aircraft in history at Kitty Hawk, North Carolina. Orville Wright flew the Flyer for 12 seconds on December 17th, 1903. Wilber Wright flew the Flyer II for over five minutes on November 9th, 1904.

1905 The Russian Revolution of 1905 leads to the reorganization of Russia and the Russian Constitution of 1906. The Tzar and his family keep their rule for a time. There is still unrest in that country.

1905 Physicist Albert Einstein (1879-1955) proposes his **Theory of Relativity** in a paper while he is working at the patent office in Germany. This theory is one of the pillars of quantum mechanics which lead to the quantum theory.

Benjamin Britten – **(1913-1976)** British composer who wrote the Young Person's Guide to the Orchestra.

1914-1918 World War I was fought in Europe. The United States and Canada join with the French and British to win against Germany and Austria.

1917 The Russian Revolution of 1917 comes from the defeat of Russia in World War I. It leads to the creation of the Soviet Union and the overthrow and execution of Tsar Nicolas Alexander and his family.

Leonard Bernstein – **(1918-1990)** American composer and conductor who wrote music for the musical West Side Story.

Vítězlava Kaprálová – **(1915-1940)** Czech composer and conductor who wrote a piano concerto, symphonic music, music for movies, chamber, and choral music.

1920's The LP Record or "long-playing" record was introduced by the three major record companies Edison, Victor and Columbia. They expanded the length of the vinyl disc record from four minutes to eight minutes in length.

Thea Musgrave – **(1928-   )** Scottish composer and conductor who wrote The Seasons, a Clarinet Concerto and Turbulent Landscapes for orchestra.

50 Famous Composers

1929 The Wall Street Crash of October 29th, 1929 (Black Tuesday) happened when the New York Stock Exchange collapsed. Many people lost all their money, their homes and even their lives. The Great Crash was the worst in US history and led to the Great Depression. The US government set new rules and restrictions for banks.

1929-1939 The Great Depression was a time of terrible poverty in the United States and world-wide. Many people were out of work and did not have homes or enough food.

Joan Tower – (1938-) American composer who wrote Purple Rhapsody for Viola and the Fanfare for the Uncommon Woman.

1939-1945 World War II was a global war fought between the Allied Forces (Great Britain, France, United States and Soviet Union) and the Axis Powers (Germany, Italy, and Japan). Germany takes over most of Europe and is advancing on the Soviet Union and the United Kingdom. The United States joins the war. The Allied Forces win after many sacrifices and battles.

1945 The Atomic Bomb. The United States Army and Air forces detonated the first uranium fission atomic bomb on Hiroshima on August 6th destroying the entire city. A second atomic bomb was used on Nagasaki three days later, on August 9th after the Japanese military refused to surrender. This deadly show of force ended World War II and prevented more prolonged hand to hand combat with the Japanese, which would have cost thousands of US military lives and millions of Japanese lives. The horror of these bombs taught the World that we must never use such desperate military force in the future.

Gwyneth Van Anden Walker – (1947-) American composer who wrote a bassoon concerto and many choral works.

1950-1953 Korean War started when North Korea, backed by the Soviet Union, invaded South Korea. The United States defended South Korea and pushed back the communists.

1955-1975 Vietnam War was an undeclared war between America and the communist Viet Cong regime, which was fought in Vietnam.

1957-1974 Physicist Warren P. Waters (1922-2000) patents several early alloys and the **solid-state fused junction designs** at Hughes Aircraft that were used to improve the integrated circuit in the early 1950's. Later Waters and his team invent the **silicon wafer and the MOS Process** of etching integrated circuits onto discs with a photographic technique.

1958 Jack Kilby develops a crude model of the first **Integrated Circuit** while working at Texas Instruments. He wins the Nobel Prize in 2000 in Physics for this experiment.

1966-1976 The Surveyor Project of the United States sends seven unmanned space craft to land on the Moon. Physicist and solid-state engineer Warren P. Waters (1922-2000) develops the landing system, along with other team members at Hughes Aircraft, that successfully lands five of these crafts on the Moon in 1967.

1969 The Apollo 11 Mission is the spaceflight that landed the first two people on the Moon. Americans Neil Armstrong and pilot Buzz Aldrin landed the Apollo Lunar Module Eagle on the Moon on July 20, 1969.

1990-1991 Gulf War I was fought between Iraq and the US and allied forces. Iraq had invaded Kuwait to take control of their oil. The US invaded Iraq and prevented them from destabilizing the Middle East and oil interests.

2003-2011 Iraq War was fought between Iraq and the US and allied forces. Iraq had been using chemical weapons on the Kurds. The US feared weapons of mass destruction, so Congress voted to go to war with Iraq. The US invaded Iraq and took over control of the country deposing their leader. The weapons were not found until after the war.

Alma Deutscher – (2005-) English composer, pianist and violinist who composed the opera Cinderella, a piano concerto and a violin concerto by the age of twelve.

2012 – Hildegard von Bingen – She was canonized a Saint on 10 May 2012 by Pope Benedict XVI. On 7 October 2012 he named her a Doctor of the Church.

2019 The wooden roof of the nearly 900-year-old Cathedral of Notre Dame in Paris, France burned completely down on 15 April 2019 in a twelve-hour fire. Fortunately, the stone outer structure survived including the two towers and the famous window. The Crown of Thorns and other priceless relics were saved as well.

2019-2020 – A Worldwide pandemic broke out in Wuhan, China and quickly spread to 213 countries on the planet killing over 3.37 million people. The Corona Virus, which could develop into the often-fatal COVID19, is thought to have been caused by bats. People had to shelter in place and wear protective face masks for fear of catching this virus. The world's economies were in danger of collapsing from the work shut down. But many lives were saved while scientists raced to develop a successful vaccine.

2020 The United States celebrated the one hundredth anniversary of women getting the vote on 16 August 1920. The 19th Amendment to the US Constitution reads "THE RIGHT OF CITIZENS OF THE UNITED STATES TO VOTE SHALL NOT BE DENIED OR ABRIDGED BY THE UNITED STATES OR BY ANY STATE ON ACCOUNT OF SEX."

BIBLIOGRAPHY
Books

Banat, Gabriel (2006). The Chevalier de Saint-Georges: virtuoso of the sword and the bow. Hillsdale, NY: Pendragon Press. ISBN 1576471098. OCLC 63703876.

Blyth, Alan (1981). Remembering Britten. London: Hutchinson. ISBN 9780091449506.

Bookspan, Martin, 101 Masterpieces of Music and Their Composers. Doubleday and Company, Inc. New York: New York, 1973.

Bowers, Jane and Tick, Judith editors, Women Making Music: The Western Art Tradition, 1150-1950. University of Illinois Press. Chicago: Ohio, 1987.

Broe, Carolyn Waters, The String Compositions of Louise Lincoln Kerr: Analysis and Editing of Five Solo Viola Pieces. Arizona State University Press. Tempe: Arizona, 2001.

Broe, Carolyn Waters, J.S. Bach's Treatment of the Viola: In His Cantatas and Brandenburg Concertos. California State University, Long Beach, California: 250 pages, 1984.

Carter, Tim; Chew, Geoffrey (n.d.). Monteverdi [Monteverde], Claudio (Giovanni [Zuan] Antonio). In Roote, Deane. Grove Music Online: (Oxford Music Online). Oxford University Press. Retrieved 21 July 2017.

Cohen, Aaron. International Encyclopedia of Women Composers, 2nd ed., 2 vols. Books and Music (USA) Inc.: New York, New York, 1987.

Conway, David (2012). Jewry in Music: Entry to the Profession from the Enlightenment to Richard Wagner. Cambridge: Cambridge University Press. ISBN 9781107015388

Cooper, Barry (2008). Beethoven. Oxford University Press US. ISBN 978-0-19-531331-4. Retrieved 15 April 2012.

Copland, Aaron; Perlis, Vivian (1984). Copland 1900 Through 1942. New York: St. Martins/Marek.

David, Hans T. and Mendel, Arthur eds. The Bach Reader, A Life of Johann Sebastian Bach in Letters and Documents. Revised ed. New York: W.W. Norton & Co., Inc., 1966.

Deutsch, Otto Erich (1965). Mozart: A Documentary Biography. Peter Branscombe, Eric Blom, Jeremy Noble (trans.). Stanford: Stanford University Press. ISBN 978-0804702331. OCLC 8991008.

Dies, Albert Christoph (1810). Biographische Nachrichten von Joseph Haydn nach mündlichen Erzählungen desselben entworfen und herausgegeben [Biographical Accounts of Joseph Haydn, written and edited from his own spoken narratives]. Vienna: Camesinaische Buchhandlung. English translation in: Dies, Albert Christoph (1963).

"Biographical Accounts of Joseph Haydn". In Gotwals, Vernon. Haydn: Two Contemporary Portraits. (translation by Vernon Gotwals). Milwaukee: Univ. of Wisconsin Press. ISBN 0-299-02791-0. One of the first biographies of Haydn, based on 30 interviews carried out during the composer's old age.

Downes, Edward, Guide to Symphonic Music. Walker and Company, New York: New York, 1976.

Einstein, Alfred (1965). Mozart: His Character, His Work. Galaxy Book 162. Arthur Mendel, Nathan Broder (trans.) (6th ed.). New York City: Oxford University Press. ISBN 978-0304924837. OCLC 456644858.

Forkel, Johann Nikolaus. Johann Sebastian Bach: His Life, Art, and Work at Project Gutenberg, translation by Charles Sanford Terry of Ueber Johann Sebastian Bachs Leben, Kunst und Kunstwerke (1802). New York: Harcourt, Brace and Howe. 1920 (e-version: 2011).

Gilder, Eric, The Dictionary of Composers and Their Music. Wings Books. New York: New York, 1978.

Gordeyeva, E. (ed.). M.P. Musorgsky v vospominaniyakh sovremennikov [Mussorgsky in the recollections of contemporaries] Moscow: s.n., 1989.

Grout, Donald Jay, The History of Western Music. W.W. Norton & Company, Inc. New York: New York, 1973 & 2006.

Halliwell, Ruth (1998). The Mozart Family: Four Lives in a Social Context. New York City: Clarendon Press. ISBN 978-0198163718. OCLC 36423516

Hartl, Karla and Erik Entwistle, eds. The Kaprálová Companion. A guide to the life and music of Czech composer Vítězslava Kaprálová. 240 pp. Lanham, MD: Lexington Books, 2011. ISBN 978-0-7391-6723-6

Hawkins, John. A General History of the Science and Practice of Music. London: T. Payne, 1776.

Jöckle, Clemens (2003). Encyclopedia of Saints. Konecky & Konecky. p. 204.

Jones, Isola. Observations and Insights into the Life and Vocal Work of Joseph Bologne (Chevalier de Saint-Georges). Doctoral Dissertation, Arizona State University, Tempe, AZ, 2016.

Jugenderinnerungen einer Stettiner Kaufmannstocher

Kamien, Roger. Music: An Appreciation. 9th Brief Edition. New York, New York: McGraw Hill Education, 2018.

Keates, Jonathan (1985). Handel: The Man and His Music. New York: St Martin's Press. ISBN 0-312-35846-6.

Kerman, Joseph and Tyson, Alan. The New Grove Beethoven. W.W. Norton & Company, Inc. New York: New York, 1983.

La Boëssière, Tessier (1818). Traité de l'art des armes à l'usage des professeurs et des amateurs (in French). Paris: Didot.

Lang, Paul Henry (1966). George Frideric Handel. New York: W.W. Norton & Co. LCCN 66011793/MN/r842

Lebrecht, Norman. The Book of Musical Anecdotes. The Free Press. New York: New York, 1985.

Maddocks, Fiona. Hildegard of Bingen: The Woman of Her Age (New York: Doubleday, 2001), p. 194.

Mozart's Letters, Mozart's Life: Selected Letters. Translated by Robert Spaethling. W.W. Norton. 2000.

Mozart, Wolfgang; Mozart, Leopold (1966). Anderson, Emily, ed. The Letters of Mozart and his Family (2nd ed.). London: Macmillan. ISBN 978-0393022483. OCLC 594813.

From Nannerl's Reminiscences, composed 1792 and printed in Deutsch 1965.

Neumann, Werner. Bach and His World. New York: Viking Press, 1970.

The New Grove Dictionary of Music and Musicians. 6th ed. Edited by Stanley Sadie, 20 vols. London: MacMillan Publishers, Ltd., 1980.

The New Grove Dictionary of Music and Musicians. 7th ed. Edited by Stanley Sadie, 29 vols. London: MacMillan Publishers, Ltd., 2001.

Nice, David (2003). Prokofiev: From Russia to the West 1891–1935. London.

Osborne, Richard (1993) [1986]. Rossini. London: Dent. ISBN 978-0-460-86103-8.

Pincherle, Marc, Vivaldi Genius of the Baroque. W.W. Norton & Company, Inc. New York: New York, 1962.

Pollack, Howard (1999). Aaron Copland. NY: Henry Holt and Co. ISBN 978-0805049091.

Ponder, Michael (2004). "Clarke, Rebecca Helferich (1886–1979)". Oxford Dictionary of National Biography. Oxford University Press (subscription required).

Prokofiev, Sergei (2008). Anthony Phillips (translator) (ed.). Diaries 1915–1923: Behind the Mask. London / Ithaca: Faber and Faber/Cornell University Press. ISBN 978-0-571-22630-6.

Prokofiev, Sergei (2012). Anthony Phillips (translator) (ed.). Diaries 1924–1933: Prodigal Son. London/ Ithaca: Faber and Faber/Cornell University Press. ISBN 978-0-571-23405-9.

Reese, Gustave, Jeremy Noble, Lewis Lockwood, Jessie Ann Owens, James Haar, Joseph Kerman, and Robert Stevenson. The new Grove High Renaissance Masters: Josquin, Palestrina, Lassus, Byrd, Victoria. The Composer Biography Series; The New Grove Dictionary of Music and Musicians. London: Macmillan Publishers, 1980–84. ISBN 0-393-30093-5.

Robbins Landon, H. C., Vivaldi Voice of the Baroque. University of Chicago Press. Chicago: Illinois, 1996.

Sadie, Julie Anne and Samuel, Rhian editors, The Norton/Grove Dictionary of Women Composers. W.W. Norton & Company: New York: New York, 1995.

Sadie, Stanley, The Norton/Grove Concise Encyclopedia of Music. W.W. Norton & Company. New York: New York, 1988.

Sadie, Stanley, ed. (1998). The New Grove Dictionary of Opera. New York: Grove's Dictionaries of Music Inc. ISBN 978-0333734322. OCLC 39160203.

Sadie, Stanley, The New Grove Mozart. W.W. Norton & Company. New York: New York, 1985.

Sadie, Julie Anne & Samuel, Rhian editors. The Norton/Grove Dictionary of Women Composers. W.W. Norton & Company, Inc.: New York, 1994.

Schubert, Franz. Deutsch, Otto Erich. Franz Schubert's Letters and Other Writings. Ed. Savile, trans. By Ventia, Books for Libraries Press, 1970.

Smith, Rollin (1992). Saint-Saëns and the Organ. Stuyvesant: Pendragon Press. ISBN 978-0-945193-14-2.

Solomon, Maynard (1995). Mozart: A Life (1st ed.). New York City: HarperCollins. ISBN 978-0060190460. OCLC 31435799

Schweitzer, Albert. J.S. Bach. 2 vols., English trans. by Ernest Newman. London: Breitkopf and Härtel, 1911; reprint ed., London: A. & C. Black, Limited, 1977.

Talbot, Michael (1992). Vivaldi, second edition. London: J. M. Dent. American reprint, New York: Schirmer Books: Maxwell Macmillan International, 1993.

Todd, R. Larry (2010) Fanny Hensel: The Other Mendelssohn Oxford: Oxford University Press ISBN 978-0-19-518080-0.

Wilhelmine, Margravine consort of Friedrich Margrave of Bayreuth; Helena Augusta Victoria, Princess Christian of Schleswig-Holstein. New York, Scribner & Welford, 1887.

Wolff, Christoph et al, The New Grove Bach Family. W.W. Norton & Company. New York: New York, 1985.

Newspaper, Magazine, Letters, Lectures, Journal Articles, Diaries, and Interviews

Banat, Gabriel (2000). "Saint-Georges, Joseph Bologne, Chevalier, de". The New Grove. London.

Friedrich Blume, "J.S. Bach's Youth," The Musical Quarterly 54 (January 1968): 15.

Jon Brain (22 October 2012). "Alma Deutscher, seven, writes opera The Sweeper of Dreams" (video). BBC. BBC News. Retrieved 1 August 2020.

"Cécile Chaminade". Encyclopædia Britannica. Encyclopædia Britannica. Retrieved 26 February 2014.

Chantal Incandela, "Mayer's Faust Overture," Obscure Music Mondays, Performers Edition Articles, January 6, 2020.

Cleland, JoAnn, Interview by author Carolyn Waters Broe, July 2, 2020, Arizona.

Deutscher, Alma, "Interview on 60 Minutes, CBS show," with Scott Pelley, August 11, 2019. Retrieved 31 July 2020.

Deutscher, Alma, "Why Music Should Be Beautiful," Concert preview on her YouTube channel, February 21, 2017.

Duchen, Jessica, "Chevalier de Saint-Georges: The man who got under Mozart's skin.",

Independent.co.UK: Arts and Entertainment, 7 February 2016.

The Etude Archived 2013-10-21 at the Wayback Machine, which calls Thomas "the celebrated composer and writer". Thomas appears to have left no published writing.

Grove Dictionary of Music and Musicians, "(Johann Georg) Leopold Mozart", which is part of the major article "Mozart". The section about Leopold is written by Cliff Eisen. Oxford University Press.

Hofmann, Kurt, tr. Michael Musgrave (1999). "Brahms the Hamburg musician 1833–1862". In Musgrave 1999a, pp. 3–30

Ines Bellinger, "The Musical Greatness of Bach's Hands," National Geographic, September 2019, pg. 35.

Kerr, William, interview with author Carolyn Waters Broe, April 22, 2001.

Letter from Leopold Mozart to his daughter Maria Anna from February 16, 1785. In the original: "Ich sage ihnen vor gott, als ein ehrlicher Mann, ihr Sohn ist der größte Componist, den ich von Person und den Nahmen nach kenne: er hat geschmack, und über das die größte Compositionswissenschaft." For more details of the occasion, see Haydn and Mozart.

Library of Congress, "Who Was She? Notable Women" in Music Knowledge Cards, Pomegranate Communications, Inc., Petaluma, CA.

PBS TV Documentary, "Leonard Bernstein: Reaching for the Note" originally shown in the series American Masters on PBS in the U.S., now on DVD.

Summers, Jonathan. "CECILE CHAMINADE". NAXOS. NAXos. Retrieved 26 February 2014.

Swafford, Jan (2001). "Did the Young Brahms Play Piano in Waterfront Bars?". 19th-Century Music. 24 (3): 268–75. doi:10.1525/ncm.2001.24.3.268. ISSN 0148-2076. JSTOR 10.1525/ncm.2001.24.3.268.

Taylor, A. Nannette, Louise Lincoln Kerr: Grand Lady of Music (Phoenix, AZ: Kerr Cultural Center, Arizona State University, n.d.) c. 1991.

Thompson, Regine Angela, "Fanny Mendelssohn's response to the epidemic of 1831", Women's Philharmonic Advocacy newsletter, 17 May 2020.

Virginia Woolf, "A Room of One's Own," an extended essay by Virginia Woolf, first published in September 1929. The work is based on two lectures Woolf delivered in October 1928 at Newnham College and Girton College, women's constituent colleges at the University of Cambridge."Hogarth Press", England, September 1929.

Wakin, Daniel J. (8 March 2009). "The Week Ahead: March 8–14 March: Classical". The New York Times. Retrieved 23 May 2010.

50 Famous Composers

Websites

https://aleksandramaslovaric.com/discography/mayer-violin-sonatas/

https://www.bach-leipzig.de/en/bach-archive/johann-christoph-friedrich-bach

http://www.brainyquote.com/quotes/authors/g/gioachino_rossini.html

http://www.classicfm.com/composers/bach/guides/children/#X8V3fhVmmyAkPbzW.99

http://www.classicfm.com/composers/beethoven/guides/daniel-steibelt/

http://www.classicfm.com/composers/haydn/pictures/haydn-facts-great-composer/mozart-and-haydn/

https://www.cpebach.de/en/about-bach/people-and-places/princess-anna-amalia

https://culturalcocktailhour.wordpress.com/2010/03/05/bach-and-the-nanny-goat-bassoonist/

http://www.encyclopedia.com/people/literature-and-arts/music-history-composers-and-performers-biographies/charles-camille-saint

https://www.encyclopedia.com/women/encyclopedias-almanacs-transcripts-and-maps/anna-amalia-prussia-1723-1787

https://en.wikipedia.org/wiki/Emilie_Mayer

https://www.mja.com.au/journal/2009/190/4/are-alleged-remains-johann-sebastian-bach-authentic

http://www.npr.org/sections/deceptivecadence/2010/11/24/131568241/composers-in-the-kitchen-gioachino-rossini-s-haute-cuisine

http://www.musicwithease.com/bach-pictures.html

https://www.naxos.com/

https://performersedition.com/index.php/content/obscure-music-mondays/

https://www.sfcv.org/learn/composer-gallery/saint-saens-camille

https://www.smithsonianmag.com/arts-culture/maria-anna-mozart-the-familys-first-prodigy-1259016/

http://www.violintutorpro.com/5-interesting-facts-about-johannes-brahms/

https://www.telegraph.co.uk/news/worldnews/australiaandthepacific/australia/11848915/Mozarts-sister-composed-works-used-by-younger-brother.html

https://en.wikipedia.org/wiki/1812_Overture

https://en.wikipedia.org/wiki/Anna_Amalia,_Abbess_of_Quedlinburg

https://en.wikipedia.org/wiki/Antonio_Vivaldi

https://fr.wikipedia.org/wiki/Antonio_Vivaldi

https://en.wikipedia.org/wiki/Camille_Saint-Saens

https://en.wikipedia.org/wiki/Carl_Philipp_Emanuel_Bach

https://en.wikipedia.org/wiki/Felix_Mendelssohn

https://en.wikipedia.org/wiki/Francesca_Caccini

https://en.wikipedia.org/wiki/George_Frideric_Handel

https://en.wikipedia.org/wiki/Gioachino_Rossini

https://en.wikipedia.org/wiki/Haydn%27s_head

https://en.wikipedia.org/wiki/Johann_Christian_Bach

https://en.wikipedia.org/wiki/Johann_Sebastian_Bach

https://en.wikipedia.org/wiki/Johannes_Brahms

https://en.wikipedia.org/wiki/Joseph_Haydn

https://en.wikipedia.org/wiki/Josquin_des_Prez

https://en.wikipedia.org/wiki/Leopold_Mozart

https://en.wikipedia.org/wiki/Ludwig_van_Beethoven

https://en.wikipedia.org/wiki/Maria_Anna_Mozart

https://en.wikipedia.org/wiki/A_Midsummer_Night%27s_Dream_(Mendelssohn)

https://en.wikipedia.org/wiki/Modest_Mussorgsky

https://en.wikipedia.org/wiki/Claudio_Monteverdi

https://en.wikipedia.org/wiki/Pictures_at_an_Exhibition

https://en.wikipedia.org/wiki/Pyotr_Ilyich_Tchaikovsky

https://en.wikipedia.org/wiki/The_Carnival_of_the_Animals

https://en.wikipedia.org/wiki/Violin_Concerto_(Brahms)

https://en.wikipedia.org/wiki/Wilhelm_Friedemann_Bach

50 Famous Composers

https://en.wikipedia.org/wiki/Wilhelm_Friedrich_Ernst_Bach

https://en.wikipedia.org/wiki/Wolfgang_Amadeus_Mozart

https://en.wikisource.org/wiki/A_Dictionary_of_Music_and_Musicians/Haydn,_Joseph

http://kidsmusiccorner.co.uk/composers/classical/cpebach/

http://kidsmusiccorner.co.uk/composers/classical/mendelssohn/

http://kidsmusiccorner.co.uk/composers/classical/tchaikovsky/

https://wiki.kidzsearch.com/wiki/Johann_Christian_Bach

http://www.tlsbooks.com/

http://www.tlsbooks.com/bachbook.pdf

http://www.tlsbooks.com/beethovenbook.pdf

http://www.tlsbooks.com/handelbook.pdf

http://www.tlsbooks.com/haydnbook.pdf

http://www.tlsbooks.com/mozartbook.pdf

https://alchetron.com/Rebecca-Clarke-(composer)-1269346-W

http://www.encyclopedia.com/people/literature-and-arts/music-history-composers-and-performers-biographies/cecile-chaminade

http://www.notablebiographies.com/supp/Supplement-Ca-Fi/Farrenc-Louise.html

http://www.persimmontree.org/v2/spring-2009/an-interview-with-thea-musgrave-scottish-american-composer/

https://en.wikipedia.org/wiki/Amy_Beach

https://en.wikipedia.org/wiki/Cécile_Chaminade

https://en.wikipedia.org/wiki/Clara_Schumann

https://en.wikipedia.org/wiki/Rebecca_Clarke_(composer)

https://en.wikipedia.org/wiki/Duchess_Maria_Antonia_of_Bavaria

https://en.wikipedia.org/wiki/Elisabeth_Jacquet_de_La_Guerre

https://en.wikipedia.org/wiki/Fanny_Mendelssohn

https://en.wikipedia.org/wiki/Flute_Concertino_(Chaminade)

https://www.gwynethwalker.com/letrep.html

http://hrhprincesspalace.blogspot.com/2015/01/todays-princess-anna-amalia-of-prussia.html

https://en.wikipedia.org/wiki/Hildegard_of_Bingen

http://lepetitrenaudon.blogspot.com/2010/08/cecile-chaminade-1887-1914-les-annees.html

https://en.wikipedia.org/wiki/Lili_Boulanger

https://en.wikipedia.org/wiki/Louise_Farrenc

https://en.wikipedia.org/wiki/Mademoiselle_Beaumesnil

https://en.wikipedia.org/wiki/Marianna_Martines

https://en.wikipedia.org/wiki/Wolfgang_Amadeus_Mozart#CITEREFHalliwell1998

https://en.wikipedia.org/wiki/Nadia_Boulanger

https://en.wikipedia.org/wiki/Piano_Concerto_(Schumann)

https://en.wikipedia.org/wiki/Robert_Schumann

https://en.wikipedia.org/wiki/Wilhelmine_of_Prussia,_Margravine_of_Branden-burg-Bayreuth#Works

Dr. Carolyn Waters Broe

About the Author
CAROLYN WATERS BROE

Dr. **Carolyn Waters Broe**, American violist, conductor and composer has been the featured soloist with orchestras in California and Arizona. She has made several CD recordings and performed with numerous celebrities. Broe received her Bachelor of Music Performance degree from Chapman University, her Master of Fine Arts in Music History from California State University, in Long Beach, and earned her Doctor of Musical Arts in Viola Solo Performance from Arizona State University in 2001. Her viola teachers include Jerry Epstein, William Magers, Adriana Chirilov, and Louis Kievman. She studied conducting with John Koshak and attended master classes with Leonard Bernstein, Herbert Blomstedt, and Seiji Ozawa.

Carolyn Broe conducts the **Four Seasons Orchestra of Scottsdale**, which was nominated in two Grammy categories for 2000. She conducted Four Seasons Orchestra on tour in Vienna, Austria for the Haydn Festival in 2009. Broe conducted the Paradise Valley Community College Orchestra for ten years as well as serving as their Violin and Viola Instructor. She is the violist with the Four Seasons String Quartet and Sweetwater Strings. She has written two books including "J.S. Bach's Treatment of the Viola" and "The String Compositions of Louise L. Kerr". Carolyn holds several awards including: The Dream Catcher Award of 1995 from Indian Women in Progress; the Ten-Year Service Award of 2003 from Paradise Valley Community College; and the Phoenix Office of Arts and Culture "Artist Award" in 2005. Carolyn was nominated twice for the Arizona Governor's Arts Awards in 2003 and 2004 for education and community service. She recently toured to China as a violist with the American Festival Orchestra. Carolyn Broe is the Principal Violist with the Scottsdale Philharmonic Orchestra. She is currently teaching private violin, viola, cello and piano at her home studio in Scottsdale, Arizona.

CPSIA information can be obtained
at www.ICGtesting.com
Printed in the USA
LVHW062210021122
732257LV00005B/41